Visual Arts Library
Main D804.R9Z3
Zawodny, J./Death in the forest

3 2660 00008459 3

D1679167

WITHDRAWN
From School of Visual Arts
Library Collection

INTERNATIONAL
STUDIES
OF
THE
COMMITTEE
ON
INTERNATIONAL
RELATIONS
University of Notre Dame

DEATH

❧ "I have been accused of woolly-mindedness for entertaining even hope for man. I can only respond that in the dim morning shadows of humanity, the inarticulate creature who first hesitantly formed the words for pity and for love must have received similar guffaws around a fire. Yet some men listened, for the words survive." ❧

LOREN EISELEY

IN THE FOREST

The Story of the Katyn Forest Massacre

by

J. K. ZAWODNY

UNIVERSITY OF NOTRE DAME PRESS

Copyright © 1962 by
J. K. Zawodny

First printing, 1962
Second printing, 1965
Third printing, 1972
Fourth printing, 1980

Library of Congress Cataloging in Publication Data

Zawodny, Janusz Kazimierz
  Death in the forest

  Bibliography: p.
  1. Katyn Forest Massacre, 1940. I. Title.
D804.R9Z3   940.5405   62-16639
ISBN 0-268-00849-3
ISBN 0-268-00850-7 (pbk.)

Manufactured in the United States of America

To
PUNIA

Acknowledgements

I SHOULD LIKE to express my deep appreciation to the institutions and persons who were helpful in accomplishing this study.

The Princeton University Faculty Research Committee financed part of the research, traveling, translations, typing, and materials. Professor Ernest R. Hilgard, Stanford University, gave sympathetic support to the writing.

Professor Philip W. Buck of the Department of Political Science, Stanford University, expended much time and effort in editing the final draft. Professor Charles Fairman of the Harvard Law School provided comments concerning my treatment of the Katyn case at the Nuremberg trial.

Professor S. Świaniewicz, residing in London, read my manuscript. His comments were particularly valuable as he was the only survivor of the Katyn Forest Massacre, taken away from the vicinity of the slaughter literally minutes before the execution. The manuscript was read also by Kazimierz Skarżyński, Secretary General of the Polish Red Cross 1939-1945. Now living in Canada, he was present at the Katyn graves during the exhumations performed by the International, German, and Polish Red Cross medical teams. Mr. Józef Czapski, Polish Commissioner for the Affairs of Former Prisoners of War in the U.S.S.R. in 1941, presently in France, was kind and patient enough to answer all my queries. Again, he was in a position to offer valuable first hand information as a former prisoner from Camp Starobelsk. The Honorable Stanisław Mikołajczyk, presently in the United States, former Prime Minister of the Polish Government-in-Exile in London, 1943-1945, spent considerable time giving me the benefit of his experience and rich memories related to the Polish-Soviet relations in the period of the Katyn affair. Mr. Józef Mackiewicz, Polish journalist, residing in Germany, who at one time visited the Katyn graves, and who has done a great deal of research on the subject, was willing to answer inquiries. Dr. Wiktor Sukiennicki (United States) read the manuscript and gave his valuable and expert suggestions. He was the author of the main Polish source collating the evidence available to the Polish Government-in-Exile. Dr. Zdzisław Stahl (London) undertook to answer my questions.

Professor Vernon Van Dyke, Chairman of the Department of Political Science at the State University of Iowa, encouraged my research on the Katyn affair when I was a graduate student. The reference desk staff of the Hoover Institution on War, Revolution, and Peace, Stanford University, and particularly Miss Irene Kozlov, was gracious in rendering co-operation and assistance in locating the materials.

Mrs. Helen Kmetovic of Palo Alto, California, and Mrs. Dorothy Hutchins, Half Moon Bay, California, typed the manuscript.

But above all—thanks to my wife, Lorraine. To the qualities of her heart this manuscript owes its completion.

J.K.Z.

Introduction

MORE THAN 15,000 Polish soldiers, among them 800 Doctors of Medicine, were murdered in one operation. Originally they had been taken into captivity by the Soviet Army in 1939. There was a possibility, however, that the prisoners, while still alive, had been taken from Soviet custody by German forces in 1941.

Some of the bodies were found in German-held territory. The ropes with which their hands were tied were Soviet-made, but the bullets with which the men were killed were of German origin.

The Soviet and German governments accused each other of the massacre. To obtain or remove the evidence, the intelligence services of several nations carried on a merciless secret contest in the Katyn Forest, Poland, Germany, Italy, England, and the United States. Men disappeared; so did files, including one from the United States Military Intelligence Office. In the process a key witness was found hanged, diplomatic and military careers were destroyed in the United States, personnel of the International Military Tribunal at Nuremberg lied by omission, and so did some of the greatest Allied leaders of the Second World War.

This book attempts to reconstruct, in detail, the fate of the prisoners and to provide the answers to these questions:

(1) Who killed these men?
(2) How were they killed?
(3) Why were they killed?

The research on this subject has been done by the author at the Library of Congress, The Hoover Library at Stanford University, and the Library of Princeton University. Available data in Russian, Polish, German, and English have been surveyed and, when they contributed to the clarification of the case, included.

J. K. ZAWODNY
*Center for Advanced Study
in the Behavioral Sciences*

Stanford, California
1962

Contents

INTRODUCTION	ix
ABBREVIATIONS	xiii
I. The Prisoners Who Vanished	3
NOTES	11
II. The Graves in the Forest	15
NOTES	25
III. The Inconvenient Allies—Alive and Dead	29
NOTES	45
IV. The Soviet Commission Investigation	49
NOTES	56
V. Nuremberg: Crime and Punishment in International Politics	59
NOTES	74
VI. Analysis of the Evidence	77
NOTES	95
VII. Reconstruction: To the Edge of the Graves	101
NOTES	124

VIII. Reconstruction: Marked to Live and Marked to Die	127
NOTES	162
IX. Problems Caused by Katyn after the War	169
NOTES	191
APPENDIX	199
BIBLIOGRAPHY	201
INDEX	219

Abbreviations

German Report — Germany. *Amtliches Material zum Massenmord von Katyn* (Official material concerning the Katyn massacre). Im Auftrage des Auswärtigen Amtes auf Grund urkundlichen Beweismaterials zusammengestellt, bearbeitet und herausgegeben von der Deutschen Informationsstelle. Berlin: Zentralverlag der NSDAP, F. Eher Nachf., 1943. 331 pp.

Hearings — U.S. House of Representatives. Select Committee on the Katyn Forest Massacre. *The Katyn Forest Massacre.* Hearings before the Select Committee to Conduct an Investigation of the Facts, Evidence and Circumstances of the Katyn Forest Massacre. 82nd Cong., 1st and 2nd Sess., 1951-1952. Washington: U.S. Government Printing Office, 1952. 7 parts. 2362 pp.

I.M.T.	International Military Tribunal. Secretariat. *Trial of the Major War Criminals before the International Military Tribunal. Nuremberg, 14 November 1945-10 October 1946.* Nuremberg, Germany, 1947. Vols. I, II, III, IV, V, VII, IX, X, XIV, XV, XVII, XVIII, XXII, XXIII, XXIV.
M.S.Z.	Poland. Ministerstwo Spraw Zagranicznych. *Stosunki Polsko-Sowieckie od Września 1939 do Kwietnia 1943. Zbiór Dokumentów* (Polish-Soviet relations from September 1939 to April 1943. Collection of documents). London: 1943, 317 pp. (Najściślej tajne—Top secret).
P.S.Z.	Poland. Komisja Historyczna Polskiego Sztabu Głównego w Londynie. *Polskie Siły Zbrojne w Drugiej Wojnie Światowej.* Tom 1: *Kampania Wrześniowa 1939*, cz. 1, 2; Tom 3: *Armia Krajowa* (Polish forces in the Second World War. Vol. I: The September campaign of 1939, parts 1, 2; Vol. III: The Home Army). London: Instytut Historyczny im. Generała Sikorskiego, 1950-1951.
Polish Report	Poland. Polish Government-in-Exile, Council of Ministers. (Author, Dr. Wiktor Sukiennicki). *Facts and Documents Concerning Polish Prisoners of War Captured by the U.S.S.R. during the 1939 Campaign.* (Strictly confidential). London, 1946. 454 pp.

Soviet Report	U.S.S.R. Spetsial'naya Komissiya po Ustanovleniyu i Rassledovaniyu Obstoyatel'stv Rasstrela Nemetsko-Fashistskimi Zakhvatchikami v Katynskom Lesu Voennoplennykh Pol'skikh Ofitserov. (Special commission for ascertaining and investigating the circumstances of the shooting of Polish Officer prisoners by the German-Fascist invaders in the Katyn Forest). *Nota Sovetskogo Pravitel'stva Pravitel'stvu SShA; Soobshchenie Spetsial'noi Komissii.* (Note of the Soviet Government of the U.S.; communication by the Special Commission). Moscow: Supplement to *Novoe Vremya*, no. 10, 1952. 20 pp.
Stalin's Correspondence	U.S.S.R. Ministry of Foreign Affairs. *Correspondence between the Chairman of the Council of Ministers of the U.S.S.R. and the Presidents of the U.S.A. and the Prime Ministers of Great Britain during the Great Patriotic War of 1941-1945.* 2 vols. Moscow: Foreign Languages Publishing House, 1947.

DEATH IN THE FOREST

I

The Prisoners Who Vanished

THE GERMAN PUBLIC believed that the Second World War began with a number of Polish attacks on the German frontier. A typical episode was the attack on a radio station deep in German territory on August 31, 1939. "Poles" had commenced military activity by shooting their way in and out of a radio station, and, having seized it, broadcast an abusive speech in Polish and German. One dead Pole was found at the door of the station; his glassy eyes, blood-smeared face and the wreckage of the station were mute testimony to the raiding action which lasted three or four minutes. The German press marvelled at the remarkable knowledge of the terrain and of the building displayed by the "Poles" and announced that after a furious gun battle with the police, one of the raiders was killed and all others arrested.

Details of the raid on the German station became known after the war. The leader of the raiding party testified to the actual circumstances at the Nuremberg trial of war criminals. His name was A. H. Naujock. He was not a Pole, but a German, a long-standing member of the SS.

In the late summer of 1939 A. H. Naujock had been ordered personally by Heydrich, Chief of Sipo and S. D. (organs of the German security system), to attack the radio station at Gleiwitz and to allow a Polish-speaking German to make an inflammatory speech in Polish and German. Naujock and his band were to be dressed in Polish uniforms for the action; and, some "Polish" bodies were to be left at the station as indisputable evidence of Polish aggression.

At noon on August 31, 1939, the coded order from Heydrich to attack the station reached Naujock at Gleiwitz. At the same time a German criminal, according to Mr. Naujock, was delivered to him by the Gestapo of Gleiwitz. The man was "alive but completely unconscious" and dying from some kind of injections, introduced into his veins by Gestapo doctors; "blood was smeared across his face." Six raiders attacked the station at 8 p.m. Shots were fired. As planned, a short speech announcing the seizure of the station and of the city by the Poles was made. Naujock and his assistants then escaped, leaving behind the already dying and bloody "Pole," where they "had him laid down at the entrance to the station." [1]

The particular significance of this episode lies in the fact that at dawn the next day, the steel of German bombs was ripping apart homes and bodies in all the major cities of Poland. In fact, both the German and Soviet armies attacked Poland. After thirty-five days of struggle, organized Polish resistance collapsed and the Polish Government fled to Romania.

It is now known that the German and Soviet Governments co-ordinated their action on the basis of prearranged plans for the territorial dismemberment of Poland.[2] Accordingly, the country was divided into two spheres of interest by the "Ribbentrop-Molotov line," with a gain for Germany of 72,866 square miles and for the Soviet Union of 77,620 square miles of Polish land. Subsequently, the Supreme Council of the U.S.S.R. incorporated these lands into the Soviet Union.

Reichminister Hans Frank (ultimately hanged by verdict of the International Military Tribunal), the ruler of German-occupied Poland, considered himself the German King of Poland, "*der Deutsche König von Polen.*"[3] He acted accordingly and was not a merciful sovereign.

In Soviet-occupied Poland an immediate mass deportation of Poles commenced. Whole families were put forcibly into trains and dispatched toward northern Soviet territories. A sober and cautious estimate of the total number of the deportees can be established as approximating 1,200,000.[4] This number does not include 230,670 Polish soldiers, from privates to generals, captured in the eastern part of Poland by the Soviet Army. Subsequently this latter group was augmented by reserve officers living in the occupied territory who were arrested in their homes, and by officers and men who had sought refuge in Lithuania and Estonia and who, after seizure of these countries by the Soviet Union, were handed over to Soviet authorities. The total number of Polish prisoners-of-war in Soviet hands was within a few hundreds of 250,000. Among these men were 10,000 officers.[5]

Some 15,000 of the prisoners, including approximately 8,300 to 8,400 officers, completely disappeared from the earth. Their fate became a matter of international controversy and an open wound for Poles. It is the purpose of this book to trace the fate of these men.

In June 1941 when German armies attacked the Soviet Union, the Russian Government allied itself with the nations already fighting the Nazis. Becoming one of the Allies, the Soviet Government had to behave like one. Among other diplomatic moves, the Soviet Union, with the skillful and subtle assistance of the British Foreign Office, re-established diplomatic relations with the Polish Government-in-Exile. This government had reconstructed itself after its flight to Romania, then moved to France where it led Polish soldiers in fighting against German armies on French soil, and, finally, after withdrawal of British forces from the Continent, it had evacuated to England.

The first formal diplomatic agreement signed (London, July 30, 1941) by General Władysław Sikorski, on behalf of the Polish Government, and the Soviet Ambassador to Great

Britain, Maisky, stated solemnly that "the Soviet-German Treaties of 1939 relative to territorial changes in Poland have lost their validity. . . ." More pertinent here, this agreement included a special "Protocol" concerning Polish prisoners in the Soviet Union which granted "amnesty to all Polish citizens who are at present deprived of their freedom on the territory of the U.S.S.R., either as prisoners-of-war or on other adequate grounds."[6] Immediately, plans were made by the respective governments to organize from these former prisoners a Polish Army in Russia.[7]

Through the newly re-established Polish Embassy in the Soviet Union attempts were made to inform and gather Polish prisoners. A point of concentration was established in Buzul'uk and to this place a steady stream of emaciated Poles flowed. They had been released from 138 major prison and labor camps, and, happy with their freedom, they were eager to remove themselves from Soviet supervision. To command this re-created army, Soviet authorities freed from imprisonment a Polish officer, General Władysław Anders.[8]

One of the first problems, among many the general had to face, was the organization of this multitude, the influx of which ran into thousands daily. Anders needed officers badly, but officers rarely appeared. Of fourteen Polish generals captured by the Soviet Army only two appeared, in a state of exhaustion; the remaining twelve were missing. From 300 high-ranking staff officers only six came to Buzul'uk, and there was no news of the other 294. After the influx of men finally stopped and counts had been completed, there were about 15,000 missing persons, among them 8,300 to 8,400 officers.[9]

The Poles became concerned, particularly when a relatively small party of prisoners from Camp Grazovec reported that they had been removed by Soviet authorities from three large camps located at Kozelsk, Ostashkov, and Starobelsk. Scrutiny and cross-checks of the reports by the men from Grazovec established that the missing 15,000 were the inmates of those three camps until the spring of 1940. None of these prisoners, however, reported to the Polish units which were forming. They could not be found anywhere; and Soviet authorities denied any knowledge of them.

General Anders, pressed by the necessity of staffing his new army and by inquiries from the families and friends of the missing men, instituted a search of his own, establishing "a search office" with the sole purpose of locating the absent prisoners. Captains Jan Kaczkowski and Józef Czapski were most active in gathering information, collating it, and following the slightest hint or bit of gossip which might lead to the prisoners. The search office received thousands of letters from the families of missing Poles, inquiring as to their whereabouts. One thing was clear from these letters—the men from the three camps stopped writing home in the middle of April 1940.[10]

Captain Czapski, a former prisoner in Camp Starobelsk, knew personally many of the missing officers, particularly from this camp. He also knew from personal experience that this camp had been totally evacuated in the spring of 1940. He was sent to Grazovec with a small party of men and afterward joined General Anders. Where the other several thousand men from Starobelsk were taken, he did not know. Nobody knew, including the Soviet authorities, who refused even to guess. Polish inquiries were met either with silence or evasive answers.

Captain Czapski, whose knowledge of Russian was very good, with General Anders' assistance and support combed the Soviet Union for every possible clue. At one time he contacted *Glavnoe Upravlenie Lagerei* (Central Administration Office of Labor Camps) commanded by General Nasedkin. The general had never heard of the missing Poles. This particular mission was protested by N.K.V.D., *Narodnyi Komissariat Vnutrennikh Del* (Peoples' Commissariat for Internal Affairs). The Commissariat insisted to General Anders that Czapski was not to be permitted to move so freely in the Soviet Union.[11]

Czapski then prepared a factual memorandum compiling information concerning the last known whereabouts of the unaccounted-for prisoners and pressed for an interview with the N.K.V.D. policy makers. His efforts were successful and on February 2, 1942, Czapski was granted an appointment with N.K.V.D. General Raikhman at Lubianka prison in Moscow. To him the Polish officer submitted the memorandum and requested information about the missing men.[12]

Raikhman read the memorandum and "phlegmatically answered that he did not know anything about the fate of the missing people." However, in spite of the fact that it "was not his department," he did promise to give definite information. Czapski waited in Moscow for a week, to be awakened by a telephone ringing at midnight. It was Raikhman, who informed him that he was "leaving Moscow the next morning and [would] not be able to see him at all." He advised Czapski to contact Mr. Vyshinsky (Vice Chairman of the Council of People's Commissars). Mr. Vyshinsky had already been approached by Professor Kot, the Polish Ambassador to the Soviet Union, on many occasions.[13] Czapski felt that he had run into a blind alley.[14] He could not obtain any information from Soviet authorities, although it appeared from the facts already gathered that only they could shed light on the fate of the vanished Poles.

By that time the information showed that the absent officers and men had been in Kozelsk, Ostashkov, and Starobelsk camps until April 1940. Men had left the camps in small groups under strong guards of N.K.V.D., were marched to the nearest railway stations, and loaded into trains. Some traces of transports from Kozelsk were found around Smolensk by painstakingly putting together data gathered from the surviving Poles from the three camps. Traces, however, ended several miles west of Smolensk. Polish officers made inquiries in this area, but nothing could be found.[15]

The officers who had disappeared constituted a loss of about 45 per cent of the total of the Polish Land Army Officers' Corps at that time. The Poles intensified their search on the diplomatic level.

The Polish Ambassador to the Soviet Union, Tadeusz Romer (who superseded Professor Kot), testified that more than fifty formal inquiries were addressed to the Soviet Government on the subject of the missing men, but no information was received. On October 15, 1941, General Sikorski, representing the Polish Government, addressed a special note to the Soviet Ambassador in London, Bogomolov, stating that "the fate of several thousand Polish officers . . . who have not been found in Soviet military camps, continues to remain uncertain. Their presence in the Polish Army camps is indispensable." A month later, Bogomolov replied that "all Polish officers on the territory of the U.S.S.R. have . . . been set free"[16] This the Poles scarcely believed, and decided that a direct appeal should be made to Stalin. On November 14, 1941, the Polish Ambassador, Professor Kot, had an audience with Stalin. The Ambassador came to the point: " . . . my request to you, Mr. President, is that you will give instructions for the officers, whom we need for the organization of the army, to be released. We possess records of when they were removed from the camps."

The discussion of the subject closed when Stalin, telephoning to the N.K.V.D., asked if all Poles had been released from prison, listened to the reply, then added: "I have with me here the Polish Ambassador, who tells me not all." [He again listened to the reply, then put down the receiver and returned to the conference table.][17]

General Sikorski decided to talk to Stalin personally and flew from London to Moscow. The two leaders met at the

Kremlin on December 3, 1941. To the persistent question, "Where are the men?" Stalin replied, "They escaped." General Anders, who was also present, asked, "Where could they escape to?" "To Manchuria," Stalin replied. Though Sikorski had flown thousands of miles over enemy-controlled territory to reach Moscow this was all the information he obtained.[18] The escape of 15,000 men in 1941 across Russia "to Manchuria" was hardly a serious possibility.

The case attracted the attention of foreign offices of Allied governments. On May 27, 1942, Admiral William H. Standley, United States Ambassador to the Soviet Union, informed Mr. Andrei Vyshinsky that "the Soviet Government has delayed giving effect to certain clauses of the Polish-Soviet Agreement, particularly in regard to . . . the release of Polish prisoners-of-war." Vyshinsky promised to convey the Ambassador's views to his government. When months elapsed and no news was forthcoming, Standley again referred to the missing Poles while talking with Molotov (the People's Commissar for Foreign Affairs). The latter replied angrily that "there are too many people interesting themselves in Polish politics." [19] The British Ambassador's inquiries likewise yielded nothing.

The search produced contradictory and confused statements from Soviet officials. Mr. Vyshinsky on one occasion assured the Poles that "we have records of everyone, alive or dead. I have promised the details and I will produce them," and several months later stated with equal strength of conviction "unfortunately we have no such lists." [20] Lists were available for the more than one million Poles herded into the Soviet Union, but not for the 15,000 who had vanished.

Informal pleas and inquiries did not yield much for the Poles. Ilya Ehrenburg, the eminent Soviet writer, doubted whether the search could show results.[21] He pointed to Czapski's low military rank and implied that this kind of information could be secured only at the highest level. N.K.V.D.

General G. S. Zhukov used his position, within the limits of propriety, to intercede informally on behalf of Poles. Some liberations of Poles still detained took place through his intervention. But when approached by Polish Major-General Bohusz-Szyszko, Chief of the Polish Military Mission in Moscow, on behalf of two officers listed among the 15,000 missing, Zhukov told him bluntly, "Please do not ask me about these men, because in this particular case, I cannot help you." [22]

The search continued from July 1941 until April 1943. For a year and eight months no efforts were spared, no contacts overlooked to obtain from Soviet authorities information about the missing men—all in vain. Not a single clue was discovered.

In the last week of February 1943 the teletypes of German Communication Regiment 537 stationed several miles west of Smolensk, deep in Soviet territory, reported that German field police had found the bodies of Polish officers within the area of their bivouac. They did not know precisely how many, but they were sure there were thousands. The dead were dressed in high leather boots, with leather belts across their chests, many of them with medals for merit and valor. Each man had been shot through the head. They were found in several mass graves in Soviet soil, but the bullets which had killed them were of German manufacture.

NOTES TO CHAPTER I

1. International Military Tribunal. Secretariat. *Trial of the Major War Criminals before the International Military Tribunal. Nuremberg, 14 November 1945-10 October 1946.* Nuremberg, Germany, 1947. Vol. XIV, 242-244; II, 450-451; III, 233-235; V, 33; X, 515-516; XVII, 155; XXI, 511; XXII, 17; also Documents GB-54, 795-PS, 2151-PS. In the following pages this source will be cited as *I.M.T.*; see also *Völkischer Beobachter.* Süddeutsche Ausgabe. Sept. 2/3, 1939, p. 6.

For details of the organization of this and other border troubles on the Polish-German frontier in 1939 see the content of 223 folders prepared especially for Himmler. They consist of precise drawings of objects to be defaced in Germany and Poland in order to create the feeling of Polish provocations. Names of German agents to commit the provocations, assessment of the effectiveness and impact on German and Polish populations are included. An evaluation of the files can be found in Edmund Osmańczyk, *Dowody Prowokacji. Nieznane Archiwum Himmlera* (The evidence of provocation. Himmler's unknown archive) (Warszawa: Czytelnik, 1951), pp. 1-48.

2. Confirmation of this may be found in the Treaty of Non-Aggression between Germany and the Union of Soviet Socialist Republics signed in Moscow, August 23, 1939 (*one week prior to the German attack on Poland*). The Secret Additional Protocol to the Treaty states in article no. 2:

"In the event of a territorial and political rearrangement of the areas belonging to the Polish state the spheres of influence of Germany and of the U.S.S.R. shall be bound approximately by the line of the rivers Narew, Vistula, and San" (*Polish rivers dividing Poland approximately in half*). Author's italics. U.S. Department of State, *Nazi-Soviet Relations, 1939-1941: Documents from the Archives of the German Foreign Office*. Edited by Raymond James Sontag and James Stuart Beddie (Washington: U.S. Government Printing Office, 1948), p. 79.

3. Curzio Malaparte, *Kaputt*. (New York: E. P. Dutton Co., 1946), p. 64.

4. Poland. Komisja Historyczna Polskiego Sztabu Głównego w Londynie. *Polskie Siły Zbrojne w Drugiej Wojnie Światowej*. Tom I: *Kampania Wrześniowa*, cz. 1, 2; Tom III: *Armia Krajowa* (Polish forces in the Second World War. Vol. I: The September campaign of 1939, parts 1, 2; Vol. III: The Home Army). London: Instytut Historyczny im. Generała Sikorskiego, 1950-1951, III, 34. Hereafter cited as *P.S.Z.*

5. Poland. Polish Government-in-Exile, Council of Ministers. (Author, Dr. Wiktor Sukiennicki). *Facts and Documents Concerning Polish Prisoners of War Captured by the U.S.S.R. during the 1939 Campaign*. (Strictly confidential.) London, 1946, p. 15. Hereafter cited as *Polish Report*.

6. Poland. Polish Government-in-Exile, Polish Embassy in Washington. *Polish-Soviet Relations, 1918-1943. Official Documents*. 1944, p. 108; also Andrew Rothstein, *Soviet Foreign Policy during the Patriotic War: Documents and Materials, June 22, 1941-December 31, 1943*. Vol. I (London: Hutchinson and Co., Ltd., 1946), 81. Doctor Wiktor Sukiennicki called my attention to possible implications of the word "amnesty" as applied to the prisoners-of-war.

7. For information concerning the exchange of diplomatic documents and a description of circumstances pertaining to this specific

subject consult the following primary sources: Poland. Ministerstwo Spraw Zagranicznych. *Stosunki Polsko-Sowieckie od Września 1939 Roku do Kwietnia 1943. Zbiór Dokumentów* (Polish-Soviet relations from September 1939 to April 1943. Collection of documents) (London: 1943 [Najściślej tajne—Top secret]), pp. 45, 115, 128, 130-134, 164, 205, 227, 237. Hereafter this source will be cited as *M.S.Z.* English translations of the full texts of the diplomatic notes exchanged between the two governments on this subject can be found in: Poland. Polish Government-in-Exile, Polish Embassy in Washington. *Polish-Soviet Relations, 1918-1943. Official Documents.* 1944, pp. 126-157. One may also consult, General Sikorski Historical Institute. *Documents on Polish-Soviet Relations 1939-1945. Vol. I, 1939-1943* (London, Melbourne, Toronto: Heineman, 1961), 112-540.

8. Władysław Anders, *Bez Ostatniego Rozdziału. Wspomnienia z Lat 1939-1946* (Without the last chapter. Memoirs of the years 1939-1946) (Newton, Wales: Montgomeryshire Printing Co., 1949), p. 65.

9. *Polish Report*, pp. 133-134; also chapter VI below, note 1.

10. Testimony of Jan Kaczkowski. U.S. House of Representatives. Select Committee on the Katyn Forest Massacre. *The Katyn Forest Massacre.* Hearings before the Select Committee to Conduct an Investigation of the Facts, Evidence and Circumstances of the Katyn Forest Massacre. 82nd Cong., 1st and 2nd Sess., 1951-1952 (Washington: U.S. Government Printing Office, 1952), part 4, p. 629. Hereafter cited as *Hearings*.

11. Józef Czapski, *Wspomnienia Starobielskie* (Memoirs of Starobelsk). Italia: Oddział Kultury i Prasy 2 Korpusu, Biblioteka Orła Białego, 1945, *passim;* also by the same author *Na Nieludzkiej Ziemi* (The inhuman land) (Paris: Instytut Literacki, 1949), pp. 102-106.

12. For a photostatic copy of the original memorandum and its English translation see *Hearings*, part 4, pp. 944-950.

13. Stanisław Kot, *Rozmowy z Kremlem* (My conferences with the Kremlin) (London: Jutro Polski, 1959), pp. 79-81—see note 21; 85-86; 88-89; 94-95; 105; 116-117; 125-127; 294. Stanisław Kot, *Listy z Rosji do Gen. Sikorskiego* (Letters from Russia to Gen. Sikorski) (London: Jutro Polski, 1956), p. 61; Ambassador's telegram to General Anders, p. 275; telegram to the Polish Embassy in Washington, pp. 283-284; telegram to General Sikorski, pp. 294-295; telegrams to General Sikorski concerning American and British Ambassadors in Moscow, p. 323.

Significant excerpts from Ambassador Kot's personal verbal and written inquiries addressed to Stalin, Molotov, and Vyshinsky are available in English in the following source: Poland. Polish Government-in-Exile. *Report on the Massacre of Polish Officers in Katyn Wood. Facts and Documents.* For private circulation only (London: 1946), pp. 18-30.

14. Captain Józef Czapski's statements since 1942 on the subject of the missing men show remarkable consistency. There is no reason to doubt their veracity. *Polish Report*, pp. 195-206; *Death at Katyn: An Account of a Survivor*. 3rd edn. (New York: National Committee of Americans of Polish Descent, 1944), pp. 1-48, *passim;* Czapski, *Na Nieludzkiej Ziemi* (The inhuman land), pp. 133-144; *Hearings*, part 5, pp. 1230-1244; Czapski, *Wspomnienia Starobielskie* (Memoirs of Starobelsk), *passim*.

15. *Hearings*, part 4, p. 618.

16. Diplomatic correspondence between the Polish and Soviet governments on the subject of the missing prisoners, *M.S.Z.*, pp. 54, 59, 106, 307, 317; also 51, 60, 81, 135, 175, 115.

17. *Polish Report*, pp. 180-181. Verified with Ambassador Kot's notes. Kot, *Rozmowy z Kremlem* (My conferences with the Kremlin), pp. 126-127.

18. Minutes Sikorski-Stalin meeting, *M.S.Z.*, pp. 81-95.

19. Admiral William H. Standley and Rear Admiral Arthur A. Ageton, "Murder, or High Strategy? The U.S. Embassy, the Kremlin, and the Katyn Forest Massacre," *United States Naval Institute Proceedings*, LXXVIII, no. 10, 1056-1057.

20. *Polish Report*, p. 211, note 1; pp. 172, 222.

21. Czapski, *Na Nieludzkiej Ziemi* (The inhuman land), pp. 131-133; Józef Czapski, "*Znów Katyń*" (Katyn Again), *Kultura*, no. 3/173, Marzec 1962, p. 6.

22. *Hearings*, part 4, p. 661.

II

The Graves in the Forest

IN THE PERSONAL diary of the German Minister of Propaganda, Goebbels, the following entry may be found under the date of April 9, 1943: "Polish mass graves have been found near Smolensk. The Bolsheviks simply shot down and then shoveled into mass graves some 10,000 Polish prisoners...."[1] Presumably it was a German war correspondent who had brought the gruesome discovery to Goebbels' attention. On April 13, 1943, at 9:15 a.m., New York time, the German radio broadcast a propaganda broadside aimed at cracking the unity of the Allies. It announced to the world that Polish officers had been murdered by the Soviets. On the basis of the German statements, it appeared that one Allied government had murdered nearly half of the officers' corps of another.

The Soviet response, after two days, was disseminated by all possible means of public communication. The Soviet Information Bureau issued a statement April 15, 1943, announcing that "... Polish prisoners-of-war who in 1941 were engaged in construction work west of Smolensk and who ... fell into the hands of the German-Fascist hangmen ..." had subsequently been executed.[2] A Soviet reconnaissance plane appeared above the territory where the Germans had discovered the graves and hovered over the area.[3]

The Katyn Forest lies about ten miles west of Smolensk. The area originally belonged to two families: Koźlinski and

Lednicki. The latter had owned the land from 1896 to 1917. After the Revolution of 1917 the area was under the jurisdiction of Soviet political police. According to German and Polish sources, about 1929, signs were posted around the forest, "Special zone of G.P.U. Unauthorized persons forbidden to trespass." [4] In 1931 one area of the forest was encircled with barbed wire, and according to Soviet citizens living in the vicinity "additional warning posters were hung." A large house was built (approximately half a mile from the site of the graves) which was used as a rest home for officials of the political police. From 1940 until the Soviet withdrawal the whole area was patrolled by N.K.V.D. men with dog escorts.

In 1941 the area was seized by German troops and at the time of the discovery of the graves, February 1943, a German unit was billeted in the former N.K.V.D. villa. Immediately after the discovery of the graves the German Military Field Police, with propaganda officials discreetly lurking in the background, took command.

No one who had lived under the German occupation was apt to believe the German description of the discovery, nor would the Allies. At the time of discovery about half a million Poles were fighting against Germany.[5] Their contribution to the war effort was well known among the free peoples. The Poles were appealing throughout the Allied camp for facts.

Public opinion pointed an accusing finger at the Germans. The fact the men had been killed with German-made bullets induced the German Government to invite an independent International Commission, the Polish Red Cross Commission, and the German Special Medical-Judiciary Commission to make a study on the spot. Moreover, if the guilt could be shifted to the Soviet Government, a rift between the Polish Government-in-Exile and the Soviet Government would follow and the Allies might be hopelessly split. Toward that purpose Himmler (Chief of the German Police and SS) and Goebbels bent all efforts.[6]

The International Commission was drawn from twelve countries other than Germany. The participants consisted of distinguished scholars and specialists in forensic medicine. There is no evidence to indicate that these men were pro-Nazi or that they were under pressure to participate in the Commission. (Postwar testimony of the Commission's members concerning the findings is discussed in Chapter IX.) Members included: Belgium, Dr. Speleers, University of Ghent; Bulgaria, Dr. Markov, University of Sofia; Denmark, Dr. Tramsen, Institute of Medicine, Copenhagen; Finland, Dr. Saxen, Helsinki University; Italy, Dr. Palmieri, University of Naples; Croatia, Dr. Miloslavich, University of Agram; Netherlands, Dr. de Burlet, University of Groningen; Czechoslovakia, Dr. Hajek, Charles University; Czechoslovakia, Dr. Subik, University of Bratislava; Romania, Dr. Birkle, Institute of Criminology and Medicine at Bucharest; Switzerland, Dr. Naville, University of Geneva; Hungary, Dr. Orsos, University of Budapest; and France, Dr. Costedoat, Medical Inspector of the Vichy Government. Dr. Orsos was elected chairman of the International Commission by his colleagues.[7]

The International Commission arrived at the Katyn Forest on April 28, 1943.[8] The Germans on the spot provided all necessary staff and facilities.[9] The members of the Commission had complete freedom of movement and were permitted to choose any corpse they wished for autopsy.[10] The members of the Commission interviewed Soviet citizens living in the vicinity of Katyn Forest, performed autopsies on nine bodies previously untouched and also examined 982 bodies already exhumed for them, and finally signed a medical report summarizing their findings.[11]

At approximately the same time a nine-person medical team (subsequently increased to twelve) of the Polish Red Cross from occupied Poland was allowed by Germans to carry on its own investigation at the spot.[12] The findings of this team are of particular importance for two reasons. First, its members were, in fact, extremely suspicious (having lived under the German occupation for the preceding three years) of German concern for Poles, living or dead. Second, there were in this team, unknown to the Germans and the rest of the group, members of the Polish Underground Movement, whose assignment was to gather data concerning the identity of the murderers and to dispatch it through the Underground radio system to the Polish Government-in-Exile in London.[13] In addition to the medical team, other officials of the Polish Red Cross were brought to the spot, and all were given Red Cross arm bands and freedom to move about, touch, inquire and take photographs. Nevertheless, the Poles persistently refused to be involved in any activity which might play into the hands of the German propaganda organization, such as, for example, speaking on the radio or making anti-Soviet statements.[14] The German authorities tried to persuade the Polish delegates to tour the camps of the Polish prisoners-of-war in Germany and to lecture about Katyn. This the Poles also refused to do. Possibly as a consequence of the failure of this strategy, the Germans transported to Katyn Forest by plane delegations of Polish and other Allied prisoners-of-war. These visits of the Polish prisoners failed to change their anti-German attitude, to the chagrin of German authorities.[15] With the Underground's approval, at least two Polish journalists and some civic leaders took advantage of German permission and transportation facilities to take a firsthand look at the place of the murder and the victims.[16] The Poles wanted to be sure that this was not one of Herr Goebbels' hoaxes. However, the graves were actually there.

Besides the International Commission and that of the Polish Red Cross, a German Special Medical-Judiciary Commission was also active. Members of the three commissions acted independently during the investigations, and arrived independently at conclusions stated in their three separate final reports.[17] Since the reports coincide in the most important details, the following description of the findings in Katyn Forest is based on all these reports, with pertinent supplements gathered from other sources.

In Katyn Forest eight mass graves were found, in depth from six to eleven feet, filled with bodies. Generally, there had been a particular system in their burial. They were lying face down, hands beside or tied behind their bodies, legs straight, one upon another in ten to twelve layers of corpses. Without exception all of the men had been shot in the back of the head. In most cases, the men had been shot once. There were some who had been shot twice; and in one case a man's skull was crushed by three shots. As a rule, the entry of the bullet was above the neck, its course upward, the bullet leaving the skull on the face side between nose and hair line. Two individual graves were located; and in them two fully uniformed Polish generals were found, each shot as the men had been. Microscopic analysis of the uniforms, with the assistance of infra-red rays, established that the men had been executed by firing a revolver against the raised collar of each victim's winter coat or directly against his head.

Many of the corpses, particularly the cadets and younger men, had their hands tied. An eyewitness to the exhumations reported:

> A typical feature of the bodies exhumed from this grave [No. 5] was the fact of the hands of all of them being tied behind their backs with a white cord tied in a double knot. Their greatcoats were tied round their heads. These greatcoats were tied with the same kind of cord at the neck level and sometimes a second knot had been made over the head of the victim. At the neck there was a simple knot and the rest of the cord was passed down the back, wound round the tied hands and then tied again at the neck. In this way the hands of the victims were pulled up to the height of the shoulder blades. Victims tied up in this way were unable to give any resistance because every move of the hands tightened the

noose round the neck thereby throttling them. They were besides, unable to make any sound on account of the greatcoats over their heads . . . such a way of tying up the victims before execution was inflicting especially refined torture before death.[18]

The technique of tying the knots was identical in all instances. The ropes were evidently methodically prepared in advance, since all of them were of the same length. Microscopic analysis of the rope—made by a German scientist on the spot—showed it to be Soviet-made. The same kind of knots was found on the bodies of several men and women dressed in the remnants of garments of Soviet origin, who also were found in a separate common grave in Katyn Forest. Close examination of these cadavers established that the persons had been killed in the same manner between five and ten years earlier—many years before the Germans had come to this area.

The mouths of some of the Poles were filled with sawdust and also with pieces of felt with strings attached at each side and passed around the cheeks.[19]

Gagged, bound, blinded by their coats thrown over their heads, the officers apparently had struggled, until subdued by thrusts of bayonets. On body number 378, identified as Lieutenant Stefan Mejster, holes from a bayonet were quite visible on the coat, jacket, two shirts, and on the arms, thighs, and the buttocks. They evidently had to be overpowered and held while the executioner shot them, otherwise the death wounds would not be so uniform on all victims. The bayonet thrusts could be easily detected and the members of the medical teams investigated these under microscopes. The wounds and holes in the material were made by four cornered bayonets. It was observed that this type of bayonet was used by the Soviet Army at that time.[20]

Intermingled with the members of the medical commissions, Allied prisoners brought to Katyn, and visitors from Poland, were foreign correspondents from Sweden, Switzerland, Spain, Norway, Holland, Belgium and Hungary, not to mention Germany. All of them moved about freely. Mr. Jaederlunt, a Swedish citizen representing the *Stockholm Tidningen* in Germany, even borrowed a saddle horse and rode in the forest without "being hampered or hindered by anyone." [21] There were many observers eager to find evidence that the German discoverers had committed the massacre. The Poles, particularly, expected the graves to yield some data which would abolish the German accusation. At this time, the Soviet Government was unable to defend itself with facts, since it did not have access to the graves.

Meanwhile the graves were giving up their evidence. The bodies were separated with iron hooks, shovels, "even picks." They had been compressed by their own weight and adhered to each other with the acids of decomposition. Each body was lifted out of the grave, given a separate number, and, according to an American officer brought to the graves as a prisoner of war, "... was searched very carefully, examined, and identified.... The articles removed from each body were placed in a large manila envelope for safekeeping. A search of the bodies was very thorough.... A typist was present recording the findings on each body." [22]

The identity of the murdered men could be established because in the pockets of their uniforms a wealth of personal data was found. The Polish Red Cross Report itemizes the types of documentary data recovered. "... Statements of typhoid injections received in a Soviet camp, personal identification documents, diaries, letters ... military aluminum identification tags, personal cards, sketches, photographs...." [23] On the basis of these materials it was rather easy to ascertain the first and second name, rank, age, profession, home address, and even, as the Report pointed out, the religious faith of the victim. The Poles present at the exhumations ascertained beyond any doubt that the documents were authentic and that they could not have been inserted prior to their visit to the graves. Bodies were removed from the graves in the presence of the Poles and members of other medical commissions, and the soggy documents were taken from the pockets. On many occasions a slit had to be made through the pockets with a thin knife, to free the papers.[24] Many Soviet daily newspapers were found on the bodies.

It was expected that there would be personal jewelry such as watches, rings, golden trinkets, or fountain pens, on the bodies, but nothing of this sort was found unless hidden in seams or in boots. Were these soldiers even robbed before their death? Or did the men change their criteria of values while imprisoned and exchange gold for something which was of more immediate importance?[25] Some of the findings were touchingly universal in their appeal. Children's letters, pictures of women with graceful, longing dedications, and assurances of love. There were also some mementos the importance of which was known only to the dead man, such as a pass to a popular Warsaw movie-house, the "Apollo," found on body number 810. The men evidently had clung to anything which was identified with their own country and their past, and the past of many of them was full of personal achievements and distinction not only in military service. Among the identified there were several hundred lawyers, hundreds of high school and elementary school teachers, twenty-one university professors, over 300 doctors, journalists, and even a priest.[26] As the Polish source points out, they were the flower of the Polish intelligentsia who had done their duty in uniform as reserve officers. There was even the body of a woman among the murdered men. She was a lieutenant of the Polish Air Force. After being captured by the Soviet Army, she had been detained together with other Polish officers and was found shot in Katyn.[27]

Here are three examples of the identified and catalogued bodies:

1) Major Stefan Pieńkowski, M.D., professor at Kraków

University. Possessions on the body: identification card, fishing license, three post cards, and a diary.

2) General Bronisław Bohatyrewicz. A personal letter, two pictures. (Found in a separate single grave.)

3) Naval officer Edwin Finger, Manager of the technical department of the Vacuum Oil Company in Warsaw. Driver's license, a picture, one gold cuff link.[28]

Although the bayonet thrusts were made by weapons manufactured in the Soviet Union, the bullets were of German manufacture. Goebbels was not comfortable about this. In his diary under the entry of May 8, 1943, he wrote: "Unfortunately, German munitions were found in the graves of Katyn. The question of how they got there needs clarification." [29]

The ammunition used by the executioners was Geco caliber 7.65 (in some cases 6.35). It was produced in Germany by the factory belonging to Gustav Genschow in Durlach. German Ordance speedily established that this type of ammunition was produced by the Genschow Company and was exported from Germany to Poland, the Baltic states, and the Soviet Union prior to 1939.[30] Polish sources confirmed the exports to Poland. Nevertheless, these calibers were also used in Germany.

The establishment of the date of the massacre was the crux of the whole investigation. The Soviet Government controlled the Katyn area until the late summer of 1941. At that time the German Army seized it. If it could be determined *when* the men were shot, the identity of the executioners would be known. Had the bodies been in the graves not longer than about twenty months, it could be assumed that the Germans committed the crime. Had the bodies been longer in the graves, it would appear that the government of the Soviet Union was responsible.

The findings of the three commissions agree that the men

were killed and buried about *three* years before the exhumations, in approximately the spring of 1940, or a little more than one year prior to the outbreak of the German-Soviet war, when the area belonged to the Soviet Union and the forest was under the jurisdiction of the N.K.V.D.

This conclusion was based on the medical examination of the bodies, particularly the decalcification of the skulls and brains and the saponification of muscles, and the most recent date found in diaries, Soviet newspapers and the documents issued by Soviet authorities—May 6, 1940. Also, after the burial of the men, spruce had been planted on the graves to hide the crime. These were considerably younger in appearance than the trees around them. Microscopic examination of cross sections of the spruce trunks showed equal annual growth in the three outer rings, while between these lines and the heart of the trees was a dark border, which according to the testimony of an expert forester named Von Herff in 1943, showed that the young trees had been transplanted on the graves at least three years before. Again the spring of 1940 is indicated. This man, testifying under oath nine years later, repeated his findings with conviction.[31]

According to the German Commission the number of bodies was 4,143; according to the Polish Red Cross Commission—4,243. To this number about 200 bodies from the partially excavated grave number 8 ought to be added in making a total of approximately 4,443 bodies.[32] The majority were officers. Privates and twenty-two men in civilian clothing were also found.

A striking fact was discovered through collation of the data: the men in the graves were from the Soviet prisoner-of-war Camp Kozelsk. The names of the murdered men corresponded with the names on the lists so persistently submitted to the Soviet authorities by the Poles. So, at last, about one third of the missing men was found.

The number of bodies discovered was not convenient for

the German propaganda purposes. Knowing that the Poles were searching for about 15,000 men, they originally had set the number of their findings as 10,000 (or in some announcements 12,000) men. A German propaganda official insisted that the Polish Red Cross Committee should give the final figure of exhumed bodies as 12,000, stating quite bluntly that the refusal "may cost one's head." Nevertheless, the Poles refused. The International Commission was not exposed to such pressures;[33] moreover, its sole assignment was to establish the cause and date of the death.

Up to the last days of the investigation the Germans employed some fifty Soviet prisoners to dig and search for other graves in the area. But more graves were not found and more bodies could not be produced, embarrassing the German propaganda effort and disproving the original claims of "10,000-12,000" murdered.

The approaching Soviet counter-offensive, "millions of flies," and a heavy choking stench were announced as the official reasons for suspending the investigation. It is also quite possible that these reasons were used merely as an excuse, allowing the German propagandists a way out. The exhumations ended on June 3, and the last bodies were buried on June 7, 1943. The International Commission had spent three days at the Katyn Forest; the Polish Red Cross Commission, five weeks.

The peace of the new graves was not to last long. Soviet motorized columns were moving toward the Katyn Forest.

NOTES TO CHAPTER II

1. Germany. Joseph Goebbels, *The Goebbels Diaries, 1942-1943* (in German). Microfilm copy of typewritten manuscript. Made by the University of California. Library Photographic Service. Positive. Collation of the original. 6792 pp. On six reels. Also *The Goebbels Diaries, 1942-1943*. Edited and translated and with introduction by

Louis P. Lochner. 1st edn. (Garden City, N. Y.: Doubleday Co., 1948), p. 318. For the convenience of the English-speaking reader Lochner's translations will be cited. These were verified against the original Goebbels diaries at the Hoover Institution, Stanford, California, and found to be reliable. (Original manuscript, April 9, 1943, p. 11.) In the following pages this source will be cited as *Goebbels Diaries*.

2. *Pravda* (Moscow), April 16, 1943, p. 1; U.S.S.R. Soviet Embassy in London. *Soviet War News*, April 17, 1943, p. 4; *Daily Worker*, London, April 18, 1943, pp. 1, 4. Compare with *Völkischer Beobachter*. Süddeutsche Ausgabe. April 15, 16, 17, 18, 19, 29, 30; May 5, 6, 22, 29, 30; June 6, 1943, *passim*.

3. *Hearings*, part 5, p. 1567.

4. The peasants living in the area were acutely aware of this, since they could not gather either mushrooms or wood in that part of the forest.

5. *P.S.Z.*, vols. I, II and III.

6. Germany. *Reichsführer SS und Chef der deutschen Polizei. Persönlicher Stab. Schriftgutverwaltung* (Reichsführer SS and Chief of the German Police. Personal staff. Document administration). Himmler Files 3. Photostatic copies. Folder n. 277, pages numbered 7217-7229; *Goebbels Diaries, passim*.

7. *Hearings*, part 5, p. 1601. It may be added that Dr. Orsos, long before the discovery of the graves at Katyn, had advanced a theory that on the basis of decalcification of the brain the time of death might be established with relative precision. He had published a work on this subject in Hungarian two years prior to his arrival at Katyn.

8. Germany. *Amtliches Material zum Massenmord von Katyn* (Official material concerning the Katyn Massacre). Im Auftrage des Auswärtigen Amtes auf Grund urkundlichen Beweismaterials zusammengestellt, bearbeitet und herausgegeben von der Deutschen Informationsstelle. (Berlin: Zentralverlag der NSDAP, F. Eher Nachf., 1943), pp. 114-135. In the following pages this source will be cited as *German Report*.

9. Dr. Tramsen's testimony. *Hearings*, part 5, p. 1443.

10. *Ibid.*, p. 1589.

11. Report of the International Medical Commission, included in *German Report*, pp. 114-135.

12. *Polish Report*, pp. 229-234.

13. Certified English translations of the pertinent radiograms can be found in *Hearings*, part 4, pp. 712-718; Testimony of Kazimierz Skarżyński, Secretary General of the Polish Red Cross at that time, *Hearings*, part 3, pp. 384-415; Kazimierz Skarżyński, "Katyń i Polski Czerwony Krzyż" (Katyn and the Polish Red Cross), *Kultura*, no. 9/51, May 1955, pp. 127-141.

14. Skarżyński, *ibid.*, p. 135; Kazimierz Skarżyński. Secretary Gen-

eral of the Polish Red Cross 1939-1945. *Krótki Zarys Losów Polskiego Czerwonego Krzyża w Polsce Podczas Okupacji Niemieckiej* (A brief outline of the history of the Polish Red Cross during the German occupation of Poland 1939-45). Manuscript from the personal archives of Mr. Skarżyński. Made available to the author in January 1961, 3 cards; Kazimierz Skarżyński. *List do por. Heizmana w Sprawie Projektu Roztoczenia Sprawy Katyńskiej na Forum Publicznym* (A letter to Ltn. Heizman concerning presentation of the Katyn affair to the general public). Manuscript from the personal archives of Mr. Skarżyński. Made available to the author in January 1961, 4 cards; Kazimierz Skarżyński. *Oświadczenie, Złożone Przezemnie w Sądzie Polowym Polskim w Londynie, we Wrześniu 1946 r* (Testimony submitted by me to the Polish Military Court in London, September 1946). Manuscript from the personal archives of Mr. Skarżyński. Made available to the author in January 1961, 11 cards; Kazimierz Skarżyński. *Polski Czerwony Krzyż w Katyniu* (The [mission of the] Polish Red Cross at the Katyn [Forest]). Manuscript from the personal archives of Mr. Skarżyński. Made available to the author in January 1961, 82 cards.

15. *Polish Report*, pp. 22-223.

16. A Polish journalist, Józef Mackiewicz, presently living outside Poland, periodically writes on the subject of the Katyn massacre. See bibliography for his book and articles. His impressions from the visit at the graves are to be found in English translation in Joseph Mackiewicz, *The Katyn Wood Murders* (London: Hollis and Carter, 1951), pp. 137-165.

17. International Medical Commission Report, full text, *German Report*, pp. 114-135; Polish Red Cross Commission, full text, *Hearings*, part 6, Exhibit 32, pp. 1806-1819; German Special Medical-Judiciary Commission, full text, *German Report*, pp. 38-113.

18. *Hearings*, part 6, Exhibit 32, p. 1817.

19. Testimony of a doctor, member of the Polish Red Cross Commission, verified with the observations of members of the other two commissions. *Polish Report, passim.*

20. There are eighty pictures available from the exhumation, medical autopsies and laboratory analysis. Also see *German Report:* manner of death, pp. 107-113, 303-306, 308; hands tied, pp. 309-312; bayonet thrusts, p. 313.

21. *Hearings*, part 5, p. 1566.

22. U.S. Department of Defense. Office of Public Information. *Katyn Case.* Release no. 1141-50, September 1950, p. 3.

23. The Report of the Polish Red Cross, signed by Dr. Marian Wodzinski; section 12; *Zbrodnia Katyńska w Świetle Dokumentów* (The Katyn crime in the light of documents). Z przedmową Władysława Andersa. 2-gie wydanie. (London: Gryf, 1950), p. 292.

24. A German citizen, Albert Pfeiffer, then a member of the Ger-

man military police, was engaged in this particular task. He testified under oath on April 22, 1952, during the Congressional hearings, that members of the Polish Red Cross were also engaged with him on this job. It is easy to understand why the Poles put their own men with Pfeiffer—they wanted to be sure that materials such as Soviet news, etc., could not be planted in the pockets by German staff. Hearings, part 5, p. 1319.

25. See chapter VI.
26. *Hearings*, part 6, Exhibit 32, p. 1645.
27. Eyewitness report of the exhumation of her body, Mackiewicz, *op. cit.*, p. 128.
28. Adam Moszyński, *Lista Katyńska. Jeńcy Obozów Kozielsk, Starobielsk, Ostaszków, Zaginieni w Rosji Sowieckiej* (The roll of Katyn. The prisoners of the camps Kozelsk, Starobelsk, Ostashkov who disappeared in Soviet Russia) (London: Gryf, 1949), pp. 132, 24, 47.
29. *Goebbels Diaries*, p. 354. (Original ms., May 8, 1943, pp. 12-13.)
30. *German Report*, p. 75; see also Karl Genschow's testimony, *Hearings*, part 5, pp. 1577-1580.
31. *Hearings*, part 5, pp. 1491-1495.
32. The Commission of the Polish Red Cross gives the number of bodies as 4,243. The difference is 100. The reason for this discrepancy lies in the fact that prior to the arrival of the Commission, the Germans had disinterred about 100 bodies. These were not given serial numbers. The circumstances pertinent to this discrepancy are explained in *Hearings*, part 6, Exhibit 32, pp. 1750-1752; also in Exhibit 33, pp. 1819-1823. In this connection, there are some contradictions in the *Polish Report* and the Exhibits submitted to the Congressional Committee of the United States Congress. Accepting the number 4,443 as the number suggested by the Polish sources, it is the author's opinion that (1) Katyn Forest either hides an additional grave (or graves) of about 300-350 prisoners from Camp Kozelsk, (2) grave number 8 had more than the estimated 200 bodies in it, or, (3) the estimates of the Commissions were not precise. These observations are submitted to the reader, without depreciating the value of the difficult task performed by the International, Polish and German Commissions. See also chapter VI below, also note 1, pp. 94-95.
33. See pp. 177-178 below.

III

The Inconvenient Allies— Alive and Dead

WHEN THE DISCOVERY of the graves in Katyn was announced, I was in Warsaw. It was generally believed by the Poles that this was a hoax to drive a wedge between the Soviet Union and the other Allies and that Goebbels was wielding the hammer. Then the first list of names and the pictures appeared in the daily (German-controlled) paper.[1] The name-lists were read in radio broadcasts.[2] The Polish delegations returned from Katyn spreading their observations.[3] It was true! The Underground community had its own sources at the scene for verification—they confirmed. The crescendo of German propaganda might as well not have existed. The Underground knew for certain that the Polish prisoners-of-war had been killed on Soviet territory. But by whom?

The names of sons, fathers, brothers and fiancés were identified by families from lists that came out daily. Public opinion demanded justice. Appearances were persuasive, but those Poles who were levelheaded, while convinced that the men had been shot, still were not sure as to the identity of those who had killed them.

The Polish Red Cross was deluged with letters from families wanting to bring the bodies to Poland for burial, asking for documents, and inquiring about the men missing from the other two Soviet camps, Starobelsk and Ostashkov.[4]

The German press in Poland kept Katyn before Polish public opinion every day from April 14 until August 4 of 1943. According to this press "the Jews did it!!" Jews were guilty of everything—even the Allied strength.

Of course, the Katyn affair and official German compassion for Poles did not stop daily executions and manhunts by the German police on the streets of Warsaw. The Germans' pathological hate for Polish citizens of Jewish origin exploded in Warsaw in a manner no less cruel than Katyn. On April 19, 1943, the mass murder in the Warsaw ghetto commenced. It lasted for four weeks.

These were the circumstances in which the German propaganda was telling the Poles that the Soviet Union was the only menace and the Germans were their real protectors.

The German administration was of such a character that their propaganda failed to convince.[5] The Poles did not take the bait, did not officially collaborate with Germany in any area, and they refused to blame the Soviet Union for the Katyn Forest massacre, but they wanted to know who had done it, and were desperate in their intent to determine who had killed the prisoners.

Poles looked to Churchill and Roosevelt to see that truth and justice should triumph. The Underground radio stations pulsated with messages to the Polish Government-in-Exile. The occupied country demanded justice; the government in London had to act.

During the same period, German propaganda outside Poland was aimed at creating division among the Allies. Himmler wanted to accomplish this by contacting Poles in London and maneuvering them into direct accusation of the Soviet Union. Von Ribbentrop, the German Minister of Foreign Affairs, had a more sophisticated plan. Whatever the Polish reaction might be, German propaganda would provide "evidence" that it was instigated by the English Government. In this way the Katyn affair not only would split Soviet-Polish but also Soviet-British relations. Goebbels was elated. Hitler himself ordered that "the affair be given widest possible use."

On April 14, 1943, a relatively unkown German public official named Bohle wrote Himmler a "strictly secret" letter proposing that General Sikorski, the head of the Polish Government-in-Exile, be invited to inspect Katyn as a private person, and that representatives of the Allied governments be invited also. It was obvious, Bohle said, that the Allies would refuse to come, and that they also would prevent Sikorski's coming, even if he wanted to come. This might provide some material for propaganda to further assist in splitting the Allies. Himmler acknowledged the letter politely but with the air of a man who knows it all. He was pleased with the idea "particularly since myself, I have already thought about it ...," he wrote. Eight days later Himmler wrote to Ribbentrop, "It occurred to me ...," then repeated what had been, basically, Bohle's suggestion.

Herr Ribbentrop was cool to the idea. In his reply dated April 26, 1943, he admitted that such propaganda could gain some advantage. However, he pointed out that the principles guiding German foreign policy in regard to the Polish Government-in-Exile were such that they prevented any contacts with the Poles. These principles were so important that they could not be impaired for "immediate gains of propaganda." [6]

On April 19, 1943, a member of Ribbentrop's personal staff named Megerle sent a codified telegram to the German legations in Budapest and Geneva requesting them to look for "about four" Poles among the emigrés, who would be willing to go to Katyn, and give at least an outward impression of co-operating with German authorities. The telegram specified that they ought to have "anti-bolshevik or anti-Semitic convictions." [7] Officials at the legations sought in vain among thousands of Polish emigrés in Switzerland and Hungary to find even four willing to play such a role.

Meanwhile, the Poles in London acted, even before the first

radiograms sent by the Underground members in the Polish Red Cross Commission reached them.[8] It is quite possible that they had been prodded by a special telegram sent on April 15, 1943, at 7 p.m. by General Anders (who by this time had been evacuated with his army from the Soviet Union to the Middle East). In this telegram the general requested the government "to intervene in this affair with the object of obtaining official explanations from the Soviets, especially as our soldiers are convinced that the rest of our people in the U.S.S.R. will also be exterminated."[9] The soldiers were fearful about their families still in the Soviet Union. The Polish-language press in London was hopeful that "this terrible news taken up by the German propaganda will turn out—as it often has been the case in the past—to be lies."[10] On the same day, April 15, 1943, the Polish Government-in-Exile in a closed meeting decided to appeal to the International Red Cross in Geneva for an impartial investigation. The *Daily Telegraph's* diplomatic correspondent reported it the next day, and that same evening Reuters International News Agency (Globe-reuter) published the decision.[11] On April 17, 1943, one day *after* the press reported it, the Polish Minister of National Defense issued a communiqué in which he, after restating the whole problem and circumstances of the disappearance of the Polish prisoners in the Soviet Union, informed the public of the decision to appeal to the International Red Cross for investigation.[12] The fact that a correspondent had learned this decision one day prior to its official announcement was to have fatal diplomatic consequences for the Polish Government-in-Exile.

On the day of the Minister's announcement (April 17, 1943) at 4:30 p.m., a representative of the Polish Red Cross delegate in Geneva called on Mr. Reuger, an official of the International Red Cross, and handed him the formal request of the Polish Government for the investigation of the Katyn massacre. To his astonishment he was informed that less than an hour before the German delegate had done the same.[13] To outside observers this would appear to be Polish-German co-operation. The Soviet Government was waiting for this kind of a situation.

Actually, the Poles had not co-operated with the German Government. After the Reuter agency announced on April 16 the decision of the Polish Government to appeal to the International Red Cross, Goebbels, who had a daily evaluation of the Allied press submitted to him, reported this to Hitler. Both of them saw an occasion to embarrass the Poles and to create a vehement reaction on the part of the Soviet Government. Hitler sent instructions to issue "at once" a *second* German invitation to the International Red Cross.[14] The Germans had first sent an invitation on April 15, 1943, by wire and had already received a reply two days *before* the Polish representative appeared at the offices of the International Red Cross in Geneva. The second German invitation was timed to coincide with the Polish action.[15] (Though it is possible that the Poles knew from their representatives in Geneva that the Germans had appealed to the International Red Cross, there is no evidence that they acted in concert.)

The answers from the International Red Cross came quite promptly. Both governments, German and Polish, were told in separate letters that this institution was "prepared to give assistance by selecting neutral experts, *on the condition that similar appeals were received from all parties interested in this question*"[16]—meaning if the Soviet Government also extended an invitation.

However, the Soviet Government was silent and did not request an investigation. Instead, an officer of the Soviet diplomatic corps in London approached the Polish Minister of Information (Professor Kot, the former Polish envoy to Moscow), asking "on instructions from Kremlin" that the Polish Government publish a statement that the Katyn massacre was committed by the Germans.[17] This the Poles refused to do.

The Soviet daily *Pravda* on April 19, 1943, exploded the fuse so carefully prepared by Hitler, Goebbels, and Ribbentrop. The title of *Pravda's* editorial indicated its content—"Hitler's Polish Collaborators!" In it the Polish Minister of Defense was charged with "direct and obvious help to the Hitlerite provocateurs." In respect to the Polish request for the investigation addressed to the International Red Cross, the Poles were called "Polish assistants"of the "German provocateurs."

The Soviet Government emphasized the fact that the Polish delegate had appeared on the same day as the German (handing the second invitation), using this as evidence of Polish-German collaboration. The Soviet accusations that these Poles were collaborating with the Germans were picked up by the pro-Soviet press abroad.[18] For the Poles, who since 1939 had supplied to the Supreme Allied Command over one-half million soldiers in the Underground and on all Allied fronts (France, Norway, Africa, Battle of Britain, Italy, etc.), this accusation was hard to stomach. The Polish press-in-exile took a defensive attitude. It pointed out that the Soviet Union had not joined in the request for an investigation by the International Red Cross and pressed for answers as to what had happened to the rest of the Polish prisoners who had disappeared.

As the problem of the disappearance of 15,000 Allied officers and men arose, on April 21 Stalin sent "personal and secret" messages to Prime Minister Churchill and President Roosevelt. The texts of the messages were identical. Because the anti-Soviet campaign had started simultaneously in the German and Polish press and followed similar lines, this was "an indubitable evidence of contact and collusion between Hitler . . . and the Sikorski Government. . . . The Sikorski Government is striking a treacherous blow at the Soviet Union. . . . " The letters continued: "These circumstances compel the Soviet Government to consider that *the present Polish*

Government, having descended to collusion with the Hitler Government has, in practice, severed its relations of alliance with the U.S.S.R. and adopted a hostile attitude to the Soviet Union. For this reason the Soviet Government has decided to interrupt relations with that Government." [19] Although the basis for a breach of relations sounded rather weak, Stalin had one point which, in terms of diplomatic procedure, could be annoying to him as head of the Soviet Government. The Polish Government had not inquired directly of the Soviet Union about the *facts* relating to Katyn. Stalin was justified in resenting this. "The Sikorski Government has not found it necessary even to address questions to the Soviet Government or to request information on the matter," he complained.[20] The Poles, as a matter of fact, had addressed a note in this spirit to the Soviet Government on April 17, but the note was not handed to the Soviet Ambassador until three days later— for "technical reasons," they said [21] —which means that they officially delivered the note *after* they had approached the International Red Cross requesting an impartial investigation. The Poles were engaged in "politicking" themselves.

One has to realize that from the fall of 1941 until the discovery of the Katyn graves in April 1943 the Polish Government was continually addressing notes, inquiries and letters through formal and informal channels asking the Soviet Government about the missing men. The total number of these inquiries on both formal and informal levels was well over 200. The answers elicited had yielded no results. Consequently they had decided to appeal as it were, to "a higher court," an international agency of repute, to ascertain the facts. Why did they appeal to the Red Cross first and inquire of the Soviet Government later? Here was a politically shrewd step on the part of the Poles. They gauged quite well what would be the answer of the Soviet Government—the Russians would maintain, as they in fact did, that the German Government committed the crime. If the Poles then appealed to the International

Red Cross, the Soviet Union would charge them with lack of faith, disbelieving another ally, etc. By notifying the Red Cross first, the Poles hoped to avoid the trap of challenging openly the statement of the Soviet Government. But they were vulnerable from any angle.

Churchill, in response to Stalin's letter, used reasonable arguments pleading for unity and denying Stalin's accusations that the Poles had collaborated with Hitler. He was disappointed that Stalin had not consulted him before undertaking such an important step as breaking diplomatic relations. He pointed out that the exiles had been and still were willing to co-operate with the Soviet Government. At the same time he slammed his fist into the agitated Poles. "I am examining the possibility of silencing those Polish newspapers in this country [England] which attacked the Soviet Government," he wrote.[22] Subsequently, the Polish press in England was forbidden to express hostility to the Soviet Union, and Churchill advised Sikorski to make no further inquiries about the missing men. "If they are dead, nothing you can do will bring them back." [23] Roosevelt's reaction was along similar lines. He assured Stalin that he could not "believe that Sikorski has in any way whatsoever collaborated with the Hitler gangsters. In my opinion, however, he has erred in taking up this particular question with the International Red Cross." [24] But, Stalin was not to be deterred from his course of action.

At 12:15 a.m. on April 26, 1943, the Polish Ambassador in the Soviet Union, Mr. Romer, was summoned to the Commissariat for Foreign Affairs, where Mr. Molotov read to him a note reiterating mainly the points covered in Stalin's letters to Churchill and Roosevelt and, after bluntly denouncing the Polish Government for "contact and accord" with Hitler, notified him that "on the strength of the above, the Soviet Government has decided to sever relations with the Polish Government." [25] The alert ambassador refused to accept such a note, informing Molotov that it was "couched in language no ambassador can receive." This was the argument of the weaker party and was treated as such. After returning to his hotel, Mr. Romer was awakened much later the same night by sharp knocking on the door. He opened the door to be handed a letter by a messenger, who left immediately. After opening the envelope the ambassador discovered in it Mr. Molotov's note. Neither the content nor the manner of delivery of the note was according to commonly respected diplomatic custom. In addition, it was most distressing to Romer, since he visualized the difficulties such a step created in promoting unity among the Allies. He immediately consulted the British and the American ambassadors in Moscow. Both of them, however compassionate as persons, were helpless as ambassadors. The American Ambassador, Admiral Standley, revealed a Yankee spirit and sense of humor, advising Romer to take the note back "to the Kremlin gate, give it to a messenger and tell him it was sent to you by mistake." [26] This advice did not cheer the Polish Ambassador, although the attitudes of the two Allied colleagues did. When he left the Soviet Union for England he was seen off at the station by both the American and the British Ambassadors, who brought him farewell presents, as one of them said, " to show where our sympathy lies." [27]

This feeling of sympathy apparently was not shared by the Allies on the highest level of policy formation. With the Polish press forcibly silenced and the pro-Soviet papers keeping the Poles under constant fire by charging them with the slandering of the Soviet Union and collaborating with Hitler, the policymakers literally forced the Polish leaders into a position from which the American and British Governments could deal with Stalin. The day after the break of the diplomatic relations General Sikorski, the head of the Polish Government, was "invited" to participate in a chain of conferences with Churchill, Eden, and the American Ambassador, Mr. Drexel Biddle. The outcome was a statement by the Polish

Government, issued through its Telegraph Agency, that the Polish Government considered its request to the International Red Cross for the investigation of the Katyn massacre *to be withdrawn*.[28] Sikorski complained privately about British pressure but there were no alternatives available. Even this step did not change the attitude of the Soviet Government.

Behind the Soviet action was a potent diplomatic secret. On the surface it appeared that Stalin was merely annoyed with the Polish Government. One needed Mr. Churchill's incisiveness and his ability to get at the core of the matter to discover Stalin's intention and pinpoint it as the real reason for the Soviet behavior.

Several weeks prior to the announced discovery of Katyn, the "Union of Polish Patriots" was created in Russia under Soviet auspices. It was composed of Polish communists. A prominent role in its organization was played by Wanda Wasilewska, a Soviet citizen, although of Polish origin, with the rank of Colonel in the Soviet Army. Her goal was to see Poland under communistic government. The group was from the beginning under Stalin's tutelage and, according to its own pronouncements, represented the will of the Polish people. What was needed was a means of discrediting the Polish Government-in-Exile in London, in order for the group of eager Polish "representatives" to assume the functions of the Polish Government-in-Exile. The Katyn affair provided an opportunity.

Mr. Churchill, keeping the unity of the Allied camp in mind, brought the Poles in London into line, and at the same time called Stalin's bluff in plain language. Referring to the possibility of the formation of a Polish Government in the Soviet Union, he pointed out in his letter dated April 30, 1943 (four days after the Russians severed relations with the Poles), "We should not, of course, be able to recognize such a Government and would continue our relations with Sikorski who is far the most helpful man you or we are likely to find for the

THE INCONVENIENT ALLIES

purposes of the common cause. I expect that this will also be the American view." [29]

Ambassador Standley evaluated the long-range policy of the Soviet Union expertly and with foresight. A paraphrase of his telegram sent at that time to the State Department asserts: "We may, it seems to me, be faced with a reversal in European history. To protect itself from the influences of Bolshevism, Western Europe in 1918 attempted to set up a *cordon sanitaire*. The Kremlin, in order to protect itself from the influences of the west, might now envisage the formation of a belt of pro-Soviet states." [30] The subsequent seizure of Eastern European Republics by Soviet-groomed men proved his acute observation, made two years in advance, to be correct. Poland was the crucial buckle in this belt and it was necessary to "produce" a pro-Soviet government if the buckle was to hold. Unfortunately for the Soviet Government, the communistic underground in Poland was extremely weak and the Poles, whether in exile or in occupied Poland, could not easily forget Soviet-German co-operation in 1939, the seizure of Eastern Poland and the mass deportations. There was scarcely a possibility that a pro-Soviet government would emerge, particularly after the Katyn massacre. Stalin had to do it himself. The flimsily constructed "Polish Patriots" were the result. No student of politics could deny Stalin's astuteness in long-term planning.

This was a difficult time for the British leadership. Priorities had to be established in dealing with Polish-Soviet relations, but foremost among these was the winning of the war against Germany and the preventing of separate peace agreements between Stalin and Hitler. It must be remembered that only four years before, the two countries had assisted each other. Such a possibility could not be completely disregarded in 1943. Churchill was quite clear about the primary goals. Of his talk with Soviet Ambassador Maisky he said, "I did not attempt to discuss facts [about Katyn] ... we have got to beat Hitler

... this is no time for quarrels and charges."[31] Foreign Secretary Eden, while making a statement on the floor of the House of Commons concerning Polish-Soviet relations, blamed "the common enemy" for the situation and appealed to members of Parliament and public opinion. "Least said, soonest mended," he pleaded.[32] However, silence was virtually impossible to maintain. There were 55,138 Communist Party members in Great Britain at that time and about 100,000 Poles. There was no love between these two groups.

The pro-Soviet press, particularly the *Daily Worker*, continued the anti-Polish campaign week after week, generating heat so intense that the British Minister of Information castigated it for vilification of the Polish Government. At the same time the Minister assailed, by implication, the papers printed in Polish, and pointed out that both sides were contributing to disunity among the Allies.[33] The Poles in London, knowing that the anti-Polish press was Soviet-instigated, tried to retaliate. Everybody climbed on the bandwagon—inhabitants from Eastern Polish territories, to which the Soviet Union already was establishing claims, families of the deported and missing, real patriots fearing for the future of Poland, and "professional patriots" fearing for their jobs with the government. Crackpots appeared. A New Zealander in London called for a separate peace with Hitler, signing his memorandum, "King of Poland, Hungary and Bohemia, Grand Duke of Lithuania, Silesia, and the Ukraine, Hospodar of Moldavia, and High Priest of the Sun."[34]

At the same time that these attacks were being made on the Poles, Stalin was assuring Mr. Roosevelt that agencies of the Soviet Government "have always treated and will continue to treat [Poles] as comrades, as people near and dear to us."[35]

Not only British but also American officials, particularly those responsible for propaganda, found the Katyn affair most difficult to handle. It was impossible for them to silence completely their own public opinion and that of the Poles. (There were well over six million American citizens of Polish origin.) At the same time they could not say, "the Germans did it," since they were not sure, particularly in view of the data taken from the graves and the information available from General Anders' men who already had arrived in the Middle East and were talking freely about their experiences in the Soviet Union. Nor had the Soviet Union provided any evidence, except a formal statement (which was submitted as "evidence") printed in *Pravda*, that "the fascists did it," and the Kremlin refused to co-operate with the International Red Cross.

The State Department, four days prior to the breach of Polish-Soviet relations, instructed the American Office of War Information, headed by Mr. Elmer Davis, that "until further and more conclusive evidence is available, it would be inadvisable for OWI to take a definite stand in this regard [Katyn]." [36] Mr. Davis, in his broadcast on May 3, 1943, cast doubt on the German accusations calling the whole story "very fishy." But some sort of position was necessary, particularly since the whole affair was snowballing into a political problem of major proportions. According to Mr. Wallace Carroll, director of the United States Office of War Information in London, "the line" had two phases: in the first, discussion of the Katyn case was avoided except by pointing to it as an example of a German maneuver to distract attention from German losses sustained in battles. Next, the proposed action "was to talk about the German crimes against Poland and other occupied countries." [37] This was obviously dodging the issue and hardly a satisfying treatment of the story, but there were no other alternatives, except those conflicting with the aims of the OWI at that time. Parenthetically, the organs of propaganda of any country are not particularly conspicuous for the presentation of factual data. That is not their purpose, as Mr. Carroll knew. "If we told the whole truth to the Continent, we would at times encourage the Germans and discourage our friends. If we talked frankly about the Allied disagreements over Poland, for example, we would only help Goebbels to strengthen German resistance and thus sacrifice the lives of Allied soldiers." [38]

Besides, public opinion in the United States at that time was strongly bent on finding common ideas and goals between America and the Soviet Union. Even such a traditionally conservative magazine as *Life* was "selling" the Communist leaders to the American people. The issue of March 29, 1943 (just preceding announcement of the Katyn discovery) was dedicated to the Soviet Union, with Stalin's picture on the cover and a full page picture of Lenin, who, *Life* announced, was "perhaps the greatest man of modern times." [39] In its attempt to find parallels between the two countries, the magazine also informed its millions of readers that the Soviet N.K.V.D. was "a national police similar to the F.B.I." [40] It is interesting to note that during the same year, the two major American labor organizations, the C.I.O. and the A.F. of L., refused to cooperate and withdrew their support from the Office of War Information because the head of the labor desk was outspokenly communistic in his attitudes.[41] Political stereotypes were turned upside down, and the sympathies of pressure groups, so important in American politics, were losing their conventionally assumed patterns.

President Roosevelt's intentions were even more difficult to ascertain. In the very din of the Polish-Soviet fracas, while Churchill was trying hard to mend the cracks in the Allied camp, Mr. Roosevelt sent an "old friend" to Stalin with a message inviting him to meet Roosevelt somewhere in the area of Bering Straits *without Churchill*. Mr. Roosevelt mentioned that he would bring Harry Hopkins.[42] The meeting was to be so secret that the "old friend" (Mr. Joseph E. Davies) upon his arrival in Moscow not only refused to inform the American Ambassador to the Soviet Union of the content of the message, but also told the Ambassador that the President felt the Ambassador should not be present when the letter was delivered to Mr. Stalin.[43]

Propaganda officials in the United States and England were fully aware that the problem of Katyn had become not a problem of human compassion or of justice but a political problem. They had to maneuver gingerly not to step on anyone's toes. Their position was most difficult, particularly since both governments, British and American, did not make available to them the data concerning Katyn already in the governmental files. There is undeniable evidence that the intelligence agencies of the British and American governments already had substantial files on the Katyn matter. Analysis and publication of those materials probably would have shed considerable light on the circumstances of the crime. But these materials were pigeonholed and, as it happened in the American case, subsequently "disappeared" between the room of the Chief of Military Intelligence and the State Department. (This will be discussed in Chapter IX.)

The questions "Who killed the men, and what happened to the more than 10,000 still missing?" ceased to be of interest to the Allies. Only the Poles still tried to raise them, but who would listen? Goebbels, who kept a close look at the tenor and content of the Allied press, could not help chuckling in his diary, "The Poles are given a brush-off by the English and the Americans as though they were enemies." [44]

But the Soviet Union was willing to re-establish diplomatic relations with Poland for a price. According to Stanisław Mikołajczyk,[45] who became Polish Premier after Sikorski's death in 1943, the two officially pronounced conditions were: one, a change in the composition of the Polish Government-in-Exile (members of the Union of Patriots in Moscow were suggested to fill the vacancies left by those unacceptable to the Soviet Union); two, recognition of the Soviet claim to the Polish eastern territories. There was also a third condition, actually a prerequisite and the most important, although always announced in an informal fashion—the Poles were to denounce themselves for demanding the Red Cross investigation and were to state publicly that they had been wrong in doing so.

The Poles refused.

The German Foreign Ministry now made a second attempt to disrupt Allied co-operation.

A secret order from Ribbentrop's office addressed to the German embassies in Sweden, Turkey and Switzerland advised the German emissaries in these countries to spread propaganda "insinuating that the English Government incited the Poles to send their well-known note to the Red Cross." The order also stated that "the German origin of this whisper-propaganda must not be recognizable." [46]

German agents began to spread the "line" to all levels of social interaction in the neutral countries. The news was immediately reported in Moscow, London, and Washington, clouding the Katyn issue even further and sowing mistrust and confusion in three capitals.

Confusion existed even on the highest policy-making level. Between October 19 and 30, 1943, a conference of Foreign Ministers of Allied Powers took place in Moscow. Cordell Hull, Molotov and Eden participated. A communiqué from this conference was published together with a Special Declaration signed by Roosevelt, Churchill and Stalin. The Declaration was released to the press November 1, 1943. Under these circumstances it might be expected that the content of the Declaration would be the same when published in the three countries concerned. It was not so.

When referring to German atrocities, the appropriate part of the Declaration in the Russian version read as follows: "Thus, the Germans who took part in shooting *Italian officers* . . . will be brought back to the scene of their crimes and judged on the spot. . . ." [47] The American version was identical with the Soviet and also spoke about "Italian officers." [48] The British were less malleable.

The *Times* of London also published on November 2 the full text of the Declaration; however, in it there was reference to "... the Germans who took part in shooting *Polish officers*...."[49]

Seventeen days later the British Foreign Office announced "that because of mutilation in transmission the version of the declaration on German atrocities ... differed from the correct text issued by the Soviet Government." In other words, it should have read "Italian" officers and not "Polish" officers.[50]

During this time the Red Army had been repulsing the German invaders. It is not important whether the Red Army soldier fought as a communist or a Russian; he fought magnificently.

The day after the Soviet units reached the Katyn Forest area, a Special Soviet Commission appeared on the spot of the executions to begin its own investigation. The dead soldiers were to be taken from their graves again. The silent trees were to see them for the third time.

NOTES TO CHAPTER III

1. *Nowy Kurier Warszawski* (Warsaw), April 14, 1943, pp. 1-2. Published in Polish under German auspices during the occupation of Poland in the Second World War.
2. *Ibid.*, April 18, 1943, p. 1.
3. *Ibid.*, April 18, 1943, p. 2; April 19, 1943, p. 1.
4. *Ibid.*, May 6, 1943, p. 2; June 4, 1943, p. 1.
5. Germany. *Verordnungsblatt für das Generalgouvernement* (Regulations for the occupied area). Krakau, nos. 1-97. January 6-December 18, 1943, *passim*. Published in Poland by the German occupation administration during the Second World War. For a detailed description of the German administrative apparatus in occupied Poland, see Max Freiher du Prel, *Das Deutsche Generalgouvernement Polen* (The German Government of Poland) (Krakau: Buchverlag Ost G.m.b.H., 1940), pp. 1-344.
6. All the above-mentioned correspondence was found among Himmler's personal files. Germany. *Reichsführer SS und Chef der deutschen Polizei. Persönlicher Stab. Schriftgutverwaltung* (Reichsführer SS and Chief of the German Police. Personal staff. Document

administration). Himmler Files 3. Photostatic copies, in German. Folder no. 277, pages numbered 7217-7229, *passim.*

7. For fully translated telegram see *Hearings,* part 5, p. 1372.

8. First precise reports sent by the radio stations from occupied Poland came to London on April 22, 1943. Radiograms nos. 625/1, 625/2, 625/3, 625/4, 689/FFB, 690/KMS, 691/STW, 692/ZZK. The others concerning Katyn came on May 7 and 13: 692/1, 692/2, 755/1, 755/2, 755/3. *Hearings,* part 4, pp. 710-718.

9. *Polish Report,* pp. 243-246.

10. *Dziennik Polski* (London), April 15, 1943, p. 1.

11. *Hearings,* part 6, Exhibit 32, p. 1723.

12. *M.S.Z.,* pp. 308-311.

13. *Polish Report,* p. 255.

14. Excerpt from the memorandum of the State Secretary of the German Foreign Ministry, Weizsaecker. Delivered by phone to the German Ambassador in Switzerland, von Rintelen, on April 17, 1943. *Hearings,* part 5, p. 1367.

15. For the exchange of correspondence between the German authorities and the International Red Cross and for instructions given to German foreign legations regarding handling of the Katyn case, see certified translations and photostatic copies of original documents as submitted by Dr. Paul Sweet, head of the American team studying captured German documents. *Ibid.,* part 5, pp. 1337-1416.

16. The author's italics. The German Government already had received an answer in this spirit on April 16, 1943, at 7:10 p.m. This did not prevent Hitler from sending a personal envoy with the second invitation, synchronizing his arrival with that of the Pole. The Polish Government received a similar answer on April 22, 1943.

17. Professor Kot's testimony. *Hearings,* part 4, p. 927.

18. *Daily Worker* (London), April 19, 1943, p. 4.

19. U.S.S.R. Ministry of Foreign Affairs. *Correspondence between the Chairman of the Council of Ministers of the U.S.S.R. and the Presidents of the U.S.A. and the Prime Ministers of Great Britain during the Great Patriotic War of 1941-1945* (Moscow: Foreign Languages Publishing House, 1947), vol. I, 120-121; II, 60-61. Hereafter this source will be cited as *Stalin's Correspondence.* Italics under the words *"the present Polish Government"* are mine.

20. *Loc. cit.*

21. *Hearings,* part 6, Exhibit 32, p. 1722.

22. *Stalin's Correspondence,* I, 123; see also 120-129.

23. Winston S. (now Sir Winston) Churchill, *The Hinge of Fate* (Boston: Houghton Mifflin Co., 1950), p. 759.

24. *Stalin's Correspondence,* II, 61.

25. *Polish Report,* pp. 269-270.

26. Admiral Standley's testimony. *Hearings,* part 7, p. 2063.

27. *Ibid.*, part 7, p. 2072.
28. *Polish Report*, p. 279. My italics.
29. Churchill, personal and secret message to Stalin, April 30, 1943. *Stalin's Correspondence*, I, 125. This opinion about General Sikorski's co-operative attitude was shared by Mr. Sumner Welles, the American Undersecretary of State. *Hearings*, part 7, p. 2090.
30. Telegram from the American Ambassador to Moscow, Admiral Standley, to the U.S. Department of State, April 28, 1943. *Hearings*, part 7, p. 2068. He resigned his post in disgust over President Roosevelt's bypassing him in his official position with "a personal emissary" to Stalin.
31. Churchill, *The Hinge of Fate*, pp. 760-761.
32. 389 H.C.Deb. 31 (5th ser. 1942-1943).
33. *Ibid.*, p. 1218; see also 392 H.C.Deb. 1038 (5th ser. 1942-1943).
34. 389 H.C.Deb. 1248-1249 (5th ser. 1942-1943).
35. Stalin's letter to Roosevelt, April 29, 1943. *Stalin's Correspondence*, II, 62.
36. Memorandum from the Division of European Affairs, U.S. State Department, with the stamp of the Assistant Secretary, Mr. Berle, addressed to the OWI, April 22, 1943. *Hearings*, part 7, p. 1986.
37. Wallace Carroll, *Persuade or Perish* (Boston: Houghton Mifflin Co., 1948), p. 151.
38. *Ibid.*, p. 236.
39. *Life*, XIV, no. 13, March 29, 1943, p. 29.
40. *Ibid.*, p. 40.
41. *Hearings*, part 7, p. 1995.
42. Roosevelt's letter to Stalin, May 5, 1943. *Stalin's Correspondence*, II, 63-64.
43. Admiral Standley's testimony. *Hearings*, part 7, p. 2073.
44. *Goebbels Diaries*, p. 347.
45. Author's personal interview with former Prime Minister Mikołajczyk, April 1, 1958; also *Hearings*, part 7, p. 2162.
46. *Ibid.*, part 5, p. 1406.
47. *Pravda* (Moscow), November 2, 1943, p. 2. Italics mine.
48. U.S. Department of State. *The Department of State Bulletin*, IX, no. 228 (November 6, 1943), 311.
49. *Times* (London), November 2, 1943, p. 3. Italics mine.
50. *Times* (London), November 19, 1943, p. 3. Credit for noticing the British Foreign Office's subsequent correction of the version of the Declaration belongs to Dr. Wiktor Sukiennicki, Polish scholar preparing *Polish Report*.

IV

The Soviet Commission Investigation

GOEBBELS, HAVING BEEN informed that the German Army had to withdraw from the Katyn area, entered a prediction in his diary: "Unfortunately we have had to give up Katyn. The Bolsheviks undoubtedly will soon 'find' that we shot 12,000 Polish officers. That episode is one that is going to cause us quite a little trouble in the future."[1]

The Soviet Special Commission arrived in the Katyn Forest following its liberation from the German occupation. The previous commission on the spot had attempted to ascertain the circumstances, but above all who had murdered the prisoners. The Soviet Commission, judging by its title, already seemed to know who had killed the men. The official title of the team was: *The Special Commission for Ascertaining and Investigating the Circumstances of the Shooting of Polish Officer Prisoners by the German-Fascist Invaders in the Katyn Forest.*[2]

The Commission and the medical experts associated with it included a number of distinguished Soviet names,[3] but no foreign medical representatives were invited and even the Polish communists were barred from the participation in exhumations.[4]

The Commission attempted to discredit the verdicts of the three preceding commissions and the materials submitted by the Polish authorities.

The Commission began by stating that "the Katyn Forest had for a long time been the favorite resort of Smolensk people ... access to the Katyn Forest was not banned or restricted in any way." The N.K.V.D. from Smolensk had its own "rest home" in the forest. When the German Army arrived in the area, this home became the headquarters of the 537th Engineering Battalion of the German forces.

Just before the German units entered the area, according to the Commission, Polish prisoners-of-war, officers and men, were employed in road-building in the vicinity of Smolensk. The Soviet authorities tried to evacuate these prisoners by train but were unable to do so, and the Poles were captured by German forces. After their capture, they frequently escaped from German authorities, and people around the Katyn Forest and Smolensk saw them, and saw the German police looking for them, particularly in the fall of 1941. It should be recalled that the three previous medical commissions established the date of the massacre as the early spring of 1940, whereas the Soviet sources maintained that the prisoners were murdered in the fall of 1941.

According to Soviet witnesses, who testified in large numbers, the German commanding officer of the unit occupying the former N.K.V.D. rest home was Colonel Arnes. He told two Soviet women who were employed by the Germans in this house as kitchen help that they must not enter certain rooms. The same two employees on two occasions noticed blood stains on the cuffs of two German lance-corporals. They also heard trucks coming to the forest and heard shots fired. On one occasion one of the women saw about thirty Polish prisoners being led into the forest, and twenty minutes later she heard shots.

The director of the Smolensk Observatory, Professor B. V. Bazilevsky, testified that the Soviet lawyer B. G. Menshagin, appointed mayor of Smolensk by the German administration, told him that the Poles were being exterminated by the German

THE SOVIET COMMISSION INVESTIGATION 51

authorities in the Katyn area. Also Menshagin's notebook from the period of 1941 was found by the Commission. There was an entry in it to this point. Menshagin himself could not be located. He had moved toward Germany before the arrival of Russian forces at Smolensk. The Soviet Security police arrested him somewhere in the West, after cessation of hostilities.

According to the report of the Soviet Commission, the background of the shooting was as follows: In the winter of 1942-1943 the Soviet military might was growing stronger, and so was Allied unity. To offset this "the Germans decided to launch a provocation, using for this purpose the atrocities they committed in the Katyn Forest." In order to get the appropriate testimonies from the local people, and to blame the Soviet Union, ". . . the Germans beat, threatened, and persuaded them to testify." While conditioning the witnesses to testify in their favor, the German authorities proceeded with the preparation of the bodies and graves to prove that the men were murdered in the spring of 1940, or, in other words, prior to the German arrival in the area.

The Soviet Commission's account goes on to say that the Germans started by ordering all 11,000 bodies (the number given by the Soviet Commission) to be exhumed. They removed from the clothing all documents dated later than April 1940, and then returned the bodies to the graves. This occurred in March 1943. Five hundred Soviet prisoners-of-war were used to carry out this operation, and afterward they were shot. The bodies of these 500 Soviet prisoners were not found by the International, the German, nor the Polish Commissions investigating the graves. Nor did the Soviet Commission ever claim to have found them. This is remarkable considering the weight this evidence would have given the Soviet Commission's report.

The Soviet Commission concluded by saying that several weeks later the Germans again dug up the bodies of some of the

Poles and announced the discovery of the Katyn Massacre. Moreover, the Commission continues, German soldiers brought the bodies of Poles from outside the Katyn Forest and dumped them into the graves as late as April 1943. Three Soviet witnesses testified that they met on "several nights big trucks covered with tarpaulins and spreading a heavy stench of dead bodies" driving toward Smolensk in March and April 1943.

The Special Commission based all this on the testimony of witnesses. To this testimony was added evidence gathered by the medical experts. The Special Commission interviewed the witnesses from September 26, 1943, until January 24, 1944, but the medical experts investigated the graves during one week—January 16 to 23, 1944.[5]

The Soviet experts ascertained the identity of the slain men, the cause of death, and the time of burial, pronouncing their findings on the basis of the exhumation of 925 bodies. The victims were Poles, they were killed by shots in the back of the head. The Commission corroborated, so far, the findings of their professional colleagues of the preceding commissions. But here the similarities of the reports end. When it came to the most important point, the date of the burial, the Soviet doctors found that the "bodies were buried about *two* years ago . . . between September and December 1941."

Altogether, four teams had examined the graves: the International, German, Polish, and Soviet. Yet the investigating medical experts did not agree on the date of the murder.

While the Soviet doctors were working on the bodies, a group of foreign journalists came to Katyn Forest, and with them was Miss Kathleen Harriman, an American girl of twenty-five. She wrote a report of her visit to the graves which promptly reached the State Department and attracted its attention. The girl's father was Mr. Averell Harriman, at that time American Ambassador to the Soviet Union.

Apart from Miss Harriman, there were in the group about twenty journalists: one Frenchman, one Pole, the rest American and British. In the group were Mr. Werth of London's B.B.C., Mr. Lawrence of the *New York Times*, Mr. Duncan-Hooper of Reuters, and Professor Davies of the *Toronto Star*. According to Mr. Harriman, he sent his daughter along because the diplomatic corps was usually not invited to participate in press conferences and the Russians " . . . would be more likely to let her go than . . . an embassy official." [6] Miss Harriman went. The third secretary of the American Embassy in Moscow, Mr. John Melby, went also.

The group was taken to the forest, "then the party went into one of four large gray-green tents, clumping the snow and muck off their boots as they entered. It was warmer inside and the stench was overpowering. Dr. Prozorovsky ripped open a corpse numbered 808, sliced chunks off the brain like cold meat, knifed through the chest and pulled out an atrophied organ. 'Heart,' he said, holding it out to Kathy [Miss Harriman]. Then he slit a leg muscle. 'Look how well preserved the meat is,' he said." [7] Miss Harriman stayed, giving evidence of the emotional stamina of American womanhood. There was also a press briefing on the spot, during which the Polish correspondent "slept noisily." (He explained to the American embassy official that "the present investigation has no interest for the Poles in Russia since it is obvious that the Germans committed the crime." [8] His rank was that of a captain and he was editor of *Wolna Polska* (Free Poland), a paper printed by the Polish communists in the Soviet Union under the auspices of Wanda Wasilewska.) After a time the correspondents asked questions. These became more and more penetrating and, as Mr. Melby says, were "usually rude." The atmosphere of the conference was growing progressively tense and uncomfortable. "At midnight it was announced abruptly that our train would leave. . . . The members of the Commission were hasty and formal with us in their farewells, and the earlier atmosphere of at least semicordiality had disappeared." [9]

Ambassador Harriman conferred with his daughter and Mr. Melby upon their return. The outcome was his telegram addressed to the Secretary of State which stated that the "general evidence is inconclusive but Kathleen and Embassy staff member believe probability massacre perpetrated by Germans." [10] Miss Harriman followed with her personal report affirming that " . . . it is my opinion that the Poles were murdered by the Germans." She then cited the findings of the Soviet Commission. So did Mr. Melby, asserting that "on balance, however, and despite loopholes the Russian case is convincing." [11]

The Soviet medical team maintained that the bodies excavated by it had never previously been subjected to a medical examination but that they already had been searched; slits were visible in the pockets and some of them had been turned out. (All bodies except about two hundred in grave number eight had been searched by the International, Polish, and German commissions.) The Soviet group reported that it found, nevertheless, on the already-searched bodies some documents with dates ranging from November 12, 1940, to June 20, 1941. Nine of these documents are cited.

This is evidence which, if irrefutable, would completely exonerate the Soviet Government of the crime. The documents would prove that the men could not have been killed in April-May 1940, because they were still writing or receiving letters in 1941, and that the three non-Soviet medical commissions were wrong.

This is the crucial closing statement of the report: "The conclusions drawn from the evidence given by witnesses, and from the findings of the medico-legal experts on the shooting of Polish war prisoners by the Germans in the autumn of 1941, are completely confirmed by the material evidence and documents excavated from the Katyn graves."

The list of names signing the Soviet Report is headed by the Chairman of the Special Commission, Member of the

THE SOVIET COMMISSION INVESTIGATION

Extraordinary State Committee, Academician N. N. Burdenko. This gentleman, before his death, supplemented the report informally. The supplement will be included here, in an appropriate place.

The Soviet Commission's report was about fifteen times shorter than the German and twenty times shorter than the Polish reports. It does not mention three things, prominent in the statements of other commissions: the trees planted on and around the graves, the four-corner bayonet wounds on the bodies, and the origin of the ropes with which the hands were tied.

Although only 925 bodies were exhumed, the Commission arrived "by calculation" at the figure of 11,000 bodies in the graves. The manner of calculation is not stated. On the other hand, in one respect the report is more precise than the International, Polish, and German commissions—it identifies *the German officers responsible for the murder, and the official designation of the unit:* the officers were Lieutenant Colonel Arnes and his assistants, First Lieutenant Rekst and Second Lieutenant Hott. They belonged to the 537th Engineer Battalion. Under their command the executions were performed. The Commission states positively that they murdered the Poles.

Colonel Ahrens (Arnes) survived the fighting on the Russian front, and voluntarily appeared at the Nuremberg trial of German war criminals. His appearance after the war was unexpected, since it was fair to assume that the man guilty of such a hideous and well publicized crime would keep in the shadow to protect himself. The investigation of the Katyn Massacre at the Nuremberg trial was also unexpected. In fact, what happened at Nuremberg was a surprise not only to the general public but even to tough-minded international lawyers.

NOTES TO CHAPTER IV

1. *Goebbels Diaries,* p. 487.
2. This chapter is based on the report of this Commission, unless otherwise indicated. U.S.S.R. Spetsial'naya Kommissiya po Ustanovleniyu i Rassledovaniyu Obstoyatel'stv Rasstrela Nemetsko-Fashistskimi Zakhvatchikami v Katynskom Lesu Voennoplennykh Pol'skikh Ofitserov. (Special commission for ascertaining and investigating the circumstances of the shooting of Polish officer prisoners by the German-Fascist invaders in the Katyn Forest.) *Nota Sovetskogo Pravitel'stva Pravitel'stvu SShA; Soobshchenie Spetsial'noi Komissii.* (Note of the Soviet Government to the Government of the U.S.; communication by the Special Commission.) Moscow: Supplement to *Novoe Vremya,* no. 10, 1952. In the following pages this source will be cited as the *Soviet Report.* For the German translation of the note see *Neue Zeit.* Beilage, zu no. 10, 1952; in the English language consult Supplement to the *Soviet Embassy Information Bulletin,* Washington: March 23, 1952.
3. The Commission consisted of Academician N. N. Burdenko, member of the Extraordinary State Committee (chairman of the Commission); Academician Alexei Tolstoy, member of the Extraordinary State Committee; Metropolitan Nikolai, member of the Extraordinary State Committee; Lt. Gen. A. S. Gundorov, president of the All-Slav Committee; S. A. Kolesnikov, chairman of the executive committee of the Union of the Red Cross and Red Crescent Societies; Academician V. P. Potemkin, People's Commissar of Education of the Russian SFSR; Col. Gen. E. I. Smirnov, Chief of the Central Medical Administration of the Red Army; P. E. Melnikov, chairman of the Smolensk Regional Executive Committee.
4. Stanisław Mikołajczyk, *The Rape of Poland: Pattern of Soviet Aggression* (New York: Whittlesey House, 1948), p. 36.
5. *Soviet Report.* In accordance with the instructions of the special commission for ascertaining and investigating the circumstances of the shooting of Polish officer prisoners by the German-Fascist invaders in Katyn Forest (near Smolensk), a commission of medico-legal experts was set up, consisting of V. I. Prozorovsky, chief medico-legal expert of the People's Commissariat of Health Protection of the U.S.S.R. and director of the State Scientific Research Institute of Forensic Medicine; Doctor of Medicine V. M. Smolyaninov, professor of forensic medicine at the Second Moscow State Medical Institute; Doctor of Medicine D. N. Vyropayev, professor of pathological anatomy; Dr. P. S. Semenovsky, senior staff scientist of the thanatology department of the State Research Institute of Forensic Medicine under the People's Commissariat of Health Protection of

THE SOVIET COMMISSION INVESTIGATION

the U.S.S.R.; Assistant Prof. M. D. Shvaikova, senior staff scientist of the chemico-legal department of the State Scientific Research Institute of Forensic Medicine under the People's Commissariat of Health Protection of the U.S.S.R.; with the participation of Major of Medical Service Nikolsky, chief medico-legal expert of the Western front; Captain of Medical Service Bussoyedov, medico-legal expert of the [Soviet] Army; Major of Medical Service Subbotin, chief of the pathological anatomy laboratory No. 92; Major of Medical Service Ogloblin; Senior Lieutenant of Medical Service Sadykov, medical specialist; Senior Lieutenant of Medical Service Pushkareva.

6. Mr. Harriman's testimony. *Hearings*, part 7, p. 2105.
7. "Day in the Forest," *Time*, XLIII, no. 6 (February 7, 1944), p. 27.
8. Mr. Melby's report. *Hearings*, part 7, p. 2141.
9. *Loc. cit.*
10. Telegram from Ambassador Harriman, Moscow, to the President and the Secretary of State, Washington. Dated Moscow, January 25, 1944. *Hearings*, part 7, p. 2124.
11. Enclosures No. 1 and 2 to Dispatch No. 207 dated February 23, 1944, from the American Embassy in Moscow. *Ibid.*, part 7, p. 2133.

V

Nuremberg: Crime and Punishment in International Politics

GOEBBELS HIMSELF PROMPTED the decision of the German authorities that special care should be exercised in preserving the evidence taken from the graves. Thousands of letters, identification cards, photographs, and personal possessions were recovered from the bodies. These were bundled off in the western direction to avoid capture by the Russians. They were the most important, and the only tangible, German evidence after the seizure of Katyn Forest by Soviet forces.

The story of the transit of these documents is dramatic. While German authorities guarded this evidence, both the Polish Underground and the Soviet security police planned to steal it.

There were nine huge wooden cases filled with the personal possessions of the dead. The Germans decided to permit Polish specialists in forensic medicine and criminology to analyze this truckload of data. The Poles could, at their own convenience, having the documents in Poland, ascertain their origin and authenticity with precision by comparing them with other documents of the same type, or by contacting families, or other means. Evidently the Germans felt that this would be to their advantage, although the Soviet Government maintained that all documents had been falsified by the Germans.

The big crates with the material were brought to the Polish city of Kraków and deposited in the Polish Institute of Forensic Medicine. Here, under the supervision of Polish Doctor Robel and with the assistance of his Polish staff, the documents were processed and analyzed systematically and thoroughly. Needless to say, the Underground arranged access to the data and scrutinized it also. The Poles were so meticulous about the investigation of the material that the Secretary-General of the Polish Red Cross read the most important parts of the evidence himself.[1] These were the twenty-two hand-penned diaries which had been found on the dead Poles. All of them ended in April-May 1940, and some of the entries appeared to have been written literally minutes before the execution. Authenticity of these documents had to be proved by the Poles beyond all doubt, and this the German officials permitted them to undertake. The processing, checking, and verification were completed rather quickly, and many documents were copied and photographed, but the Germans were watching the materials closely and it was difficult to remove them completely from their hands. The Underground movement decided to snatch the lot from under the noses of the German guards.

The documents had proved to be authentic and could be valuable evidence of Soviet guilt. The Poles feared that the Soviet Government would either steal them or destroy them by one method or another. The Germans were not only wary of Soviet intentions with respect to the boxes of documents, but they also knew the Poles in the Underground to be a tough and tricky lot.

Mr. Skarżyński, the Secretary-General of the Polish Red Cross, collaborating with the underground, decided to build nine wooden boxes identical in appearance to those in which the materials were stored. The "Polish" boxes were to be lined with tin and to be airtight. The idea was to transfer surreptitiously the materials from the "German" boxes into the "Polish" boxes and then, in greatest secrecy, to submerge the cases in a lake. It was expected that the heavy boxes would settle to the bottom and rest there until the war was over. The Poles proceeded with the action, and part of the materials were already "transferred" when the German guards discovered the plot.

Police attention was again called to the Katyn affair. Soviet armed forces were already entering eastern Poland, pushing across the land with armored pincers aimed toward Kraków. An order was issued by the chief of German police to Dr. Beck, the German director of the Institute of Forensic Medicine and Scientific Criminology in the German Government of Poland, to destroy the materials rather than to allow their capture by the Soviet Army. Dr. Beck, after some unsuccessful attempts to hide the materials in private homes in Kraków (the stench was overpowering and people could not stand it), decided to evacuate the materials to Germany. The evidence was repacked in fourteen boxes (according to one of the German guards there were sixteen boxes),[2] loaded on two trucks, and moved west toward Germany. Dr. Beck personally accompanied the load.

Several days after the departure of the convoy, Dr. Beck reappeared in Kraków. He had broken his leg on the way and was brought back to the city for recovery. News of Beck's return spread among the Poles, who were most curious as to the destination of the convoy. While the doctor was in a hospital he was gently "pumped" for information and one day he gave it—the trucks were sent to Breslau (now Wrocław)!

When the doctor had sufficiently recovered, he proceeded to Breslau to join the trucks. Kraków was seized by Soviet units. Agents of the so-called "Lublin government" (which evolved from the "Union of Polish Patriots in Moscow") sought the documents, but they were gone. Ultimately, Dr.

Robel, the Polish doctor who had supervised the verification of the documents in Kraków, was arrested by the security organs of the Polish communist government.

The Soviet armies relentlessly rolled back the German defense. Breslau was taken. Several days later the Soviet security police were on the spot looking for the boxes. So was the Polish Underground. A member of the Polish Red Cross, hiding the real purpose of his visit, went to Breslau immediately upon its capture. After diligent snooping, he found the traces.

The boxes had reached the city and had been stored on the first floor of Breslau's university. Even a blind man could have located them by sniffing the air. Unfortunately, in the very last days of the fighting for the city, a detachment of SS came, took the boxes—and Dr. Beck, who was still guarding them—and headed west toward the central part of shrinking and burning Germany. The Polish Red Cross official looked for the doctor in the eastern section of Germany, in vain. However, the doctor had not permanently disappeared. From the information collected from him and from one of the guards, during the Congressional investigation in 1952, it is possible to trace the fate of the documents further.[3]

The duty-minded doctor, appreciating the political importance of the materials, decided to save them at any cost. With Breslau on fire, he pushed toward Berlin. This was not an easy task. The network of communications was already disrupted. Germany was cracking between two walls of steel converging from the west and east. On the way to Berlin, this time in a single truck, the documents reached Dresden. Here the Gestapo H.Q. provided a new truck. The cases were reloaded.

On toward Berlin bounced the doctor in the smelly truck, dodging Soviet planes, pushing through masses of refugees, giving priority to German armored units racing frantically from gap to gap to plug the breaking fronts. The truck reached the town of Radebeul between Dresden and Meissen. It was impossible to proceed further.

It was the beginning of May 1945. In a few days the Second World War would be over in Europe. The doctor decided to take the last measure to prevent the materials from falling into Soviet hands.

He stored the boxes at the Radebeul railway station with an explicit order to the dispatcher that in case of the approach of Soviet units, "the boxes be burned completely." He then raced toward Prague, where he thought he might contact representatives of the International Red Cross or the American Army who would accept his deposit.

He reached Pilsen and contacted the American commander of a unit there. Simultaneously news came that the Soviet units had reached the vicinity of Dresden, including Radebeul, and Dr. Beck decided not to go back. His race was over.

As for the documents, the Russians did not get them. The forwarding agent, immediately prior to the Soviet entry into the city, set fire to the boxes. It is assumed that they burned to ashes.[4] A subsequent check revealed that the forwarding agent and his family were arrested by the Soviet police and simply disappeared. At the time of Dr. Beck's testimony (1952) the agent was still missing.

One thing Dr. Beck did not know while fulfilling his decision to go to Prague. In a matter of hours after the seizure of an area by the Soviet army, security police were at Dr. Beck's stopping-places. They traced him with unfailing precision. Dr. Beck's parents' home was searched several times, as were the homes of his German friends in which he stopped on his flight from Poland and through Germany. The Soviet agents were relentless in their efforts to locate the man and the documents. In some instances they were but a few days too late. Finally, the police arrested Dr. Beck's mother, at that time sixty-two years old, and kept her in prison for more than six months to learn from her Beck's address. But her son had already escaped to western Germany and she protected his identity.[5]

Between June 26 and August 8, 1945, a special conference of the four victorious powers took place in London. Its objective was to agree "upon methods of procedure for the prosecution and trial of the major European war criminals."[6] The result was the Agreement and the Charter of the International Military Tribunal.[7] These documents were the legal foundations of the so-called Nuremberg trial which followed.

Because the governments of the United States, Soviet Union, Great Britain, and France organized the conference, they divided the areas of responsibilities for the prosecution among themselves as follows: The United States would prosecute for the war of aggression, Great Britain for the crimes committed on high seas and treaty violations, and the Soviet Union would prosecute for "crimes against humanity"—sharing this responsibility on a geographical basis with the Government of France. The Soviet Union was responsible for the indictment for crimes committed by the German armies and authorities in Eastern Europe; the French for those committed in the Western part of Europe. This meant that the massacre of the Poles in the Katyn Forest could be submitted and prosecuted only by representatives of the Government of the Soviet Union, a party which, at that time, still had not been cleared of suspicion of committing the murder. There was eager speculation whether or not the Soviet Union would bring charges concerning the Katyn Massacre. It did.

The Katyn Massacre was brought up during the drawing of the indictment by the Soviet prosecutor. Both British and American representatives protested against the inclusion; however, as the Chief American Prosecutor stated, if the Soviet prosecutors thought they "could prove the charge, they were entitled to do so under the division of the case."[8]

The Allied indictment of German war criminals was publicly announced on October 18, 1945. Chapter "C" of the indictment bore the caption, "Murder and ill treatment of prisoners-of-war, and of members of the armed forces of the countries with whom Germany was at war and of persons on the high seas." In a systematic tabulation of many German crimes of this type, the charge appears: "In September 1941, 11,000 Polish officers who were prisoners-of-war were killed in the Katyn Forest near Smolensk." Originally the Soviet indictment said "925 Polish officers," but at the last moment before the submission of the indictment the Soviet representatives changed it to "11,000 Polish officers." [9]

The first fire was drawn on February 8, 1946, during the trial, when the Chief Soviet Prosecutor, General Rudenko, assailed the Germans for the invasion of Poland and their policies of extermination.[10] This was received by the German defendants with derision. "Goering and Hess took off their headphones. Goering, when asked why he did not listen, said, 'I did not think they [Russians] would be so shameless as to mention Poland.' Dr. Gilbert, of the U. S. Army, asked, 'Why do you consider that shameless?' 'Because they attacked at the same time we did.' Baldur von Schirach laughed, 'When they mentioned Poland, I thought I'd die!' " [11]

These charges made by the Soviet Union appeared to the Germans as nothing less than ridiculous. The attack on Poland had been committed also by the prosecutor's government. It was a direct result of the German-Soviet military and political alliance in 1939. In any case, the evidence against the Germans on behalf of the murdered Poles was presented by Soviet Colonel Pokrovsky, Deputy Chief Prosecutor. What evidence? The report of the Soviet Commission.[12]

The German defense counsel, requesting the admission of some other materials, incurred Soviet objections. The Soviet Chief Prosecutor, General Rudenko, stated that "the Soviet Prosecution categorically insists on the rejection of the application of the Defense Counsel." Why? Because "our position is that this episode of criminal activity on the part of the

Hitlerites has been fully established by the evidence presented by the Soviet Prosecution. . . . " [13]

When the German counsellor offered the testimony of one Captain Böhmert, a former adjutant of the very unit accused by the Soviet Government of committing the mass murder, General Rudenko also objected on the grounds that "Captain Böhmert is himself a participant in the crimes of Katyn Forest. . . . As he is an interested party, he cannot give any useful testimony." [14] The logic of this argument is hard to follow. The witness was being disqualified because he was directly connected with the case.

The Poles in London had had an "intellectual premonition" as to the manner in which the Katyn case would be considered at the Nuremberg trial. Prior to the opening of the proceedings, eleven Polish senators and ten deputies of the Polish Government-in-Exile expressed an opinion as a parliamentary group and sent it to Supreme Court Justice Robert Jackson, Chief Prosecutor for the United States. In it they maintained that " . . . it would be ill-advised to include the Katyn case in the tasks of the Nuremberg tribunal. This case is of a special character, and needs . . . to be examined apart and treated independently. . . . " [15] It was the Polish contention that one of the accused was acting as a prosecutor. But this the senators did not say in their note. The trial proceeded.

After the Soviet Commission's *Report* was introduced to the court as evidence, Colonel Prochovnik of the Soviet prosecuting staff suggested to Dr. Stahmer (the German defense counsel) in the presence of Professor Exner (defense counsel for General Jodl) that the proceedings be shortened by not hearing witnesses at all. He proposed that written affidavits be presented in lieu of public testimony. This, of course, would prevent the testimony from reaching the public. The German counsellor refused to agree and demanded that the witnesses testify.[16] After some bickering as to the number of witnesses to be presented by the Soviet Union and Germany, it was decided that three men would testify for each.

Names of the Soviet witnesses appear in the Soviet report. One is that of Dr. Prosorovsky who performed an autopsy for the benefit of Miss Harriman during the Soviet investigation, and another that of Professor Basilevsky from Smolensk, the man who heard the rumors that the Poles were executed by German units. The third witness, Dr. Markov, created a real sensation. He was a member of the International Commission which had been organized by German authorities, and he had signed the International Commission's report accusing the Soviet Government. Now he was coming to testify on behalf of the Soviet Government.

Dr. Markov was brought from his native Bulgaria, already occupied by Soviet forces. The atmosphere was tense when the man was ushered into the courtroom. He completely reversed his previous opinions. Not only did he attack the competence and results of the investigation by the International Commission of which he had been a member, he also affirmed that the report had been signed by all the members under German duress. "The only thing which bore the character of the scientific examination was the autopsy which I carried on," he said. It was "absolutely clear" to him that the corpses had been buried one year to eighteen months. This meant that the men were shot by Germans.[17]

The Soviet prosecutor questioned Dr. Markov by making statements to which Dr. Markov subscribed. For example:

Soviet prosecutor: "You were shown already opened graves, near which the corpses were already laid out, is that right?"

Dr. Markov: "Quite right. Near these opened graves were exhumed corpses already laid out there." [18]

This procedure was repeated again and again.

Soviet prosecutor: "You signed it (the report of the International Commission) because you felt yourself compelled to?"

Here the venerated President of the Court, Lord Justice Lawrence, reacted in his quiet way. "Colonel Smirnov," said he, turning to the Soviet prosecutor, "I don't think it is proper for you to put leading questions to him." [19]

Many men among the doctors and journalists present during the work of the International Commission in Katyn Forest distinctly recalled during the U.S. Congressional Hearings that Dr. Markov had on several occasions at the Katyn graves volunteered his observations and opinions of Soviet guilt. Two of Markov's colleagues from the Commission, Dr. Neville (Switzerland) and Dr. Tramsen (Denmark), later asserted several times that the Germans did not use any coercion or pressure on the signatories to the report. They also recalled Dr. Markov's statements about Soviet guilt.[20] At Nuremberg Dr. Markov maintained that the "Germans did it." Dr. Markov's post-Katyn investigation experiences provide some clues to the new position he had taken.

Dr. Markov was arrested in Bulgaria soon after Soviet units reached this country. He was tried as an "enemy of the people" for his participation in the International Commission investigation at the Katyn graves. After several months of imprisonment he faced the "People's Court." Dr. Markov admitted before the court, "I am guilty before the Bulgarian Nation and its Liberator, Russia. . . . This is my guilt. . . ." Subsequently he testified that he was forced to go to Katyn Forest and that all members of the International Commission were compelled by the Germans to sign the report. He also maintained that all members were convinced that the evidence "was false." After this confession the public prosecutor withdrew the indictment against Dr. Markov.[21] His next public testimony was at the Nuremberg trial.

Dr. Prosorovsky maintained that he was convinced beyond "doubt that the Polish officers were buried in the fall, 1941." [22] Professor Basilevsky affirmed the Soviet report that the Katyn Forest was "a favorite resort of the inhabitants of Smolensk," and that there was "no fence at all." [23] He talked about the forest, but not about the area around the N.K.V.D. house.

Professor Basilevsky spent his leave in August 1940 in the town of Kozelsk. The slain Poles in the Katyn Forest all came from the prisoner-of-war camp at Kozelsk. In his testimony he assured the court that the Poles "were there" in August 1940; therefore, they could not have been killed in May 1940. He did not actually say that he saw them, but he said, "they were there." [24]

Curiosity was aroused when Colonel Ahrens, named in the *Soviet Report* as Arnes, the officer under whose supervision the atrocity was committed, volunteered to testify.[25]

Colonel Ahrens testified for one week under a barrage of questioning from the Soviet prosecution. He was not commander of the unit at the time of the massacre as established by the *Soviet Report*.[26] He was not even there at the date designated by the Soviet prosecutor as the time of murder. Then, the Soviet prosecution took a different line—Ahren's predecessor was responsible.

The German defense produced Colonel Bedenk. He was commander of the area prior to Ahrens. Facts against Bedenk could not be produced.[27] The German defense brought the immediate superior of both colonels: General Oberhäuser.[28] Also one of the lieutenants, whose responsibility was drafting orders for the unit, testified.[29]

According to these officers' testimony, at the end of August 1941 a German communication center belonging to the Central Army Group moved into the former N.K.V.D. house. The official designation of the communication unit was 537th Signal Regiment. Its task was to tie a web of communication among five (sometimes six) German armies spread through devastated Ukrainian and western Russian lands.

The number of soldiers and technicians operating the telephones and other apparatus was between seventeen and twenty. It was during the presence of this German unit in the area that the buried Poles were found. Its staff, however, had nothing to do with the exhumations which followed.

In spite of the efforts of the Soviet prosecution, the German officers' testimony cleared them from the Soviet accusations. What happened next? Nothing. The Katyn case "disappeared" from the Nuremberg trial. When Dr. Hans Laternser, the counsel for the German General Staff and High Command of the German Armed Forces, asked, "May I have the question put to the Prosecution, who is to be made responsible for the Katyn case?" the President of the Court, Lord Justice Lawrence, said, "I do not propose to answer questions of that sort." [30] Soviet prosecution refrained from further action.

When the final verdicts were rendered on September 30, 1946, the Katyn affair was not mentioned. Following the arrangement of charges from the indictment, the verdict dealt with the Sagan slaying of fifty R.A.F. officers, describing it as "plain murder in complete violation of international law," [31] and proceeded to the execution of Soviet prisoners during the German-Soviet war. The charge concerning Katyn was simply omitted without explanation.

The responsibility for the deaths of 4,443 to 4,800 Allied officers and men and the disappearance of an additional 10,000 in the Soviet Union was simply disregarded. At the same time, the murder of fifty other Allied officers in Germany was very thoroughly investigated and judgment rendered. As one of the members of the American prosecution staff remarked, the treatment of the Katyn case at the Nuremberg trial "looked mighty funny." [32]

On the other hand, looking at the handling of the Katyn

affair during the Nuremberg trial from the technical standpoint, one must realize that the German military elite were the defendants. They, and no one else "sat at the hard benches and faced the record of their deeds." In the case of the Katyn massacre the Germans were the accused, and their guilt was to be established. At the moment when German guilt could not be proved, it can be supposed that the jurisdiction of the court ended. It definitely was not the function of this court to establish who killed the Polish prisoners-of-war by arranging a separate investigation to look for the murderers elsewhere.

While the court had some legal technicalities as reasons for not pressing to discover who committed the crime, there seems to be no excuse for the way in which the evidence was treated during the trial. First of all, the bulk of evidence of paramount importance in the possession of the Poles was not only not sought, but was also not admitted when offered. The Poles not only had the copies of diaries and some other materials which they took from the graves without the Germans' knowledge, but could even produce a witness, Professor Świaniewicz, who had been a prisoner in Camp Kozelsk and who was still with the men what appears to have been only hours before their execution. There were several hundred officers who were evacuated with General Anders' army from the Soviet Union, from whose testimony much of the case could be reconstructed. Captain Czapski and Major Kaczkowski, the officers who tried so hard to gather all data on the missing men, were already in the West and had available a wealth of material collected in the Soviet Union, but they were not called to testify.

In the latter part of May 1946 one of the German counsellors at the trial, Dr. Otto Stahmer, asked, in writing, the former commander of the Polish Forces in the Soviet Union, General Anders, to send him material which would be useful in establishing the identity of those guilty of the Katyn Massacre. General Anders had in his possession a great deal of material. He was at that time the commander of the 2nd Polish Corps in the British Eighth Army. It was General Anders' feeling that, being a corps commander in the Allied forces, he should not render assistance directly to the counsellor of German war criminals. He, therefore, submitted a letter to the Allied Forces Headquarters, through American liaison officer Colonel John Tappin, expressing his willingness to submit important material upon an official request from the International Tribunal in Nuremberg.[33] He also answered Dr. Stahmer in this spirit.

General Anders did not receive any reply to his proposal and the trial continued without Polish evidence and witnesses. General Anders did not know whether the tribunal was ever "so advised." [34] Justice Robert Jackson, United States Chief of Counsel for Prosecution at Nuremberg, maintained that General Anders' offer never came to his attention.[35] Jackson was not even given extremely valuable materials concerning Katyn which were already in the possession of the United States Government, for example, the reports of Colonels Szymanski and Van Vliet, U.S. Army officers.[36]

Some material was given Jackson—the German report, Soviet documents placing the guilt on German forces, and "excerpts of conversations between Sikorski, Anders, Stalin, and Molotov." However, according to Jackson, "none of these was in condition to be useful as evidence." [37]

The case did not fare any better at the hands of the British Government. General Anders' British superiors knew his willingness to submit evidence at Nuremberg. They also knew, through their channels of intelligence, that the evidence was of considerable magnitude, definitive and decisive in character. Neither he nor his materials were tapped.

The representatives of the "Warsaw Government" who participated in the trial as Polish representatives said nothing. Evidence collected under auspices of the Council of Ministers of the Polish Government-in-Exile by Doctor Wiktor Sukiennicki (cited in this book as *Polish Report*) was excluded.

It was quite interesting to hear Justice Jackson defending the procedures of the Nuremberg trial with regard to the Katyn Massacre during the Congressional hearings in 1952. His position was that "we could not at the international trial wisely undertake or satisfactorily achieve the long task of separating truth from falsehood." [38] Then, he proceeded to list four reasons in support:

(1) "Responsibility for the massacre did not appear to be capable of documentary proof or substantial corroboration"; [39]

(2) "we knew of no witnesses who could supply oral proof to establish the identity of the perpetrators that would meet the high standards of credibility"; [40]

(3) "we did not need to prove Nazi responsibility for the Katyn murder in order to establish that the Nazi regime and individual defendants were guilty of conspiracy and a program to exterminate vast numbers of Poles"; [41]

(4) "we were under exceedingly heavy pressure to get along with the trial." [42]

Justice Jackson's arguments were eloquent, but they cannot stand scrutiny. "Documentary proof" and creditable witnesses were available at the time of the trial, but they were neither sought nor admitted as evidence. The material gathered by the Congressional Investigating Committee (see Chapter IX) is the best proof of this. His third point is irrelevant, and the last one about "getting along with the trial" not serious.

Justice Jackson was on much more secure ground when he pointed out to the Congressional Committee that in any case the Soviet Union Government or its personnel could not be prosecuted at the Nuremberg trial for the simple reason that not they but the Germans were indicted.[43]

Justice Jackson: "I will make a bargain with you, Mr. Congressman. If you will capture Stalin, I will try him."

Mr. O'Konski: "I will ask for that job myself to be sure he hangs. I wouldn't trust another Nuremberg Trial." [44]

Four years after the trial, the handling of the Katyn case at Nuremberg was partially clarified. The mighty lion of international politics, Mr. Churchill, did so in his memoirs. One sentence, free from legal subtleties and full of implications, is: "It was decided by the victorious Governments concerned that the issue should be avoided, and the crime of Katyn was never probed in detail." [45] Perhaps one day the records will reveal precisely who decided that, and how it was decided.

The public trial of war criminals at Nuremberg ended with the murderers from Katyn Forest unrevealed and unpunished —without protest, as Poles point out, from the Soviet Government or the Communist Government of Poland.

NOTES TO CHAPTER V

1. Kazimierz Skarżyński, "Katyń i Polski Czerwony Krzyż" Katyn and the Polish Red Cross), *Kultura*, no. 9/51, May 1955, p. 140. Mr. Skarżyński was Secretary General of the Polish Red Cross at that time.

2. Testimony under oath by Dr. Beck and one of the German guards, Karl Herrmann. The guard was evacuated with documents from Kraków on January 18, 1944, to Breslau, then to Dresden, and finally to Radebeul. References concerning the number of boxes: *Hearings*, part 5: Dr. Beck, p. 1515; the guard, pp. 1510-1511.

3. *Loc. cit.*

4. Compare Stanisław Mikołajczyk, *The Rape of Poland: Pattern of Soviet Aggression* (New York: Whittlesey House, 1948), p. 37.

5. Dr. Beck's testimony, *Hearings*, part 5, p. 1517.

6. U.S. Department of State. International Organization and Conference, ser. II. European and British Commonwealth, 1. *Report of Robert H. Jackson United States Representative to the International Conference on Military Trials, London 1945* (Washington: Division of Publications, Office of Public Affairs, 1945). Released February

1949. Of particular interest are the drafts of the Soviet and American proposals printed in parallel columns on pp. 165-184.

7. U.S. Office of Chief of Counsel for Prosecution of Axis Criminality. *Nazi Conspiracy and Aggression.* Supplement A and B (Washington: Government Printing Office, 1947), pp. 1-12.

8. Justice Jackson's testimony. *Hearings,* part 7, p. 1946.

9. *Loc. cit.*

10. *I.M.T.,* vol. VII, 154. References to the Katyn Forest Massacre at the hearings of the International Military Trial can be found in the following volumes and pages: Vol. I, 48, 54; II, 65; VII, 425-428, 468-469; IX, 3-4; XIV, 513-514; XV, 289-293; XVIII, 271-371, 539-545; XXIV, 172.

11. G. M. Gilbert, *Nuremberg Diary* (New York: Farrar, Straus and Co., 1947), p. 136.

12. *I.M.T.,* VII, 425-428; also Document U.S.S.R. 54.

13. *Ibid.,* XV, 289-293.

14. *Ibid.,* XV, 290; also XVII, 271.

15. Letter of the Polish Parliamentary Group in London, sent to Mr. Justice Jackson on February 15, 1946. *Hearings,* part 7, pp. 1976-1978.

16. *Ibid.,* part 5, p. 1551.

17. *I.M.T.,* XVII, 337, 345.

18. *Ibid.,* 336.

19. *Ibid.,* 347.

20. *Hearings,* part 5, pp. 1310, 1416, 1480, 1491, 1610; Joseph Mackiewicz, *The Katyn Wood Murders* (London: Hollis and Carter, 1951), pp. 119-122; "Katyn—ein Verbrechen der Soviets" (Katyn—a Soviet crime), *Der Spiegel,* Vol. VI, no. 1 (January 2, 1952), p. 19; *German Report,* p. 188.

21. *Zbrodnia Katyńska w Świetle Dokumentów* (The Katyn crime in the light of documents). Z przedmową Władysława Andersa. 2-gie wydanie (London: Gryf, 1950), pp. 224-228.

22. *I.M.T.,* XVII, 371.

23. *Ibid.,* 321.

24. *Ibid.,* 330; "Basilevsky was ludicrous when one correspondent asked him why he was so excited by the murder of 10,000 Poles when he also knew that 135,000 Russians had been killed in the same area. He answered that the Poles were prisoners-of-war and it was an outrageous violation of international law for them to be massacred." This statement concerning Professor Basilevsky was written two years *before* the Nuremberg trial by John Melby, the third secretary of the U.S. Embassy in Moscow, as the result of his and Miss Harriman's visit to the Katyn graves. They met Basilevsky there. Enclosure No. 1 to Dispatch No. 207, dated February 23, 1944, from the American Embassy in Moscow to the State Department, Washington.

25. Colonel Ahrens testified voluntarily also at the Congressional Hearings in 1952. *Hearings,* part 5, pp. 1252, 1257, 1258, 1275.
26. *I.M.T.,* XVII, 287.
27. Colonel Bedenk also testified during the Congressional investigation. *Hearings,* part 5, pp. 1249-1263.
28. General Oberhäuser's testimony. *I.M.T.,* XVII, 310-321.
29. *Ibid.,* 301-304.
30. *Ibid.,* 286.
31. *I.M.T.,* XXII, 472.
32. *Hearings,* part 5, p. 1548.
33. Władysław Anders, *Bez Ostatniego Rozdziału. Wspomnienia z Lat 1939-1946* (Without the last chapter. Memoirs of the years 1939-1946) (Newton, Wales: Montgomeryshire Printing Co., Ltd., 1949), p. 414.
34. General Anders' testimony. *Hearings,* part 4, p. 968.
35. Mr. Justice Jackson's testimony. *Hearings,* part 7, p. 1947.
36. *Ibid.,* pp. 1955, 1959-1960.
37. *Ibid.,* p. 1948.
38. *Ibid.,* p. 1946.
39. *Loc. cit.*
40. *Ibid.,* p. 1947.
41. *Ibid.,* p. 1948.
42. *Ibid.,* p. 1951.
43. *Ibid.,* p. 1953.
44. *Ibid.,* p. 1966.
45. Winston S. (now Sir Winston) Churchill, *The Hinge of Fate* (Boston: Houghton Mifflin Co., 1950), p. 761.

VI

Analysis of the Evidence

THE NUREMBERG TRIAL did not untangle the Katyn affair; the Germans and the Soviets each blamed the other for the atrocity. For reasons of political expediency some of the existing data in the Allied camp were suppressed or conveniently omitted from consideration. It is the purpose of this chapter to assess *all* of the available evidence.

Let us first summarize the facts. The physical presence of about 15,000 Polish prisoners-of-war, mostly officers, in Soviet Russia has been established beyond doubt. These men were imprisoned in three Soviet camps—Kozelsk, Ostashkov, and Starobelsk—following their capture in the Soviet-Polish campaign of 1939. The approximate distribution of the men in the camps was as follows: Kozelsk, 5,000; Ostashkov, 6,570; and Starobelsk, 4,000. These added up to a total of 15,570.[1]

All of these men were in the camps around November 1939. By the latter part of December 1939, they were allowed to write once a month to their families in Poland, which at that time was divided between the Soviet and German occupying military forces and administrations. In the early spring of 1940 all correspondence from the men from the three camps abruptly ceased. The Soviet Post Office began returning to the senders mail addressed to the prisoners; the explanation stamped on the envelopes was that the mail could not be delivered. Research has established an explanation for this fact.

Early in May 1940 all three camps were completely evacuated by the Soviet authorities. Four hundred forty-eight of the prisoners were gathered after a time in Camp Pavelishtchev Bor and then transferred to Camp Grazovec. They were the only men ever found alive from the 15,000.

These men continued to correspond with their families in Poland until June 21, 1941, when the German-Soviet war broke out. The prisoners from Grazovec were able to remember the approximate number and to list most of the names of their compatriots with whom they had been kept imprisoned until the spring of 1940, confirming beyond a doubt the presence of 15,000 Polish prisoners in Russia at that time. The "four hundred" from Grazovec were ultimately released as a direct result of the re-establishment of Soviet-Polish diplomatic relations in July 1941. These men joined General Anders' Polish army in Russia, reporting that they were from the Camps Kozelsk, Ostashkov, and Starobelsk. They delivered the lists of names of the unaccounted-for men who had been evacuated from these camps in May 1940 in an unknown direction. None of these 15,000 men appeared in the Polish units, nor could they be located anywhere. Among the missing were 8,300-8,400 officers.

Every attempt since the spring of 1940 to find these men had failed. Polish, British, and American diplomatic efforts to do so had been fruitless. They could not have been exchanged by the Soviet Government to the Germans because the Polish Underground Movement in a search for the missing men had thoroughly combed all labor camps, concentration camps, and prisoner-of-war camps throughout Germany and German-occupied Europe without finding even a trace of them. They were obviously not in Poland, where they would have contacted their families, who were frantically searching for them, and where their presence would be immediately known to the Underground. The search had been in vain, until the mass graves were found in Katyn Forest. All of those missing from Camp Kozelsk—one third of the men—were there.

ANALYSIS OF THE EVIDENCE

The problem is twofold: Who killed the 4,443-4,800 men in the Katyn Forest, and what happened to the remaining 10,000 missing from the Camps Starobelsk and Ostashkov?

First, who shot the men in the forest and dumped their bodies into mass graves? There are but two possibilities. They were shot either by German or by Soviet military or police units designated for this operation.

The German record of atrocities during the war [2] makes it perfectly reasonable to entertain the hypothesis that they might have shot these prisoners.

The official attitude of the German administration toward Poles in general was based on a policy directive issued by Hitler himself: "There should be one master only for the Poles, the Germans. Two masters side by side cannot exist. All representatives of the Polish intelligentsia are to be exterminated. This sounds cruel, but such is the law of life." [3] The "German King of Poland," Hans Frank, who ruled the defeated country, got the point. During a special conference arranged for German police officials in May 1940, he said that the time was ripe to implement Hitler's order. These are his words:

> The [German] offensive in the West began on May 10, 1940. On that day the center of interest shifted from the events taking place here [Poland]. . . . We must take opportunity in our hands.
> I frankly admit that it will cost the lives of some thousands of Poles and these will be taken mainly from leading members of the Polish intelligentsia. In these times we, as National Socialists, are bound to ensure that no further resistance is offered by the Polish people.
> The men capable of leadership whom we have found to exist in Poland must be liquidated.[4]

The result of the conference was German order "Operation A-B, liquidation of the Polish leadership." Through Poland rode terror in screaming green police cars. Men were jerked from their beds, taken from street cars, from their desks and classrooms. Several hours later they were dead. I myself lived in Warsaw during the German occupation, 1939-1944, and was captured twice on the streets. Favorable circumstances saved me from a street execution. Hundreds of thousands were less fortunate. No man who did not live through it will understand what it means to be hunted on the streets like an animal, for being a Pole or a Jew.

The officers killed in Katyn and those who disappeared comprised the flower of Polish society. Thousands of them had been called in 1939 from the reserve. In their civilian occupations they were university professors, doctors, scientists, artists, high-school teachers—the brain and heart of Poland. This the German administration knew. It can be said that the climate of official attitudes and actions displayed by the Germans with regard to non-combatants, prisoners-of-war, and Poles in general was such as to make the execution of the Polish officers by Germans plausible.

What about the policies and attitudes of the Soviet Union? What was its record of treatment of Poles in general and Polish prisoners-of-war in particular? Was the prevalent system of values and legal norms of the Soviet State between 1939 and 1943 of such nature as to permit the murders in the Katyn Forest? Careful study of the Polish official documents [5] and extensive interviews with the former Polish prisoners-of-war who survived Soviet imprisonment justify an unqualified yes.[6]

The conclusion must be that the policies of the German and the Soviet governments with regard to Poles during the period from 1939 to 1943 would have permitted either government to annihilate over 4,000 Poles in Katyn Forest. The executioners could have worn either swastikas or red stars on their uniforms. To ascertain the identity of the guilty, all available data as presented by the German, Soviet, Polish, and International Commissions will be examined.[7]

To paraphrase the *Polish Report*,[8] the Soviet charge that the Germans are responsible for the Katyn crime is based

ANALYSIS OF THE EVIDENCE

upon two assertions: First, that the prisoners were working in Soviet labor camps in the area near Smolensk from the spring of 1940 until July 1941, at which time they were captured by the German Army; and, second, that the Germans murdered the prisoners in the late summer of 1941, buried them in the Katyn graves, and exhumed the bodies in the early spring of 1943, when they removed documents which might prove them guilty, inserted others and returned the bodies to the graves. They then called for an investigation and again exhumed the bodies, this time in the presence of the International and Polish Red Cross Commissions.

Regarding the first assumption of the Soviet accusation, if the German armies had captured the prisoners in July 1941, why did the Soviet authorities not tell this to the Polish, American, and British officials, who were searching so intensively for the missing men? Nothing would have been simpler than to say, "We had these men, but the Germans captured them." It would have automatically discharged their responsibility for 15,000 men. From July 1941, when Polish-Soviet diplomatic relations were re-established, to April 1943, the Soviet Government "did not know" what had happened to the missing men, but at the time of the discovery of the graves it stated that the prisoners had been captured by the Germans.

It does appear likely that, had the Germans captured these men, the presence of 15,000 prisoners-of-war of Polish origin would have been reported by the German authorities to the International Red Cross, as was the case with thousands of other Polish officers and men held in German prisoner-of-war camps. Keeping these men alive from July until September 1941 certainly would have attracted the attention of the Polish Underground Movement which had its operatives covering the entire territory seized by the Germans. The Underground *was looking for these men*. It would have been impossible to hide over 15,000 men from the determined search of such an efficient underground organization as the Poles had during the Second World War. It would appear that the Soviet Government had refrained from saying "the Germans captured your men," because this could have been verified or refuted in a matter of hours.

There is no doubt that the N.K.V.D. had comprehensive documentation of the maintenance of the prisoners. The transportation, feeding, supervising of over 15,000 men and the results of their purported road-building would have left some records. According to the *Soviet Report* the prisoners worked near Smolensk under Soviet supervision from April 1940 until July 1941, when they were captured by the German Army. If so, why was the evidence of their maintenance not presented to the Poles as proof that the men were still alive *after* May 1940? Reliable documents of this nature would have refuted the assertions of the International Commission, Polish Red Cross Commission, and the German Commission—all of which maintained that the prisoners were killed in the spring of 1940—and could have been included in the *Soviet Report*.

The *Soviet Report* presented some local peasants as "witnesses" who testified that the Poles were alive when the Germans came. Some of them had testified first on behalf of the Germans, then on behalf of the Soviet Commission, pivoting toward the source of power wielded over their lives. The available data are sufficient for drawing conclusions without relying on frightened witnesses who very likely were intimidated by their interrogators.

Moreover, the Soviet Commission undermined the seriousness of its own report by appearing to resort to deliberate attempts to confuse. The Commission maintained that the Poles were captured by Germans in three camps around Smolensk. It is true that there were three camps around Smolensk in which Polish privates and noncommissioned officers worked on the adjacent roads. But these men were withdrawn from the camps about nine months prior to German invasion. What

ANALYSIS OF THE EVIDENCE

is even more important, these positively were not the men from Camp Kozelsk whose bodies were found in the Katyn graves.

The second assertion of the Soviet Government was that the Germans captured the prisoners, shot them, buried the bodies, then exhumed them, removed some documents, inserted others, reinterred the bodies, and then called for an investigation.

The *Soviet Report* gives the impression that change of control over the 15,000 prisoners could have been easily accomplished. Anyone who remembers the ferocity with which the Soviet and German armies fought will realize that such a situation was highly improbable.

Or why did the Russians not evacuate the prisoners, even on foot, which would seem to be the logical procedure when conditions are controllable? And if they were not "controllable" why did none of the prisoners escape? Here were over 15,000 men, the majority combat-proven, many of them cadet officers, young and confident, who might be expected to take advantage of a situation in which they were not controlled. None of the 15,000 prisoners from the camps Kozelsk, Ostashkov, and Starobelsk ever appeared on either side of the Soviet-German front, except for the 448 men transferred to Grazovec and 4,443-4,800 found in Katyn.

All who saw the corpses during the investigations made under both German and Soviet auspices noticed that the overwhelming majority of the dead were dressed in heavy winter coats with all the buttons fastened. According to the Soviet version, the German authorities captured the prisoners in July and killed them in or around August-September.

The isotherm map of Eastern Europe shows that the average temperature at that time around Smolensk, which includes the Katyn area, "is 65° Fahrenheit, *i.e.*, the same as on the southern shores of the [English] Channel where at that time of the year the bathing season is at its height." [9] The fact that the bodies were dressed in winter clothing was noticed by all present at the excavations.[10]

An American correspondent, who upon the invitation of the Soviet authorities spent several hours in Katyn during the Soviet investigation, says:

> When the correspondents were permitted to put questions, one asked, why, if the slaughter had been in August or September, many of the corpses wore fur-lined coats. The Russians said that fall nights were cold in Smolensk and the prisoners probably had no other outer garments. Russian censorship permitted the correspondents to cable this searching question and its none-too-convincing reply.[11]

The Soviet Commission, basing its findings presumably on witnesses' testimonies, set the dates of murder as "autumn," "August and September," "up to September inclusive," "after June." The Soviet medical experts left more room for guessing by stating the date as "June-December." This implied, contrary to the rest of the content of the report, that the men could have been killed during the winter. Actually this move provided further discrepancy within the *Soviet Report*. Ultimately, the Soviet prosecution at the Nuremberg trial set the date in the indictment at "September."

The *Polish Report* noted that with regard to the establishment of the season of the year in which the murders were committed, German, International and Polish teams maintained unanimously that they occurred in the early spring, while the Russians, leaving some room for interpretation, claimed that they occurred in late summer or early autumn. Members of the teams who placed the murders in the early spring call attention to the fact that no bugs or insects were found in the graves when opened. Had the killing taken place in the relatively warm part of the year, the presence of dead bugs or insects in the graves would have been unavoidable.

Another very important observation made by those visiting the graves was the state of preservation of the officers' boots.

They were in excellent condition. They showed little evidence of wear—even the "heels were not worn down." A peculiar cultural value existed in the Polish officer corps prior to and during the Second World War. High boots were a prestige and status symbol. Only officers and cadets were eligible to wear the hand-made, exquisitely-finished, high boots. Such boots were extremely light and graceful in design, made from the softest leather brought to perfect luster by hours of tedious polishing. They did not have much utilitarian value as combat boots, but it was "in style" in the Polish officer corps to wear them.

Shod in these boots, the Polish officers went forth to fight their short campaign. In these boots they were captured, and in these boots they were held in the three Soviet camps, where their freedom of movement was very limited, until April 1940. Then, according to the *Soviet Report*, they were employed in road-building from April 1940 until July 1941. These boots would not last through three months of Russian mud, to say nothing of sixteen months on a construction gang. This argument, however, could be questioned because many of the men wore wooden clogs attached to their boots. Perhaps the boots were in good condition because the clogs protected them? The question is important enough to be examined more closely.

Wooden clogs have been known to prisoners of the First and Second World Wars as a device for protecting the leather of the soles (an extremely hard-to-get material in European prisoner-of-war camps), but, above all, for the protection they provided from the chill of the ground during the winter, particularly when the men had to muster twice a day, morning and evening, for the official counting. This procedure took some time (from half an hour to two hours). To protect themselves against the penetrating frost during the winter months, the prisoners would attach wooden clogs to their boots. The very fact that clogs were found in the graves provides an additional argument that the prisoners were killed when the weather was cold. Nevertheless, whether the prisoners could have worked for sixteen months on construction gangs while protecting their boots with clogs, seems very doubtful. These self-made, primitively-hewn, flat pieces of wood were attached crudely to the boots by pieces of string, wire, cloth, or whatever material was at hand. One could stand on them, move carefully and slowly around, but to work on road construction in snow and mud with clogs attached would be virtually impossible, unless a man was bent on breaking his legs or neck. Finally, the majority of the men in the graves did not wear the clogs. Their shoes also were in excellent condition.

The Soviet Commission maintains that the Germans exhumed all the bodies in the early spring of 1943, then removed all the documents which could compromise them and inserted those which by implication would incriminate the Soviet Union. The International, Polish, and German Commissions have commented that the layers of bodies were fused by a sticky acid produced through the process of decomposition and that this acid, together with the decomposition of the bodies and their weight, left distinct mutual impressions upon the compressed bodies. Any movement of the bodies prior to the exhumation performed by the three commissions would definitely have ruined these impressions and would have left traces of such movement. Also, all the buttons on the underwear and outer garments were fastened, and the order of the pockets did not reveal any traces of previous search of the corpses at the time of the investigation by the three commissions.

The members of the Polish Red Cross team actually took part in the work of exhuming the bodies. They volunteered for this gruesome task for the very purpose of ascertaining beyond doubt whether the bodies had been previously handled at any time except immediately after death. They unanimously maintained the bodies had not been touched. The possibility that the Germans inserted fabricated documents after the bodies were exhumed can be precluded. This was out of the question because the bodies for autopsies were taken from the graves at random. When the members of the International Commission were performing autopsies they pointed to a corpse in the grave, and the cadaver would be lifted out and placed on the table for the examination. Dr. Naville, a Swiss citizen with over thirty years of experience in forensic medicine at the time of his membership in the International Commission, testified that he and his colleagues had complete freedom in the selection and search of the bodies. He himself removed some documents and a Russian-made box of matches from a corpse. Dr. Palmieri, from Italy, also testified that he had complete freedom in the investigation.[12]

There is another problem. If it is assumed that the Germans *did* kill the prisoners in the autumn of 1941, would it be possible for them to know in the spring of 1943 (the date when they supposedly placed false documents in the clothing of the bodies) what papers had been distributed in the Soviet camp of Kozelsk in the spring of 1940? From whom could they obtain such papers, as for example, the Soviet propaganda daily distributed in Kozelsk? Such papers were found on the bodies; it seems unlikely that they could have been placed there by the Germans.

An editor of a Polish source points out a significant circumstance which diminishes the probability of German guilt:

> The Germans would not take the risk of announcing that the murder was committed in the spring of 1940 (if they killed them in 1941), as 15,000 families could have letters written after the spring of 1940 up to June 22, 1941—one such letter could offset the whole German accusation. But nobody ... received ... a letter after the spring of 1940.[13]

One eyewitness reported that during the first investigation he was permitted to wander among the graves and the exhumed corpses and to pick up all scraps of paper in a search for dates. He said he found nothing dated later than April 1940.[14]

The prisoners who were sent to Grazovec were permitted to send and receive mail until the outbreak of the Soviet-German war, while mail from the other Poles in Kozelsk, Ostashkov, and Starobelsk ceased in the spring of 1940, and letters from their families were returned by the Soviet Post Office after that time. When the families, disturbed by their inability to contact their loved ones, wrote directly to the Soviet authorities (there was even a letter written to Stalin), the answer was either, "he was transferred to an unknown camp," or something to the effect that "his whereabouts are unknown." [15]

If the results of exhumation attested by the three commissions (International, Polish, and German) are accepted, the conclusion follows that the bodies had been in the graves about three years, which would establish the date of the murders as the early spring of 1940. Other circumstantial evidence supports this conclusion.

In the voluminous material—thousands of documents, about 3,300 personal letters, post-cards,[16] and identification papers—collected by the three commissions, the latest date found was May 6, 1940. The most important documentary evidence was the diaries written by the murdered men. These diaries will be used later in reconstructing details of the fate of the prisoners, for it should be recalled here that the diaries were investigated at the graves by the members of the Polish Underground Movement, and copies were sent to the Polish Government-in-Exile in London. The originals were also subjected to very close analytical scrutiny by the Polish staff of the Polish Red Cross, when the materials were deposited in Kraków. Finally, since pictures and copies of them were preserved, the content was authenticated by those surviving prisoners who were transferred from Kozelsk to Grazovec.

Those men, referred to in the *Polish Report*, not only confirmed that the diaries were written by the hands of their friends with whom they were imprisoned, but that accurate accounts were given of the details of everyday life and of the names mentioned by the writers.

All of the diaries end in April 1940. Surely if the authors were alive until the autumn of 1941 they would have written something during the intervening sixteen months. The diaries deal with the everyday drudgery of internment, so it might be supposed that the writers would not fail to mention such great events as the outbreak of the Soviet-German war and the arrival of the German troops. (The Soviet Government maintains that they were captured in July 1941 by the German armies.)

Against this mass of evidence stands the statement of the *Soviet Report* that nine documents (no content cited) were found on the bodies (these bodies having already been searched during the investigations by the three commissions) showing dates later than May 1940. On this basis the Report refutes the conclusions of the three commissions that the massacre was in April or the beginning of May 1940.

The *Polish Report* questions the reliability of these nine documents. It points out that "all of them had either been issued by the Soviet authorities or had passed through their hands, and they concerned either completely unknown people or individuals who were known not to have been in the Kozelsk camp." [17]

Three of these documents were letters; all had been written after April 1940, and had been mailed from Poland. (The Soviet Medical Commission, when showing the bodies to the foreign correspondents and Miss Harriman, had them already prepared on the tables. This was not the procedure with the foreign representatives during the investigation under the German auspices. There, the men could roam freely among the graves, pick a body for investigation at the very moment the grave was opened. Because this procedure was not used during the Soviet investigation, insertion of documents at the second exhumation was possible.)

In one instance the Soviet Commission reported finding "an unmailed postcard in the Polish language addressed Warsaw, Bagatelia [Bagatela] 15, apartment 47, to Irene Kuczinska, and dated June 1941. The sender is Stanisław Kuczyński."[18] Stanisław Kuczyński indeed was a Polish soldier, but he was never interned in Kozelsk Camp, as were the rest of the murdered men. He was removed by the N.K.V.D. from Camp Starobelsk in 1939, and nobody has heard from him since.[19]

There are, however, five points of paramount importance which the Soviet Commission does not even mention.[20] First there were the trees. The young spruce were planted on the graves intentionally. They were younger and smaller than the other trees around them. They stood out so distinctly that the members of the three commissions soon learned to discern the locations of the graves by merely looking at the height of the trees. Wherever they saw small trees of the same height grouped together against a background of older forest, they looked for the bodies under them—successfully.[21]

A microscopic analysis of these spruce trees established that they were five years old at the time of the investigation (1943); but the arrangement of rings, when the trunks were cross-sectioned, indicated that they had been planted on the graves three years before. This points to the spring of 1940.[22] At that time the Soviet Government had complete jurisdiction and control over the area.

When the German Commission announced the result of the microscopic analysis of the trees, and the Poles and members of the International Commission verified it, this evidence became indestructible. The argument could not be evaded or refuted by political maneuvering. Even Mr. Churchill reacted to it with unusual intensity by sending a personal message:

"Prime Minister to Foreign Secretary: I think Sir Owen O'Malley should be asked very secretly to express his opinion on the Katyn Wood Inquiry. How does the argument about the length of time the birch [?] trees had grown over the graves fit in with this new tale? Did anybody look at the birch trees?" [23] Hundreds of men had looked at the trees, and it was evident that they were younger and different in height than the rest of the trees around. The Soviet Commission omits this problem entirely.

A second point of equal importance is this. The bodies of the men in the graves in many instances were bunched together in the same order they left Camp Kozelsk in the spring of 1940.[24] The men left Kozelsk in about twenty separate transports. In each of the transports there were from 50 to 344 men. (The largest, convoy number 13, departed April 20, 1940.) The officers remaining in the camp made an exact list of their friends' departure, noting the dates and the number of men in each of the transports. Some of these lists survived and were supplemented by the prisoners from Kozelsk who were sent by the Soviets to Camp Grazovec, and ultimately joined General Anders' army. In some of the diaries recovered from the graves were listed the names of those locked in the same freight car during the transport. They were found grouped together in the graves.[25]

The *Polish Report* reasons from this evidence that if the officers were employed for over one year subsequent to their departure from Kozelsk, it would be improbable that they would be grouped in the graves in the same order in which they departed. Accepting the Soviet thesis that the men, following their removal from Kozelsk, were placed in three camps, worked in teams on the roads, then underwent the Soviet withdrawal and capture by the German armies, it seems doubtful that during all these times no reshuffling or regrouping of the men would take place.[26]

The Polish argument could be further strengthened here

by using a sociological analysis. The men were captured in the fall of 1939 and departed from Kozelsk in the spring of 1940. That means they had about six months of time to develop a network of informal affiliations and loyalties. On the basis of Polish cultural values the officers probably would form traditional groups—the cavalrymen would be together, and the young Polish equivalent of "West-Pointers" would do the same, as in fact they did in German prisoner-of-war camps. When assembling the transports from Kozelsk, the Soviet authorities gathered the men at random. There was no pattern in their choice of members of the convoys. It is safe to assume that if they had been alive for the next year, the men would have reshuffled themselves according to their personal bonds and loyalties, particularly after the German capture. Yet, the bodies as a rule were in the same randomly assembled groups (layer upon layer in the graves) as they were when departing from Kozelsk.

It might be appropriate also to mention here that in grave number eight there were approximately 200 bodies dressed differently from the rest of the officers. The men in this grave did not wear either overcoats, sweaters or warm underwear, as the remaining men did. The German, International and Polish Red Cross Commissions duly noted this fact, but were unable to establish the reason. Painstaking research by Polish authorities provided an explanation. One of the last convoys left Kozelsk in the beginning of May. The weather had changed abruptly, becoming very warm, the "sun beating down." The men dressed themselves lightly, because they had to march from the camp to the nearest railway station on foot.

In the very last party which left Kozelsk there were the approximately ninety-five men who went to Pavelishtchev-Bor and subsequently to Grazovec. Some of these survivors are living today in England. They testified and, as has been mentioned, submitted lists of the departing men. Their information about the names and number of lightly-clothed men departing in May from Kozelsk tallies with the finding of the same number of bodies correspondingly dressed in grave number eight, and explains why the men were dressed differently. In addition, Soviet camp daily papers from Kozelsk dated May 1940 [27] were found on these bodies.

The *Soviet Report* is silent on this subject. It also takes no note of the fact that the rope so meticulously cut into pieces of the same length, with which the hands of the younger victims were tied, was beyond doubt of Russian origin.[28] Nor was anything said about the wounds made on the bodies with four-cornered bayonets, which were used only by the Russians in 1940.[29]

It must not be forgotten that the Soviet Government blocked the offer of the International Red Cross to investigate the Katyn matter. (It may be recalled that the International Red Cross had stipulated that it would investigate *only* if *all* interested parties requested it to do so.) The Germans not only were willing to invite the International Red Cross but promised every assistance. The Soviet Government did not ask for an investigation by the International Red Cross when Katyn was in possession of the Germans, nor did it invite that organization when the Soviet Commission started its own investigation. As a matter of fact, the Soviet Government did not invite any doctors or experts from the Allied countries. It even barred the Polish communists from participation.[30]

The preceding evidence is supported by results of the autopsies. The members of the International Commission, on the basis of microscopic analysis and evaluation of the degree of saponification of the brains, established that the bodies must have been in the graves for a minimum of three years, which again points to the date of the murders as spring of 1940. Such recognized medical authorities as Dr. Orsos (at that time from Hungary), Dr. Palmieri (Italy), and Dr. Miloslavich (presently residing in the United States) agreed on this point during the investigation in 1943, and publicly confirmed their views in 1952.[31] It also should be mentioned that the German authorities apparently attempted to preserve the evidence,[32] which suggests that they did not fear investigation.

It has been argued that the very manner of shooting the prisoners indicates that Soviet authorities committed the crime. This argument does not appear valid. On March 24, 1944, in the Ardeatine caves near Rome the German executioners shot over 300 Italians,[33] in a manner resembling that used in the Katyn Forest.

The last factor to be considered in an analysis of the evidence is the number of bodies reported by the Soviet and German Commissions. This is an exceedingly difficult subject due to the fact that each party involved—German, Soviet, and Polish authorities—juggled the numbers to prove their point.

The *German Report* admits that the number of bodies actually exhumed was 4,143, but nevertheless talks about 10,000 to 12,000 murdered in the Katyn Forest.[34] This number, larger than the number of bodies actually discovered, was claimed in order to be consistent with the original German propaganda estimate made prior to the exhumations. This original estimate of "10,000 to 12,000" had been based on German knowledge that the Poles were looking for well over 10,000 missing prisoners.

The Soviet Commission, although it exhumed only 925 bodies, set the number at 11,000. The Soviet Commission's aim was to discharge in this way the responsibility for additional thousands of prisoners from the Camps Ostashkov and Starobelsk, who, in fact, did not seem to be buried in Katyn graves.[35]

The Poles aimed at an adjustment which would bring the numbers of those interned in Camp Kozelsk and those found in the graves into agreement.[36]

By reconciling all available data, however, it can be safely assumed that the total number of Polish prisoners murdered in the Katyn Forest was between 4,443 and 4,800. In the light of all assembled data [37] it would appear that the charge, "In September 1941, 11,000 Polish officers who were prisoners-of-war were killed in the Katyn Forest near Smolensk," [38] taken from the indictment of the Nuremberg trial of 1946, was seriously at fault.

In this sentence four misstatements were submitted by the Soviet prosecution:

(1) That the men were murdered in the month of September. (The preceding review of the evidence points clearly to April or May.)
(2) That they were murdered in 1941. (The evidence points to 1940—when the territory of Katyn was solely under the Soviet control.)
(3) That 11,000 bodies were found in the Katyn Forest. (The number must lie between 4,443 and 4,800.)
(4) That the victims were all officers. (The bodies of non-commissioned officers and privates were also found.)

The Soviet prosecution was in possession of facts which refuted their charges as summarized above at the time they made the charges.

Finally, the German leaders should not be accused of this crime. They could have committed the Katyn Massacre, but they did not do it.

The Katyn Massacre was perpetrated by Soviet Security Police (N.K.V.D.) and under the auspices of the Soviet Government. In the following chapters the circumstances of the murder will be reconstructed in detail.

NOTES TO CHAPTER VI

1. "Memorandum Concerning the Polish Prisoners of War from Starobelsk, Kozelsk and Ostashkov, Who Did Not Return." Dated Moscow February 2, 1942. Submitted on the same day to N.K.V.D.

General Raikhman by the "Commissioner for the Affairs of Former Prisoners of War in the USSR, Captain of the Cavalry, Józef Czapski." English translation. *Hearings,* part 5, pp. 1238-1240. Among the several official sources printed under the auspices of the Polish Government-in-Exile which give the number of prisoners in the three camps, the original numbers as compiled by Captain Czapski in his memorandum for the N.K.V.D. are accepted by this writer throughout the book. There are two reasons for this: One, Czapski's figures were assembled and made known *prior* to the discovery of the Katyn graves. This precluded any possibility of their subsequent manipulation in order to tailor the figures, particularly those from Camp Kozelsk, to the number found in the graves in order to make the Polish case stronger. Two, there are some inconsistencies in the data provided by Polish official sources, particularly with regard to number of prisoners in Kozelsk. Compare Czapski, *loc. cit.,* with *Polish Report,* pp. 21, 22, 77, 78, 103, 332; also pp. 133, 324; also compare with *Zbrodnia Katyńska w Świetle Dokumentów* (The Katyn crime in light of documents). Z przedmową Władysława Andersa. 2-gie wydanie. Gryf, 1950, pp. 25-28; also see *Hearings,* part 6, Exhibit 32, p. 1684. In summary, the data regarding the number of men in Camp Kozelsk submitted by official Polish sources present discrepancies, some resulting from dropping civilians and privates from the list, some apparently due to typographical errors. (See *Hearings,* part 5, pp. 1238, 1240 concerning the number in Camp Ostashkov.) Some errors exist because of the exceedingly difficult task of assembling the data.

Partially reconstructed lists of the names of prisoners who were kept in the Camps Kozelsk, Ostashkov, and Starobelsk until the spring of 1940 are printed in Adam Moszyński, *Lista Katyńska. Jeńcy Obozów Kozielsk, Starobielsk, Ostaszków, Zaginieni w Rosji Sowieckiej* (The roll of Katyn. The prisoners of Camps Kozelsk, Starobelsk, Ostashkov who disappeared in the Soviet Union) (London: Gryf, 1949), pp. 1-317.

2. A first-hand report of the mass murder of Jewish children, women, and men committed on Russian territory in a manner resembling that of the Poles in Katyn Forest is included in Robert H. Jackson, *The Nuremberg Case* (New York: Alfred A. Knopf, 1947), pp. 58-62 and especially note 45, pp. 169-170; for the burning of six hundred women and children in the church at Oradour-Sur-Glane, see The Royal Institute of International Affairs. Survey of International Affairs, 1939-1946. *Hitler's Europe,* edited by Arnold M. Toynbee and Veronica M. Toynbee (London, New York, Toronto: Oxford University Press, 1954), p. 424; for the murdering of Soviet civilians, see *Pravda,* March 13, 1943, p. 3 (Mass murders at Don and Rostov, pictures included); also V. Molotov, *The Molotov Paper on*

ANALYSIS OF THE EVIDENCE

Nazi Atrocities (New York: The American Council on Soviet Relations, 1942), p. 29; executing Allied prisoners-of-war, for details consult *I.M.T.*, XXIV, 463; U.S. Office of Chief Counsel for Prosecution of Axis Criminality. *Nazi Conspiracy and Aggression.* Supplement B (Washington: Government Printing Office, 1947), p. 1322; Paul Brickhill, *The Great Escape.* (New York: W. W. Norton and Co., 1950), *passim;* Von Eichborn's testimony, *I.M.T.*, XVII, p. 309; U.S.S.R. Soviet Embassy in London. *New Soviet Documents on Nazi Atrocities* (1943), p. 96.

3. *I.M.T.*, XIV, Doc. U.S.S.R.–172, 513.

4. Excerpts from Frank's diary (in German). *I.M.T.*, XXIV, 440-459.

5. The following sources published by the Polish Government-in-Exile provide extensive material on this subject: *M.S.Z., passim; Official Documents Concerning Polish-German and Polish-Soviet Relations 1933-1939* (London and Melbourne: Hutchinson and Co., Ltd., 1940), *passim; Polish Report, passim;* P.S.Z., I and III, *passim;* Polish Embassy in Washington. *Polish-Soviet Relations, 1918-1943. Official Documents.* 1944, *passim;* consult also Władysław Anders, *Bez Ostatniego Rozdziału. Wspomnienia z Lat 1939-1946* (Without the last chapter. Memoirs of the years 1939-1946) (Newton, Wales: Montgomeryshire Printing Co., Ltd., 1949), *passim;* Stanisław Kot, Polish Ambassador to the Soviet Union, *Listy z Rosji do Gen. Sikorskiego* (Letters from Russia to Gen. Sikorski) (London: Jutro Polski, 1956), pp. 79-525; *Zbrodnia Katyńska w Świetle Dokumentów*, particularly chapter XII, concerning the evacuation of Polish prisoners from Soviet camps and prisons during the Soviet-German campaign.

6. Approximately 150 officers, noncommissioned officers, and privates were interviewed on the subject of the conditions of capture and imprisonment by the Soviet Government. Interviews were at random, open-ended, some in depth. The interviewees were Polish soldiers who had been captured by the Soviet Army in 1939 and Polish deportees from Soviet-seized territory who survived and joined General Anders' units, created as the result of the Sikorski-Maisky agreement in 1941. Anders' army was subsequently evacuated to the Middle East and then to Italy where it distinguished itself as the 2nd Polish Corps fighting under the command of the British 8th Army. The writer interviewed the men in Italy in 1945-1946 and in England in 1947-1948.

7. German. *Amtliches Material zum Massenmord von Katyn* (Official material concerning the Katyn massacre). Im Auftrage des Auswärtigen Amtes auf Grund urkundlichen Beweismaterials zusammengestellt, bearbeitet und herausgegeben von der Deutschen Informationsstelle (Berlin: Zentralverlag der NSDAP, F. Eher Nachf.,

1943), *passim*. This source has been cited throughout the book as *German Report;* U.S.S.R. Spetsial'naya Komissiya po Ustanovleniyu i Rassledovaniyu Obstoyatel'stv Rasstrela Nemetsko-Fashistskimi Zakhvatchikami v Katynskom Lesu Voennoplennykh Pol'skikh Ofitserov. (Special commission for ascertaining and investigating the circumstances of the shooting of Polish officer prisoners by the German-Fascist invaders in the Katyn Forest). *Nota Sovetskogo Pravitel'stva Pravitel'stvu SShA; Soobshchenie Spetsial'noi Komissii.* (Note of the Soviet Government to the Government of the U.S.; communication by the Special Commission). Moscow: Supplement to *Novoe Vremya*, no. 10, 1952, *passim*. This source has been cited throughout the book as *Soviet Report;* see also note 5 *supra*.

8. In analysis of the evidence, the data collected by the Polish authorities in the Soviet Union in the period 1941-1943 and presented in the *Polish Report* have been very helpful.

9. *Hearings*, part 6, Exhibit 32, p. 1632.

10. *Ibid.*, part 5, p. 1455.

11. "Day in the Forest," *Time*, XLIII, no. 6 (February 7, 1944), p. 27.

12. *Hearings*, part 5, pp. 1610, 1621.

13. *Zbrodnia Katyńska w Świetle Dokumentów* (The Katyn crime in light of documents). 1st ed., p. 331; 2nd ed., pp. 378-379. There is no evidence that such a letter has been found between the printing of the first and the second edition. Nor up to the time of writing this book (1962).

14. Joseph Mackiewicz, *The Katyn Wood Murders* (London: Hollis and Carter, 1951), p. 145; compare his testimony in *Hearings*, part 4, p. 877.

15. *Hearings*, part 6, Exhibit 32, p. 1633; part 3, pp. 338-339.

16. Mackiewicz, *op. cit.*, p. 148.

17. *Polish Report*, p. 451; *Hearings*, part 6, Exhibit 32, p. 1783.

18. *Soviet Report*, p. 19.

19. *Hearings*, part 4, p. 874. Captain Kuczynski was a professional cavalry officer. He had a Bachelor of Science degree in Architecture. This officer tried to enhance the sense of cohesion among the prisoners by personally unselfish and noble behavior. A genuine and gifted leader, he was taken away from the camp either at the end of November or in the beginning of December of 1939.

20. These points are, in substance, raised by the *Polish Report*.

21. Deposition made by a member of the Polish delegation to Katyn. *Hearings*, part 6, Exhibit 32, p. 1809.

22. *German Report*, p. 59; *Hearings*, part 5, p. 1320.

23. Winston S. (now Sir Winston) Churchill, *Closing the Ring* (Boston: Houghton Mifflin Co., 1951), p. 691. The trees in question were spruce.

ANALYSIS OF THE EVIDENCE

24. *Polish Report*, pp. 54-74; also an eyewitness report of the head of the Polish Red Cross, Kazimierz Skarżyński, "Katyń i Polski Czerwony Krzyż" (Katyn and the Polish Red Cross), *Kultura*, no. 9/51 (May 1955), p. 136.

25. *Polish Report*, pp. 439-442; *Hearings*, part 6, Exhibit 32, pp. 1795-1796.

26. The argument suggested by the *Polish Report*, p. 442.

27. *Hearings*, part 6, Exhibit 32, p. 1632.

28. *Polish Report*, p. 448; Dr. Beck's testimony. *Hearings*, part 5, p. 1518; a Swedish correspondent's statement, p. 1563; see also part 6, Exhibit 32, p. 1629.

29. *German Report*, microscopic analysis (photograph), p. 313.

30. It is interesting to note that when several months later the Polish authorities investigated the German extermination camp Majdanek in Poland, Dr. Prozorovsky (the head of the Soviet medical team in Katyn) went to Poland upon the invitation of the Warsaw government, to investigate the obvious. It appears to be a kind of double-standard. Soviet authorities forbade Polish communists to check the causes and circumstances of the massacre of their fellow citizens in Katyn, but went to confirm the German atrocities in Poland about which nobody had any doubt at all.

31. Dr. Orsos' testimony. *Hearings*, part 5, pp. 1957-1602; Dr. Palmieri's testimony, p. 1619; Dr. Miloslavich's testimony, pp. 323-324.

32. See chapter V, pp. 59-63.

33. Subsequently the executioners dynamited the entrances to the caves.

34. *German Report*, pp. 16, 17, 33, 36, 42, 47, 92.

35. *Soviet Report*, pp. 2, 17.

36. See note 1 *supra*.

37. For a list of the most important sources published in German, English, Polish, and Russian bearing on the Katyn Massacre, see the primary sources in the Bibliography. These are arranged according to countries of origin.

38. *I.M.T.*, I, 54.

VII

Reconstruction: To the Edge of the Graves

IT WAS MENTIONED earlier that, although thousands of the prisoners from the camps Kozelsk, Ostashkov, and Starobelsk disappeared, about 448 of them—from all three camps—were found. Why and how they were selected by the Soviet authorities to be spared will be discussed in the next chapter. As the result of the re-establishment of Polish-Soviet relations in July 1941, these prisoners were released from Camp Grazovec, in which they had ultimately been assembled.

Many of these men were approached and interviewed by General Anders' special office, and after they were evacuated from the Soviet Union, also by the Polish authorities in exile. Those who subsequently lived in England, France, and the United States in 1951 were also questioned by the investigating committee of the United States Congress.[1] The assembled information supplied by them makes it possible to reconstruct in detail the life of the Polish prisoners in the Soviet camps. Many of these survivors were the very last to leave the camps, so it is possible to learn from them the manner in which prisoners had departed from the camps. From the diaries of the men from Kozelsk, the conditions of their travel and the manner of arrival at the site of their slaughter can be learned. Gruesome as these details are, they shed light on the possible motives of the executioners.

Immediately after capture (autumn 1939), 250,000 Polish prisoners were assembled in about 138 camps, some on newly Soviet-occupied Polish territory, some in the Soviet Union. Ultimately, transfers were arranged by the authorities, and the officers were placed in two camps—Kozelsk and Starobelsk. After each prisoner was interviewed and investigated, the members of the Polish intelligence service, military police, border guards, and even local policemen captured on Soviet-occupied territory were separated from the rest and confined in Camp Ostashkov. In all three camps, but particularly in the latter, noncommissioned officers and privates were among the prisoners.

This study is concerned only with the men who were held in these three camps from November 1939 until May 1940, because they were the ones murdered. As will be explained below, there were Polish prisoners in these camps before and after this period, but we are interested only in those who were assembled there for these six months and then evacuated in a direction unknown to them.

Life in the three camps was more or less the same. Food was meager, but enough to sustain a man. Some consideration was given to the higher ranks: they had more room allotted and, in some instances, generals had their own batmen who volunteered from the Polish ranks. In certain areas, such as management of the camp kitchens, self-government was encouraged by the Soviet authorities. However, when a real leader emerged, who raised the general state of morale, he was arrested and kept incommunicado. (Major Zalewski was arrested for these reasons on the night of December 22, 1939, in Camp Starobelsk.)

A representative of the State Jewelry Trust visited the camps, buying the prisoners' jewelry and fountain pens. Wrist watches commanded a good price, pocket watches much less. Any fountain pen, regardless of its make, brought twenty rubles. With money gained from these sales the prisoners could buy additional food from a traveling camp-store. Many officers, although hard pressed, refused for sentimental reasons to part with personal objects. Frequently the officers would pool their rubles, make purchases and divide the goods among their roommates whether they had contributed to the pool or not.

In some instances the younger and healthier men were called upon to perform some work for the benefit of the camp, such as shoveling snow, or hauling foodstuffs. As a rule the officers from the rank of major up were not compelled to work.

Religious services had to be held surreptitiously, as did any kind of discussion having the slightest political implication. Still, morale was rather high, although it fluctuated with the kind of rumors which, as inevitable in such situations, swept the camps from time to time. The underlying hope was that the Allies would not forget them and somehow would do something to prevent them from rotting behind the barbed wires of Soviet camps.

In several respects, however, life in these three camps differed from that in prisoner-of-war camps in any other country at that time: the camp administration and the guards were the dreaded N.K.V.D. security police and not army units; all the men were very thoroughly interrogated over and over again by the N.K.V.D. officers; a well-planned and co-ordinated indoctrination was carried out in all three camps with the aim of converting the officers and men into communists.

The indoctrination, as a whole, failed. The Poles with their values—strong sense of duty toward country, "officers' honor," and *esprit de corps* —not only did not take the bait, but their cohesion, when attacked from without, initially strengthened. Rank-imposed duties and obligations were maintained, as was the discipline. The social and army structure not only did not break down but was more strongly cemented. The Poles not only refused to embrace the communistic doctrine overtly, but also refused to do so in private when, confronted only by the interrogators, they were free from the possible pressures of their colleagues. They talked about "honor," "independent Poland," and "principles of the West." They were proud to have been the first to say "no" to Hitler; they were proud that Warsaw, like a castle in the Middle Ages, fought for about two weeks after the whole Polish territory was overrun by German and Soviet armies. By March 1940 the interrogations of officers and ranks were completed. The Poles could not be ideologically indoctrinated, but the N.K.V.D. decided that 448 could probably be used.

In the first week of April, the Soviet administrations in all three camps, by innuendoes, implications, a word dropped here and there, started a rumor. The prisoners were being returned to Poland! The rumor spread. Excitement rose. They were going home!

It should be remembered that this was the period of German-Soviet co-operation. The prisoners assumed that they would be able to return to their homes either in the Soviet- or the German-occupied zone of Poland. Here and there a cautious word was dropped privately by an N.K.V.D. officer, "You are going toward home"; "to the West."[2] In fact Katyn Forest lay west of the Kozelsk camp. Some men in Kozelsk were uneasy, and felt a kind of psychic discomfort about leaving the camp. They were overridden by the enthusiasm of the rest of the men. They were going home, the N.K.V.D. said so.

Immediately following the circulation of the rumors, the first lists of those to depart were announced. Early in the morning an N.K.V.D. man went through the buildings occupied by prisoners, reading names. The men immediately assembled and returned to the administration any kind of equipment given them by the camp authorities. Then they were taken to another building where their possessions were carefully checked. From that time they were not allowed to communicate with the remaining fellow-prisoners. Thereafter they were transferred in closed trucks to the nearest railway station. As in the case of one of the transports from Kozelsk, the men were marched eight miles to the nearest railway station under close guard by the N.K.V.D. men, equipped with firearms and dogs. Some officers, observing the guards' rough behavior and the dogs, had second thoughts about their destination. If they were going home, were such security precautions necessary?

The generals were removed in the earliest groups. By virtue of their rank and prestige, they were the mainstays of the formal and informal social structure of the camps. When the generals were leaving Kozelsk, the officers assembled into a long "guard of honor" in two rows facing each other. The generals passed between the cheering and exuberant lines of officers. As one of the survivors reported, the N.K.V.D. men also gave them a "real ovation." The placating and hospitable attitude of the camp administration went so far as the preparation for the departing men of an especially good meal. For the trip, they also were given bread and three herrings each, all wrapped in white paper. In terms of conditions at the camps, white paper was a luxury as unobtainable as champagne would be at Sing Sing. Nothing was too good for the departing men, so long as the remaining officers watched and so long as they were within the compound. At Starobelsk a military band played cheerful farewell tunes. But the moment they were outside the gates, treatment aimed at security and preventing escape began. The N.K.V.D. stopped cheering.

The prisoners left the camps in groups of 50 to 360 men. Those remaining tried to perceive the basis on which the departing had been chosen. But there was no distinguishable pattern. Aside from the fact that the generals left in one of the first groups, age, rank, professions, and regimental affiliations were mixed, and assembly was completely unpredictable. It was obvious that the names were picked at random, except for one thing: the officers with traits of good aptitude for leadership were removed in the first groups. For example, Captain Bychowiec, a fine infantry leader, proven in battle against German forces, was removed from Camp Kozelsk in the first departing group. (Captain Bychowiec was found in the Katyn graves, body number 4106.) Even brothers were separated: the Machleyds and Jaroszyńskis at Camp Starobelsk, for example. Only in one case was an exception made; a son and his father pleaded to be sent "home together." Their wish was granted by the camp's administration and they were allowed to leave together. At Starobelsk, when officers tried to change their group assignment, they were told, "All of you will meet soon."[3]

It has been possible to reconstruct partially the order in which the groups departed from these camps. Such a list, giving the dates of the groups departing from Kozelsk, the approximate number of officers in each group, and their names, is available.[4]

The men from Kozelsk left during April, as was the case in the other two camps. Those omitted from the early morning calls for departure became gloomy and restive. They felt that they were being left out, and shared their frustrations with each other. In their casual contacts with camp officials they expressed their disappointment. Some of the camp officials, when approached without witnesses, were consoling, and in Starobelsk one of the N.K.V.D. men said to a complaining prisoner: "I can only tell you that you are the lucky ones." At Kozelsk, after more than 3,500 prisoners already had left, a young cadet was departing with a small group. He was approached by an officer of N.K.V.D., who said, "Well, you had good luck."[5] A prisoner was cheered by the camp doctor at Kozelsk, a rather kind and compassionate woman, "You are lucky you were not removed from the camp."[6] All these statements added to the confusion.

These comments did not make much sense to the prisoners

even when they found themselves in a separate assembly point to which they were brought from all three camps. At that time they pooled these comments. At the same time they realized that they were unable to re-establish contact with their friends from the camps, who had departed in other groups.

Evidence exists which makes it possible to reconstruct events of the journey to the Katyn Forest. A distinguished professor of economics, a reserve officer called to duty in September 1939, was one of the prisoners in Kozelsk. He was included in one of the groups departing for "home" and reached the railway station Gnezdovo, a mile and three-quarters from the Katyn graves, where the prisoners were transferred from the train to trucks. At this spot he was taken from the train by the N.K.V.D. and sent to Smolensk prison. His story is fantastic and ended happily for him. He was ultimately released from a hard labor camp and evacuated from the Soviet Union. At the time this book was published (1962) he was residing in London. From him, we have the following account of what happened after the men arrived at the station near Kozelsk. (He was kind enough to read this manuscript and to verify the details.)

> The convoy was composed of five (perhaps six) prison trucks [railway carriages].... We calculated that there were about 300 of us. We were put into separate compartments. In my compartment were fourteen people....
> We left Kozielsk [Polish spelling] in the late evening.... At sunrise we were at Smolensk. We stood there for a few minutes only, then the train moved on in a northwesterly direction. It was a bright, sunny day. From the shadows of the telegraph poles we realized that we were traveling northwest. This fact was greeted with joy, as many began to believe they were really taking us to Poland. After traveling for several kilometers the train halted. The rumor spread that we were to be unloaded....
> ... After about half-an-hour's wait a Colonel of the N.K.V.D. entered our truck, called out my name, announced that I was to

be separated from the convoy and ordered me to collect my things. He personally conducted me to an empty prison truck, where I was locked into one of the compartments. A special guard stood in the corridor before barred doors. Shortly after I heard some sort of noise in an adjacent truck, the hum of a motor and the cries of the prisoners. Prison trucks are so constructed that the walls of compartments have no windows, except for a small square of glass right under the ceiling. By climbing on the highest shelf (intended for luggage) it is possible to see out. I therefore pretended that I wanted to sleep and climbed on to it. Soon the guard was standing with his back to the door of my compartment and looking out of the window (the corridors of the prison trucks have windows). So I was able to look out. We were standing outside the station. Before us was a big square partly covered with grass. At right angles to the railway ran a road, skirting the left side of the square. The horizon was covered with a wood. The square was surrounded by N.K.V.D. guards with bayonets and rifles. The distance between the guards was about ten feet. In the square stood a passenger bus, its windows smeared with cement. . . . The entrance to the bus was at the back; it came right up to the trucks [the translator consistently in this testimony uses the word 'truck' for railway carriage] so that the prisoners were able to enter it directly from trucks. On both sides of the entrance to the bus stood N.K.V.D. men. Two of them had bayonets on their rifles. About thirty people got into the bus. It drove off in the direction of the woods and after a certain time (about half-an-hour) returned to collect the next party. The whole thing was supervised by a Colonel of the N.K.V.D., the same one who took me away from the convoy. . . .

After the unloading was completed, I was handed over to a Captain of the N.K.V.D., who turned out to be the governor of the Smolensk prison. In a special prison car he took me to the so-called 'internal' N.K.V.D. prison, in the cellars of the Smolensk N.K.V.D. office.[7]

The manner in which the prisoners from Kozelsk traveled to the station Gnezdovo also can be reconstructed from diaries and notes taken from the graves. Here are relevant excerpts from a diary found on a body which could not be identified (envelope 424). The writer left Kozelsk in a group of 277 officers on April 8, 1940.[8]

April 8,
We were loaded at the station into a prison-train under heavy guard. . . . We are moving in the direction of Smolensk. . . .

April 9,
Tuesday—Today weather like that during the winter. . . . Snow on the fields. . . . It is impossible to deduce the direction of our motion. . . . Treatment is rough. . . . Nothing is allowed. . . . 2:30 p.m. we are arriving at Smolensk. . . . Evening, we arrived at the station Gniazdowo [Polish spelling]. It appears that we shall get off . . . a lot of military men around. Since yesterday we have had only a piece of bread and a sip of water.

The diary ends on this statement.

The diaries indicate that prisoners of all groups except the first, at the moment they were put into the prison-carriages at Kozelsk station, knew that they probably would be going through Smolensk and disembarking at the station Gnezdovo. They knew it because some of the men in the preceding parties had scratched their names and the names of the stations they passed on the walls of the carriages. The same carriages were used over and over again to transport the men from Kozelsk. In some instances the travelers could decipher the signatures, and those who wrote diaries in the trains (they traveled from one to three days depending evidently on the intensity of railway traffic) duly copied in their notebooks what they read on the walls. When the survivors from Kozelsk later were transferred in these same carriages, they too saw the inscriptions on the walls and ceilings, such as "We are getting off at Gnezdovo station." The diaries consistently mention Smolensk as the major station passed and Gnezdovo as the point of leaving the train. In the personal calendar of Second Lieutenant Jan Bartys this laconic note can be found: "We have just arrived at Gnezdovo station and I see the N.K.V.D. men standing from the railway station up to the woods."

What happened when a group of prisoners arrived at the

station can be reconstructed from two sources: the diaries recovered from the graves and a witness, a Soviet citizen named Krivozertsov, at one time the only Soviet eyewitness available in the West, who testified voluntarily.

Major Solski's diary seems to be the most detailed and was kept up to the last minutes before the execution. The quoted excerpt refers to his arrival at the Gnezdovo station and transportation to the forest.

> April 9,
>
> From the morning this day has started in a peculiar way. Departure was in a prison-motorcar with little cells (horrible). We have been brought somewhere to a forest; it looks like a summer resort. Here a thorough personal search. Rubles, belt and pocket knife were taken.

Here the record ends.[9]

More detailed information with regard to the transportation of the prisoners from Gnezdovo station to the Katyn Forest was supplied by the witness, Krivozertsov. He lived about two miles from Gnezdovo station and voluntarily left his village in 1943, with the withdrawing German forces, taking with him his mother and young nephew. In June 1945 he reported to the Polish military authorities in Germany, in order to testify. He, together with his sister, who was carrying manure for a garden, had to pass Gnezdovo station in April 1940, and saw prisoners in uniforms packed in small groups into a special type of prison-motorcar without windows. Another man, by the name of Khrustalov, also employed in carrying manure, recognized the prisoners as Poles, because of their characteristic uniforms.

Krivozertsov, since he lived in this area, stated he knew the guards at Katyn, as he had to pass them very often on the local roads. He testified that the guards and the drivers of the three or four special cars transporting the prisoners were from the Smolensk and Minsk N.K.V.D.; furthermore, he knew personally the driver of one of these vans.[10]

TO THE EDGE OF THE GRAVES

It appears that the Poles were unloaded at Gnezdovo station in small groups of twenty to thirty into from one to four buses, a group at a time. From there they were taken to the place of execution.

It was obvious from the bayonet wounds, gags in the victims' mouths, their bound hands, and the throat-choking ropes on some of the bodies, that the younger men fought just before being shot. The older men were not bound or gagged.

A French volunteer, serving with the German forces against the Soviet armies, presumably reported in 1943 that he talked to a Soviet village elder from the Katyn area, who was called with others by the N.K.V.D. to cover the graves with dirt. The elder stated that the Poles had to lie, face down, near the graves and two N.K.V.D. men were walking along, one shooting the officers by putting the gun to their skulls, another loading the gun.[11]

The Polish doctor, Wodziński, head of the Polish Red Cross medical team, who performed autopsies at Katyn, thinks it more probable that the men were compelled to get down into the graves and to lie on the already dead or dying and then the revolver was put against their skulls and the fatal shot fired.[12]

There is also the opinion that the prisoners had to kneel at the edge of the grave, then were shot in the manner mentioned above. In any case, shooting was done by "specialists." In the thousands of victims the shots were placed in the same small area of the occipital bone in the back of the head. There are no reliable data to establish who dug the graves. Some sources maintain that this work was done in advance by Soviet citizens, N.K.V.D. prisoners from Smolensk.[13] As the N.K.V.D. officer had predicted, the victims met again.

What of the more than 10,000 men from the camps of Ostashkov and Starobelsk? Twenty years have passed since they left their camps in the month of April 1940. None of them has ever given a sign of life. What happened to them?

This much is known. They left their camps in the same manner and in small groups as had the men from Kozelsk, at the same time, and under the surveillance of the N.K.V.D. Their transports were painstakingly traced from station to station during 1941 by operatives of the special Polish search office acting under the auspices of the Polish Embassy and General Anders.

No clue was overlooked. Subtle questions were casually dropped to station-masters, railway men, and railway guards. All information was centrally evaluated and pursued when warranted. There was much fruitless effort, but some results emerged.

The transports of officers and men from Camp Ostashkov ended at the stations of either Bologoe or Viazma. The railway-carriages with prisoners from Camp Starobelsk reached the station at Kharkov. Arrival dates at these stations were in April 1940. This was the end of the trail.

The special Polish search office continued to gather information from the Polish population streaming toward General Anders' army from the labor camps and other places to which they had been sent. There were persistent rumors which, after a time, were corroborated by completely unrelated sources. Soviet citizens made depositions under oath, repeating a story which they had overheard, or claimed (in one instance) to have witnessed. In the spring of 1940, the story ran, several thousand prisoners in Polish uniforms were loaded on two barges (one source says three barges), towed several miles out to sea and then purposely sunk by artillery fire with the prisoners aboard. This supposedly happened on the White Sea. It has been impossible to verify this story.

Seventeen years later on July 7, 1957, a German paper of a rather popular character, "7-Tag" (editorial offices: Stephanienstrasse 16, Karlsruhe, W. Germany), published a copy of a document, which, if it is not forgery, gives a clear statement of the fate of the remaining prisoners. The document allegedly came from the N.K.V.D. office in Minsk. There are some indications that the archives of the Minsk N.K.V.D. were captured by German units, as well as some parts of the Communist Party archives at Smolensk. (The latter, however, deal mainly with the period prior to 1938.) While the archives from Smolensk ultimately found their way to the United States,[14] the papers from the Minsk N.K.V.D. have not been located. It is possible they were hidden somewhere in Germany, and that the documents cited could have come from among them.

Besides this, the Soviet witness previously mentioned, Krivozertsov, maintained during his lifetime that the N.K.V.D. from Minsk also participated in the Katyn Forest Massacre. The area of Katyn Forest lies between Smolensk and Minsk.

The document in question was purportedly typed on the official stationery of the Minsk's N.K.V.D., under the heading SECRET. It was addressed to the main office of the N.K.V.D. in Moscow and dated June 10, 1940. Here is its content in English translation:

Report

In accordance with the order of the Main Office of the N.K.V.D. dated February 12, 1940, the liquidation of the three camps for the Polish prisoners-of-war in the area of c. [cities] Kozelsk, Ostashkov, and Starobelsk was completed. The action of liquidation of the above-mentioned camps was terminated on June 6 of this year. Delegated by the Central Office, Comrade Buryanov was responsible for the over-all organization.

On the basis of the above-mentioned order, Camp Kozelsk was liquidated first in the period from March 1 to May 3 in the area of Smolensk by the organs of the Minsk N.K.V.D. As screening units, local formations of the army were used, particularly that of the 190th Infantry Regiment.

The second action on the basis of the above-mentioned order was performed by the organs of the Smolensk N.K.V.D. in the area of the town Bologoe, under the protection of the 129th Infantry Regiment (from Veliki Luki) and completed on June 5th.

The undertaking of the third action, that of the camp Starobelsk, was assigned to the N.K.V.D. from Kharkov, and this was done in the area of the village Dyergatche, being completed on June 2 under the protective screen of the units of the 68th Ukrainian Infantry Regiment of the local forces. In this instance, the N.K.V.D. Colonel, Comrade B. Kutchkov, was responsible for the action.

The copies of this report are being submitted to the attention of the N.K.V.D. Generals Raikhman and Zarubin.

The Chief of the Office
N.K.V.D.
Minsk raion
       (Tartakov)   Secretary of the Department
Copy verified with the original.

The dates, the naming of the camps, and the organizational framework suggest that the document is authentic. For example, General Raikhman was the very man who granted an audience to Captain Czapski in the N.K.V.D. office in Moscow when the latter was searching for the missing Poles. Similarly, General Zarubin was the person checking through personal interviews on the progress of indoctrination of the Polish officers at Camp Kozelsk. A Polish journalist, very much interested in the Katyn affair, was able to ascertain in 1958 that indeed the 68th Infantry Regiment was stationed, at the time given in the document, in the area of Kharkov.[15]

The Katyn affair and the problem of missing officers have been so clouded by the manipulation of Soviet, Polish, and German propaganda that even a trained social scientist has to exercise the utmost care to separate reliable evidence from manufactured stories. If the document is authentic, the questions regarding the fate of the remaining 10,000 men might be further elucidated. However, it is not possible to confirm it beyond doubt, because in 1957 the details which are verifiable could have been discovered by the German source and incorporated in a false document.

At present it is impossible to set forth reliably the manner and the place of death of the remaining 10,000 officers and men. On the basis of the available circumstantial evidence it seems reasonable to guess that, like their compatriots from Kozelsk, they were murdered by units of the N.K.V.D. immediately after their removal from the camps. Only the authorities of the Government of the Soviet Union can supply details concerning the circumstances of their death.

From the more than 15,000 prisoners, 448 men were selected to survive. What was their final fate?

Toward the end of the period of evacuation of the three camps relatively small groups (from 16 to 150 men) of those who had not gone "home" were assembled in the same manner as had been the other groups. Action brought a definite relief of tension among them, for they had felt left out and abandoned. The N.K.V.D. chief of Camp Starobelsk, with a solicitous smile, bade farewell to one of the groups from Starobelsk with a comment overheard by Captain Czapski, "You are going to the place I wish I could go."

When the gates of the camp closed after the departing, again the indifference of the guards to the discomforts of the officers indicated the change of atmosphere. The men were crowded into cages—like the compartments of the trains. In many instances the prison-carriages were those in which the previous groups had departed earlier from the other camps. This was further evidence that the removal of officers and men from the camps was centrally co-ordinated. Groups of survivors departing from Starobelsk on May 12, 1940, were squeezed into a carriage which had over its walls inscriptions and names of the officers from Camp Kozelsk, including sentences like this: "We leave the train near Smolensk." Katyn Forest lies 8-10 miles west of Smolensk.

According to the survivors, treatment by the guards was brutal. Some of the cramped men collapsed in the compartments; one went berserk. In many instances they were not permitted to relieve themselves during the trip. The men were fed herring and water exclusively. It was a trip toward the unknown.

The pounding of the railway wheels, lack of light, and the physical sufferings increased their anxiety. These men did not know that they were the luckiest—they were to live.

When the first group of survivors arrived at their new camp called Pavelishtchev Bor, the camp was empty. During the months of April and May the prisoners from Kozelsk, Starobelsk, and Ostashkov were trickling in, disappointed and unhappy at still being "on Soviet soil." On May 20 the last transport of nineteen men came from Ostashkov.

Table I

TRANSPORTS ARRIVING AT PAVELISHTCHEV BOR [16]

Departure	From	Arrival at Pav. Bor	Men in Transport
April 25, 1940	Starobelsk	May 1, 1940	63
April 26, 1940	Kozelsk	April 26, 1940	150
April 29, 1940	Ostashkov	May 4, 1940	60
May 12, 1940	Kozelsk	May 14, 1940	95
May 12, 1940	Starobelsk	May 17, 1940	16
May 13, 1940	Ostashkov	May 18, 1940	45
May 16, 1940	Ostashkov	May 20, 1940	19
		Total	448

A swarm of N.K.V.D. political investigators descended upon the camp. In addition to those who were originally attached to the old camps and who came with their prisoners to Pavelishtchev Bor, there were new ones. Intensive interrogations continued. Instead of 15,000 men, the interrogators had only 448 to concentrate upon. Even so, the number of inquisitors was increased. Checking on the values and ideas of the prisoners was intensified. Increasing pressure upon the prisoners began to break down cohesion among the men.

Some officers commenced to voice publicly pro-communist sentiments. Thirty others decided to cease not only to be Polish officers, but even Poles. They claimed German ancestry. Informal groups with diverse loyalties developed strong antagonisms. The cultural values which had united the officers began, under the stress of continuous interrogations, to lose their force. The group commenced to disintegrate. At this point the interrogators pitted them one against another.

The prisoners at Pavelishtchev Bor represented a broad cross-section. They were officers, cadets, noncommissioned officers, privates, some policemen, and even a handful of civilians, among them an old, likeable Jew (a wood merchant) and "a murderer released from a Polish prison." This further accentuated diversity. During this time some individual Poles were placed under guard and removed from the camp. It has been established that those removed were taken to various prisons to be interrogated further by N.K.V.D. specialists for specific information regarding their civilian occupations.

On June 13, 1941, the remaining prisoners were removed to Camp Grazovec. After some arrests, there were now about four hundred.[17] Traveling again in train prison-carriages, they arrived after five days at the new camp. Those of the investigators who originally were with the prisoners in Kozelsk, Starobelsk, and Ostashkov came along. The investigations continued here also, but their character changed. Now the approach adopted by the prison administrators and their interrogators was that of paternalistic and understanding benefactors extending helpful hands.

Life was much easier than before. Officers received twenty rubles, and rank, ten rubles a month. The prisoners were permitted to grow vegetables and to organize study groups. The administration's policies were fairly flexible in accommodating to the wishes of the men, particularly with respect to recreation. Books were allotted—"in kilograms [about 30 lbs.] per month." A Russian woman was employed as a recreation worker and initially she confined herself to this kind of duty. Most importantly, the men were allowed to write and receive letters, which they had not been permitted to do in Pavelishtchev Bor.

Expectation of letters from home improved morale among the prisoners considerably. However, they were forbidden to mention the names of fellow-prisoners, or the name of their camp, and the return address on all mail was given as "Post Box No. 11/c-12, Moscow, U.S.S.R."

Finally the first letters from German and Soviet-occupied Poland arrived. They had one thing in common: anxious questions about fellow-prisoners from Kozelsk, Ostashkov, and Starobelsk. They had not written since early spring. What had happened? This baffled the officers in Grazovec. They were the only officers detained, for some unkown reason, in Russia. The others should have been home since April. Letters went back and forth containing ingenious subterfuges to evade camp censorship. Ultimately the camp authorities realized that this was happening. A special supplementary instruction was issued—there were to be no answers to inquiries about the missing men. At the same time, one of the N.K.V.D. officers, Alexandrovitch, offered to collect and deliver the letters to the missing men (many families were sending letters to the missing men in care of officers in Grazovec with whom they were acquainted). The letters collected in this way by Alexandrovitch were never answered.

From among the thirty "new Germans" who were straining to speak in their new native tongue, twelve were released through the intervention of the German ambassador to the Soviet Union. The remaining eighteen evidently were not German enough.

Toward the end of August 1940, ten weeks after the prisoners' arrival at Grazovec, a new approach was made informally by the N.K.V.D. officers throughout the camp. It was subtly suggested by them that the prisoners were soldiers, and that they could leave the barbed wires behind. Poland and the Soviet Union had common interests. They could even start to organize a Polish army in Russia.

The woman who had served as a recreational officer developed a deep interest in international politics. She shared her views with the officers, whether they wanted them or not. A push toward some kind of united political action on the part of the officers was becoming more and more intense.

Fifty officers who had shown some interest in communism at Pavelishtchev Bor came into the open. They organized the "Red Corner," a place within the camp where they could hold discussions, study the history of the Communist Party, and celebrate communist anniversaries. This struck the majority of the men as both tragic and funny. Here were men in the uniform of the Polish Army, eighteen voicing German views and fifty spouting slogans and parroting the style of Soviet propaganda. All these men were their former colleagues and friends: "former" because the majority isolated them from social intercourse within the camp. The lines were plainly drawn.

The "Reds," supported by the administration, initially gained sympathizers, but eventually the groups became stable in their loyalties and did not mingle. This was not all. Fist fights broke out and the "Reds" were severely beaten. From 15,000 prisoners the Russians had selected 448 men as potential communist leaders of a future "Red Polish Army," and most of them not only did not wish to join but were attempting to beat up the studious fifty from the Red Corner.

The N.K.V.D. arrested several officers within the camp for "anti-Semitism," and several were taken away for "more intensive investigation." This further solidified the lines. The majority blamed the members of the Red Corner for the arrests of fellow officers. The atmosphere in the camp was tense.

Interestingly enough, at one point all Poles—pro-Reds, anti-Reds and the "new Germans"—felt unified in their attitude. The fate of a dog was the reason.

A gentle old mongrel found his way through the wires and was adopted by the men in the camp. Scraps of food were saved for him and unusually tender attention was bestowed upon him by the prisoners. The dog reciprocated with a loyal heart, as only a dog can. Moreover, adopting the feelings of the majority of the prisoners, he started to dislike the N.K.V.D. men. At one point he barked at the senior officer of the N.K.V.D. The prisoners, seeing the N.K.V.D. man infuriated, and anticipating trouble for the dog, tried to hide it. Soon a body of N.K.V.D. guards trooped into the camp searching for the dog. They found him and took him away. For the next two days the prisoners searched for the dog, hoping that it would return. On the third day they found it.

The body of "their" dog was tied to a log, lying stiffly in a pool of blood. Its bones were broken; the dog had been "literally massacred with clubs." The death of the dog and the manner of his killing incensed the prisoners and, according to Captain Czapski, "rallied all of them for a while."

On September 10, 1940, seven high-ranking officers were told to pack. They were going to Moscow. All seven were diligent students from the Red Corner. About five weeks later six more officers from the Red Corner followed them to Moscow. Both groups traveled by passenger train. What happened in Moscow to those men will be discussed in the next chapter; however, some of these thirteen men were subsequently rejected in Moscow and sent back to a special camp. They found their way to Grazovec again in June 1941.

Meanwhile, life in Grazovec was becoming more stable. The N.K.V.D. officers were still going through the motions of indoctrinating the stubborn majority. They told the Poles that they would be imprisoned until the end of the war. Of course, there was a way out. It led through the Red Corner, and this price the majority refused to pay.

Life was monotonous but bearable until June 1941. This was the month of the German attack on the Soviet Union. The marriage of convenience between the two governments had ended. The outbreak of the war and speedy progress of the German armies across the Soviet plains affected life in Grazovec. The number of prisoners in the camp was increased to approximately 1,400-1,700. The additional men were brought from the territories evacuated before advancing Germans. Camp Grazovec lost its character of selectivity in admission.

The war with Germany intensified N.K.V.D. efforts to enroll the Poles under Soviet banners. There was nothing subtle about it—offers were made to the prisoners. If they volunteered as paratroopers, they would be dropped behind the German lines. The anti-German feelings of the Poles were played upon rather skillfully. Promotions in rank, freedom from camp life, the possibility of being dropped in Poland, and the chance to fight against the Germans were offered. These inducements led several dozen of the Poles to enroll in the Red Army and leave the camp. The rest did not budge.

The Central Office of the N.K.V.D. in Moscow evidently became impatient with the meager results of recruitment; and one day a special commission arrived at Grazovec to check on the reasons for the failure. The commission later announced its findings—there was a secret anti-Soviet organization in the camp, composed of "fascists." The commission evidently had to show some evidence for the assertion, and on July 21, 1941, the N.K.V.D. arrested ten officers as members of the "organization." These men were taken away. (Ultimately they survived the prison sentences which were imposed on them and were released after the Sikorsky-Maisky agreement. They joined General Anders' army in Russia.) Although "the organization" was officially dissolved, there were still no volunteers for the Red Army. The commission left for Moscow in disgust. Thereafter, no more interrogations were held in the camp, and there was little food.

The food rations were cut to ridiculous amounts. The prisoners caught sparrows and crows for subsistence. Withdrawal of food was interpreted in the camp as an attempt to break resistance by lowering morale, which was, in fact, rising. The men obtained information, in one way or another, concerning the Polish Government-in-Exile, the hundreds of thousands of Polish soldiers fighting beside the British armies and in the

Underground against German forces, and the American contribution to the war effort. News of this kind restored cohesion in the camp. The "Germans" were now in a most unpleasant situation; they were double prisoners—as former Poles and as present Germans. The Poles, hungry and emaciated as they were, instead of joining the Red Army became cocky to the point of threatening riots unless the N.K.V.D. alleviated their circumstances.

It may be recalled that following the outbreak of the German-Soviet war, diplomatic relations between the Soviet Union and the Polish Government-in-Exile were resumed. General Sikorski, on behalf of the Polish Government, and Soviet Ambassador Maisky, representing his Government, signed an agreement to this effect on July 30, 1941, in London. A special protocol was attached to this agreement. The protocol assured the immediate release of Polish prisoners in Russia.

On August 14, 1941, Polish General Bohusz-Szyszko, who had arrived from London, signed a military agreement with the Soviet Government in Moscow. The agreement allowed the formation of Polish forces on Soviet soil under the command of General Anders (whom the N.K.V.D. had just released from its famous Lubianka prison in Moscow). Eleven days later Generals Bohusz-Szyszko, Anders, and N.K.V.D. General G. S. Zhukov flew into Camp Grazovec. The prisoners welcomed the two Polish generals in the most enthusiastic manner. There was cheering followed by patriotic speeches, and mass voluntary enrollment in the Polish forces commenced immediately. All the men joined with two exceptions—"the German" group of eighteen, and as the Polish source states, a "not much larger" group from the Red Corner.

On September 1, 1941, the N.K.V.D. guards were withdrawn from Camp Grazovec and the Poles took over its administration as a military unit.

One of the last acts of the N.K.V.D. was to present to the Polish authorities the testimonies of the remaining eighteen men who claimed German origin. Subsequently one of them hanged himself—the rest were ultimately supposed to have been taken away by the N.K.V.D. to the labor camps in the northern territories.[18]

The Polish flag fluttered above the camp. For some reason, the Soviet authorities started to distribute among the officers a considerable sum of money, ranging from 2,000 to 10,000 rubles, depending upon rank.[19] N.K.V.D. personnel had to leave the camp.

In a free atmosphere, gathering information about the missing 15,000 Poles commenced. The Katyn Forest graves had not yet been discovered. The Polish Embassy in Moscow under the guidance of the Ambassador, Professor Kot, and General Anders' office, with Captains Kaczkowski and Czapski, started to pool the available information in a systematic fashion with the results already described.

In this chapter some of the circumstances of life and death of the 15,000 Polish prisoners-of-war in the Soviet Union have been reconstructed. From the total number only 448 survived in Camp Pavelishtchev Bor. From these about 400 arrived at Camp Grazovec. Approximately 4,443-4,800 were subsequently found in Katyn Forest. It is the writer's opinion that the approximately 10,000 men remaining were also murdered in a manner and place known only to the officials of the N.K.V.D. (now the M.V.D.), who participated in the extermination, and the highest authorities of the Soviet Government.

One question remains: why were these men murdered and 448 spared?

NOTES TO CHAPTER VII

1. Unless indicated otherwise, data in this chapter are from official Polish sources. This is because only the Polish Government-in-Exile had the opportunity to interview the survivors systematically, to copy the diaries from the graves, and, only the Government-in-Exile

had access to the personnel lists of the Polish Officers' Corps, 1939. It is obvious that since the missing men were Poles, it was the Polish Government-in-Exile which was the most concerned with the case, and therefore had the richest accumulation of materials. This, however, does not mean that Polish sources have been treated uncritically in this book.

In order to avoid extended footnotes, credit for the materials is given here. The three main sources used in this chapter were: Poland. Polish Government-in-Exile, Council of Ministers. (Author, Dr. Wiktor Sukiennicki). *Facts and Documents Concerning Polish Prisoners of War Captured by the U.S.S.R. during the 1939 Campaign.* (Strictly confidential). London, 1946 (referred to throughout this book as the *Polish Report*), *passim*; *Zbrodnia Katyńska w Świetle Dokumentów* (The Katyn crime in the light of documents). Z przedmową Władysława Andersa. 2-gie wydanie. (London: Gryf, 1950), *passim*; Exhibits 32 and 33, submitted in 1952 by the Polish Government-in-Exile to the Congressional Select Committee to Conduct an Investigation of the Facts, Evidence, and Circumstances of the Katyn Forest Massacre. *Hearings*, part 6, pp. 1623-1823, *passim*.

2. Remarks similar in content were made in all three camps by N.K.V.D. officers.

3. From the private correspondence of the former Prime Minister of Poland, Stanisław Mikołajczyk. A personal letter from Wacław Komarnicki, a former inmate of one of the camps, to Mr. Mikołajczyk, January 29, 1948.

4. *Polish Report*, pp. 49-50; *Hearings*, part 6, Exhibit 32, p. 1654.

5. The name of the cadet was Furtek. See his report in writing, *Dziennik Polski* (London), no. 854 (April 21, 1943), p. 2; nine years later, Furtek's testimony was the same. *Hearings*, part 4, p. 509.

6. The name of the prisoner was Gawiak. See his testimony in *Hearings*, part 2, pp. 94-95.

7. Compare testimony of the witness "B." *Hearings*, part 4, pp. 603-611.

8. According to the testimony of the last Commander-in-Chief of the Polish Underground Movement, General Bór-Komorowski, fifteen of the diaries were copied by a member of the Underground who was "planted" among the Poles visiting the Katyn exhumations. The copies of the diaries were delivered to Warsaw's Underground H.Q. at the end of May 1943. Subsequently they were sent by special underground courier—Colonel Rutkowski, nicknamed "Redhead"—to London. The courier, after harrowing experiences, arrived in London in July 1944 with the copies of the diaries intact. *Hearings*, part 4, p. 711.

9. It was possible to locate a Polish Colonel Grobicki, who had been Solski's personal friend at Kozelsk. Colonel Grobicki survived

by being taken to Camp Grazovec. *Hearings*, part 2, p. 174. The colonel verified and corroborated much of the information embodied in Solski's diary. The diary contains ninety-five pages. It is quite detailed and the author has no doubt as to its authenticity. The pages are full of the intimate details about the living in Kozelsk: "Bugs showed in our room"; "they took the dogs away from our camp." He complained about "sciatic pains." The diary is saturated with love and longing for Solski's wife "Danka" and his small daughter "Ewusia."

10. Krivozertsov's fate is most interesting. After being interviewed by the Polish authorities and the British Intelligence, the man found his way from Germany, through Italy, to England. There, on October 30, 1947, his body was found hanging in an orchard. His best friend, also Russian, disappeared. The British authorities announced his manner of death to be "suicide." Many Poles and Englishmen who had known Krivozertsov have not been willing to accept the official British version of his death. For further details concerning this case, consult Joseph Mackiewicz, *The Katyn Wood Murders* (London: Hollis and Carter, 1951), pp. 176-195; also by the same author "Tajemnica Śmierci Iwana Kriwozercowa, Głównego Świadka Zbrodni Katynskiej" (The mystery of the death of the main witness of the Katyn crime, Ivan Krivozertsov), *Wiadomości*, VII, no. 15/15 (April 20, 1952), p. 1; *Hearings*, part 3, pp. 369-372 and part 4, pp. 764, 828-838.

11. *Völkischer Beobachter*. Süddeutsche Ausgabe. April 16, 1943, p. 1; *Nowy Kurier Warszawski* (Warsaw), May 23, 1943, p. 1.

12. *Nowy Kurier Warszawski* (Warsaw), May 31, 1943, p. 1.

13. Another version is that the officers dug the graves themselves. *Nowy Kurier Warszawski* (Warsaw), May 23, 1943, p. 1.

14. For an analysis of these archives see Merle Fainsod, *Smolensk under Soviet Rule* (Cambridge: Harvard University Press, 1958), pp. 1-484. The archives can be obtained through The Adjutant General, U.S. Army, Washington, D. C.

15. Józef Mackiewicz, "Czy Nowa Rewelacja w Sprawie Katynia?" (Is this a new revelation concerning Katyn?), *Dodatek Tygodniowy "Ostatnich Wiadomości*," X, no. 40 (October 12, 1958), p. 3.

16. From the *Polish Report*, p. 113.

17. For the complete list of officers, cadets, noncommissioned officers, privates and civilians who arrived at Grazovec, see *Hearings*, part 4, pp. 526-548.

18. Józef Czapski, *Na Nieludzkiej Ziemi* (The inhuman land) (Paris: Instytut Literacki, 1949), p. 10.

19. *Ibid.*, p. 35. Another Polish source gives the amounts, "2,000-5,000 depending upon rank."

VIII

Reconstruction: Marked to Live and Marked to Die

THE MOST PLAUSIBLE explanation of why nearly 15,000 prisoners-of-war were exterminated in one organized action by the security agencies of the Soviet Government may be stated in a series of propositions:

1. The prisoners were murdered because according to the prevailing values of Soviet officialdom at the time, they were enemies of the Soviet Union.

2. Their physical destruction guaranteed elimination forever of a considerable segment of the hostile military and professional elite of Poland, thus creating a leaderless vacuum into which Soviet-groomed men could move in the future. Actually this is what occurred, particularly in the period of 1945-1956.

3. According to the N.K.V.D. evaluation, the prisoners could not be induced to adopt pro-Soviet attitudes. Later, at the highest level of policy making, an order was issued to "liquidate" the prisoners. Such an order was given, in all probability, by Stalin through Beria (the chief of the N.K.V.D.) or by Beria himself with Stalin's approval.

4. There is also a possibility that Stalin's order was misinterpreted by Beria.[1] In any case, the men were exterminated in

an action centrally guided by the main office of the N.K.V.D. in Moscow.

Stanisław Mikołajczyk, former Prime Minister of the Polish Government who escaped from Poland in 1948, maintains that between 1939 and 1941 the German and Soviet governments had a mutual understanding concerning Polish prisoners in the Soviet Union: "I know positively that there was an agreement between the Germans and the Russians concerning the exchange of Poles and Ukrainians and that the Germans would not accept the Polish officers offered in that exchange." [2]

Churchill also mentions that thousands of Poles were handed over to the Germans for forced-labor purposes prior to the outbreak of the German-Soviet war.[3] In fact, Polish prisoners were exchanged "both ways." Regardless of the outcome of these German-Soviet bargains, the fact remains that the officers were treated as a group separate from the noncommissioned officers and enlisted men. Although they were kept in the same camp as others, the officers were investigated with particular care by the N.K.V.D. A German refusal to accept them could be understood easily, because the Germans could not use the officers as laborers, being bound by the Geneva Convention Relating to the Treatment of Prisoners of War of July 27, 1929. To feed unproductive thousands of officers was not in the best interest of Germany, where the population's food was already rationed.

We know the importance attached by the Soviet administrative apparatus in Stalin's era to the pronouncements of Lenin and his interpretation of the communist doctrine. The fact that the majority of men who were massacred in Katyn were officers might be, in the light of the doctrine, the reason for their death. According to the doctrine, war is not a conflict between individuals or states but *between classes*—the oppressors and those who are being oppressed—bourgeois against the proletariat. If the war promotes the interest of the proletariat, according to Lenin, such a war is "progress, irrespective of the victims and sufferings which it entails." [4]

Professor T. A. Taracouzio, in his book, *The Soviet Union and International Law*, written in 1935 (five years before the Katyn Massacre) interprets the effect of the theory of class struggle upon the treatment of prisoners taken by the Soviet Army in the event of a military clash between Russia and a capitalist state:

> The chief aim which the Soviet State would pursue in this conflict would be a socialist revolution in that state. . . . According to the principle of proletarian solidarity, the enemy enlisted man, when taken into captivity by the Soviets, might well expect a "brotherly" welcome . . . whether political "reeducation" along the lines of Communist philosophy, or an invitation to join the proletarian ranks immediately. . . . The situation would not be at all the same were officers taken prisoners, however. Obviously, it could not be expected that officers, who in the majority of cases do not belong to the proletariat, would be converted to communism by mere theoretical instruction. Hence the officers would always be considered by the Soviet authorities as class enemies.[5]

To support this reasoning Professor Taracouzio cites two examples. The first, The Joint Decree of the Revolutionary Military Council of the Soviet Republic and of the People's Commissariat for the Interior, of May 7, 1920, regarding prisoners taken during the Civil War, states:
"While the enlisted men taken into captivity could be recommended for immediate enlistment in the Red Army by Revolutionary Military Councils, the fate of the officers was left to the discretion of the All-Russian Extraordinary Commission, the 'Cheka.' " [6]

The second example illustrates again that all officers of foreign armies could be classified by the Soviet authorities with the bourgeois elements, on the basis of their rank. The Soviet Agreement with Hungary on Repatriation of War Prisoners, of July 28, 1921, in Article 6, clause 2, states: "The Hungarian officers and bourgeois elements (bourgeoisie), . . . are to be exchanged for the persons enumerated in the annex hereto." [7]

It can be proved that at the time the Red Army entered the Polish borders in September 1939, it was guided by the same policy concerning officers. Alternately with bombs, Soviet planes dropped leaflets on the Polish forces, directing the soldiers to revolt against their officers. This is an excerpt from such a leaflet: "Soldiers!! Do not believe your officers. The officers and generals are your enemies. . . . Soldiers! Destroy the officers and generals. . . ." [8] These leaflets were signed by General Timoshenko and dated September 1939. Many Polish officers who survived capture by the Soviet Army testified to the Polish authorities that they survived because they "had disguised themselves as . . . privates during their enforced stay in Russia." [9] It was commonly agreed among the Polish prisoners that the possession of an officer's rank was a definite handicap in Soviet prisoner-of-war camps.[10]

The Soviet concept of the "class struggle" led the Soviet N.K.V.D. authorities to the very meticulous classification of all Polish citizens. Secret instruction Number 0054 of the N.K.V.D. Commissar in Soviet-occupied Polish territory, dated 1940, classified persons "who because of their political or social past life, chauvinism or religious convictions . . . are the enemies of the Soviet Republic." [11] This classification embraced twelve categories of enemies of the Soviet Union, with "all former officers of any army except the Soviet Army" ranked as fourth in importance. It seems that the very fact of being an officer of the Polish Forces at that time (1940) automatically classified a man not only as a class enemy but also as an enemy of the Soviet Union.

The Soviet authorities were unrestricted legally in the treatment of the Polish officers, because the Soviet Union had not subscribed to the Geneva Convention Relating to the Treatment of Prisoners of War, of July 27, 1929.[12] Hence, the approach toward officers was guided exclusively by Soviet laws, political trends, or expediency.

Polish General Olszyna-Wilczyński, commander of the military district of Grodno, issued an order to his troops not to fight against the oncoming Soviet forces. Acting on the assumption that they were friendly, he rode forward to greet them. Upon meeting a Soviet unit he "was dragged out of his car, put against the door of a barn and shot to death." [13] The fact that he was an officer evidently sufficed as a reason. This was not an isolated case.

Whether officers fought or surrendered without fighting they were immediately arrested. Even reserve officers living in territory seized by the Soviet Army, who had not been called to the colors and were still engaged in their civilian occupations, were sought out and immediately detained. One such reserve officer was arrested together with his teen-age son, and both were sent to the officers' camp. (The son was sent to Grazovec Camp and survived.) These men were grouped together with the professional officers in the camps of Kozelsk, Starobelsk, and Ostashkov.

Not only the officer's rank incriminated many of these men in the eyes of the N.K.V.D., but also their professions. When Mr. Pohorecki, President of the Polish Supreme Court, pointed out to an N.K.V.D. general during interrogation that he was not connected with any military organization, the general remarked that the very fact that he was a President of a Supreme Court of a bourgeois state was enough to put him in prison.[14]

The criterion of profession was evidently the reason for lumping together with the officers, priests, ministers, and rabbis, some of whom were not chaplains. Many of them were subsequently removed from the camps (in Kozelsk, on Christmas Eve, 1939) because officers were receiving uplift of morale and spirit from their activities. In Kozelsk there were about a hundred men of God of various denominations. (At least one of them was identified in the graves of Katyn.) In Starobelsk the number was twenty-five. How many were at Ostashkov cannot be reliably established.[15] Only one of all these, a priest, arrived at Grazovec.

It was certainly not a coincidence that all the staff of the Polish Institute of Gas Warfare was annihilated to a man. Eighty per cent of the alumni of the Department of Armament of Warsaw Polytechnic were destroyed, as were more than 80 per cent of the personnel of the Polish Technical Institute for Armament.[16]

Such classification and destruction of specialized potential talents which could be turned against the Soviet Union would explain the presence of the several hundred civilians in the three camps. Such men were selected for arrest in Eastern Poland, were kept imprisoned with the military personnel and shared their fate. It was established that in Camp Kozelsk there were about 150 such men. ("Civilians" does not include officers in the camps who were dressed in civilian clothes.)

This approach might also explain the presence of several thousand privates and noncommissioned officers in the three camps. They evidently were interned not because of their rank, but because of their military or civilian functions. Regardless of rank, those connected with law enforcement or intelligence were kept together with the officers. The logic of this arrangement seems obvious. The law these men represented was capitalist law, and about whom did they collect intelligence? It is not well known that the Polish intelligence and counter-intelligence service prior to 1939 was one of the best in Europe. For example, its agents penetrated the Polish Communist Party on all organizational levels so well that, in 1938, the Soviet leaders decided to dissolve the Communist Party in Poland as the only means of saving the remnants of its membership from complete registration by the Polish security agencies.

The prisoner's political position *versus* the Soviet Government was evaluated by testing it against four categories. According to the N.K.V.D. nomenclature, each of these four could hide the potential present "enemies of the Soviet Union." The categories were: rank, professional function or affiliation,[17] standing in society, attitudes toward the Soviet Union in particular and communism in general. Many men were caught in all four. This is not surprising considering the fact that among the men, particularly the reserve officers imprisoned in the three camps, there were more than fifty who were on university lecturing staffs, more than a thousand lawyers, many writers, civic leaders, and journalists,[18] and approximately 800 doctors of medicine.[19]

Even the doctors disappeared. Of those from Camp Kozelsk, 146 were identified in Katyn. Which of the categories fitted these men no one will know until N.K.V.D. files are accessible, but to murder 800 doctors of medicine in one centrally organized action is without precedent. In any case, the Soviet Government captured in one sweep a considerable percentage of the Polish intellectual and professional elite, apparently with premeditation.

The problem of guarding these prisoners and finding a solution for reconciliation of their status and Soviet law belonged to the security police, the N.K.V.D.[20] The chief function of the N.K.V.D. was to eliminate acts of a treasonable nature by covert class enemies. Its prerogatives were boundless. A man could become a class enemy because the N.K.V.D. said he was.[21]

The organization guarding the prisoners acted as both warden and judge. The normal N.K.V.D. procedure with prisoners of any type was personal investigation of each case, in this instance, each prisoner.

The initial objectives of the N.K.V.D. personnel seemed to be three: to drain the prisoners of information important to the Soviet Government, to apply mass indoctrination, and to classify the prisoners and select possible collaborators.

The procedures of interrogation, search for information,

and classification were the usual functions of the N.K.V.D. What was unusual was the attempt to manipulate political attitudes by mass indoctrination. The N.K.V.D. assumed a new role in regard to the prisoners—that of teacher, or more properly, propagandist. No one could have anticipated that the experience gained by the communists on these Poles would be further developed on German prisoners and used eleven years later on American prisoners in Chinese hands, during and after the Korean war.

Interrogation began soon after the men arrived at the three camps. All the prisoners were photographed, at Starobelsk each several times. There were interviews with interrogators almost nightly. A man never knew when he might be called to report for investigation. Neither did he know how long he would be examined. Those questioned always felt that they had to tell more and more—there was never enough information for the inquisitors.

When they were asked about the future, the faces of the N.K.V.D. interrogators were professionally inscrutable. The tensions among the prisoners mounted from the outset. These inquiries never ceased. They continued until two or three weeks before the men were let out of the compound. The length of interrogations was also unpredictable. Sometimes they were very short, sometimes they continued for 72 hours, the interrogators taking turns.

The mood and approach of the interrogators constantly changed in the most unpredictable fashion. At one time, the N.K.V.D. officer would lead a polite political discourse with the cool detachment of a scholar. At another time, with the same prisoner, the excited interrogator would shout threats and vilifications at the shaky and exhausted man, then abruptly change to a sympathetic, fatherly friend. The same personal data were taken time after time. As a rule they were interpreted in such a way as to prove that the prisoner was serving a "bourgeois" cause and also taking part in the "counterrevolution against the Soviet Union." This was the standard accusation presented against each of the prisoners.[22] Political opinions, especially, were most carefully gathered during these interviews.

The prisoners, as a rule, told the truth about themselves. Most of them were proud of their backgrounds, achievements, and the positions they held. Furthermore, they discovered that the N.K.V.D. was collecting data on them from other sources. One of the officers was dumbfounded when his N.K.V.D. interrogator described to him the furniture arrangement of his home in eastern Poland.

The majority said what they thought. They were not convinced that Soviet life was better, nor did they want Poland to become a part of the Soviet Union.

Most interrogations were polite, but at one time in Ostashkov several dozen pupils from N.K.V.D. schools were brought in to practice interrogation. These young men made up in zeal what they lacked in experience, and some beatings and abuses occurred.[23]

Occasionally subtle overtures were made to enroll some of the prisoners as agents to be sent to the part of Poland under German occupation.[24] There is no evidence that any of these offers were accepted. It is possible, however, that within the camps the N.K.V.D. men were able to establish something of a network of informers recruited in one way or another.

In many instances a sophisticated officer would be amused at the topics which came up during the interrogation. Here is a description of such a situation by one of the prisoners:

> On one occasion I was being questioned by three officers—one a stout, perfumed N.K.V.D. man, the others, two Army officers of very primitive mentality. They learned that I had worked for eight years in Paris as an artist, a fact which seemed to them extremely suspicious. "What instructions were given to you by your Foreign Minister when you were leaving for Paris?" demanded

my inquisitioner, the N.K.V.D. man. I replied that the Minister didn't even know I was going to Paris. "Well then," he continued, "what did the Vice-Minister tell you?" "He didn't know about it either," I said. "I went to Paris as a painter, not as a spy." "Do you think," he persisted, "that we do not understand that you, as a painter, could have prepared a plan of Paris and sent it to your Minister in Warsaw?" I was absolutely unable to convince him that a plan of Paris could be brought for fifty centimes on any street corner in Paris and that Polish artists going to Paris were not spies drawing secret plans. Not one of them could be persuaded that anyone was ever allowed to go abroad except on an errand of espionage.[25]

After some time the file on each man consisted of the following types of data (apart from some of the personal documents taken away from prisoners):
(1) photographs,
(2) fingerprints,
(3) official reports of the interrogations,
(4) reports and evaluation of the camp authorities,
(5) testimony of fellow prisoners,
(6) extracts of works published by a prisoner,
(7) extracts from biographies pertinent to prisoner's past, and
(8) copies (or originals detained by censor) of letters from or to families or friends.[26]

Though a file of these dimensions had been built up on each of the prisoners, gathered between the fall of 1939 and spring of 1940, the Soviet Government persistently maintained in July 1941 that it did not know anything about these men. This "know nothing" attitude was maintained until the Germans announced that they discovered the graves.

While some of the investigators did not appear sophisticated, the over-all policy of conditioning of prisoners was. Its objective was to create a state of insecurity and a feeling of unreality ("confusion neurosis") in which the man's values and ideals are "doubted and ultimately shattered." Then, according to Pavlov's theory of conditioning, the man given the proper set of stimuli would learn to respond automatically and with predetermined results. The main idea of such premeditated processing of the prisoners was to control their responses. As one of the psychiatrists interested in the conditioning of prisoners, Dr. Joost A. M. Merloo, says, "when you control responses—you control the individual." At least in Pavlovian interpretation.

The N.K.V.D. hoped that a prisoner would lose his own identity. Then, responding automatically to the stimuli supplied by the propaganda apparatus, he would change his political attitudes and become converted to the values fostered by the interrogators.[27] (A general comment might be warranted here. It seems that when the procedures for conditioning prisoners are systematically worked out they can be applied by relatively unsophisticated personnel.)

The captured men were already in a state of tension and anxiety. In thirty days their world had been destroyed. They had been uprooted from their cultural setting and removed from their families. They were imprisoned and did not know what to expect from their captors.

The camp authorities did nothing to alleviate the prisoners' anxiety. To the contrary, they did everything to increase it, as a part of the conditioning process. Any props which might support the prisoners' morale were systematically kicked from under them.

They were told on every occasion that Poland no longer existed. Polish culture was contemptuously ridiculed. At any level of communication between administrative personnel and the prisoners the Poles' values were attacked, often crudely, and occasionally in a subtle manner causing reflection. But above all, one idea was hammered into the prisoners: they were wrongdoers for not being communists. On one occasion in Kozelsk, Polish Lieutenant Colonel Chałacinski organized a discussion group. This had been explicitly forbidden by the camp authorities. The colonel was arrested, and the Soviet authorities announced it in the following manner: "The former Lieutenant Colonel Chałacinski of the former Polish Army has been sentenced to 10 days arrest for patriotic activity on behalf of former Poland." [28]

The men were attacked as a group and as individuals at the same time. The target was to split the group into separate particles and to destroy identity and identification symbols of each of them, one by one. Subsequently, the men would be "rebuilt" on the N.K.V.D. model. All efforts of the N.K.V.D. were bent toward these goals.

The prisoners' mail was not only censored but withdrawn at times. The men at Camp Kozelsk had permission to write once a month, but could not admit that they were prisoners. Their outgoing letters were stamped "Gorki Rest House." The return address was given as "Kozelsk, Province of Smolensk, Post Office Box 12." [29]

To break the network of loyalties and affiliation, the men in Starobelsk were constantly and individually shifted from one barracks to another. Hardly did they begin to develop a closer relationship among themselves than they were scattered. None knew when he would be moved. This happened repeatedly.[30] Attack was also directed against the possible emergence of potential leaders. In Starobelsk high-ranking officers were kept within the compound but in a separate enclosure, so that the rest of the men would not have contact with them.

Men with ability for leadership, when recognized, were immediately singled out by the N.K.V.D. and shipped from the camp. This happened to Lieutenant Kwolek in Starobelsk. A born leader, with serenity of soul and iron determination, Kwolek soon became a center of popular affection and respect. At one point he made a huge cross out of wood and hung it on the wall. The N.K.V.D. pounced on him then and there.

No praying was allowed, yet the officers did so in spite of

the consequences. Mass prayers were recited aloud, resulting in a "tremendous uplift."[31] The authorities retaliated by forcible removal of active chaplains of all denominations from the camps. In Starobelsk, Catholic priest Aleksandrowicz and Rabbi Steinberg, both genuinely loved, were removed several days prior to Christmas, 1939. They never reappeared.[32] Some of the N.K.V.D. officers attempted, in a sense, to assume the chaplains' role by playing cheerful, available father-confessors.[33] Also, some of the men developed interest in spiritualist seances.[34]

In an apparently consistent policy of blocking the avenues for the men's feelings of loyalty and attachment, even dogs were purposely removed from the camps. The poor animals crept under the barbed fences for scraps of food. The prisoners adopted them joyously and shared their meager meals with them. Removal of the dogs was felt deeply by the men.

More subtle devices to increase anxiety were also applied. An N.K.V.D. officer "lost" in Camp Starobelsk a document in which the route of transport of the officers from the camp was mapped. It led from Starobelsk to Poland. The document raised hope of returning to Poland among many prisoners.

On one occasion the prisoners were awakened during the night with inquiries of "Who knows Greek and Romanian?"[35] This implied to the men that they would be traveling through the Balkans and further increased their confusion and apprehension.

The result of the nightly interrogation and the "processing" described above was an increasing state of tiredness, tension, insecurity, and anxiety among the prisoners. The physical deprivations, such as insufficient food and dismal cold, and crowded living conditions, contributed further to these fears and tensions. The intensity of the application of all these discomforts and pressures was varied. There was a method in this, too. The psychological pressures were put on and off, like an ebb and flow, with an equally eroding effect.

Soon after the prisoners' arrival huge billboards had sprung up all over the camps. On them, vividly painted, was the Soviet Constitution translated into Polish. The articles guaranteeing various "freedoms" gave the officers a subject for unprintable comments. Kozelsk and Starobelsk had camp movies. In the case of Starobelsk the theater was in the former church, which prior to the officers' arrival had served as a granary. The movies were Soviet productions with propaganda undertones. During one of the showings in Kozelsk when a crude and offensive antireligious scene was projected on the screen, the men left the room in protest. After this incident, when the audience had filed into the room, the doors were locked and those inside had to sit throughout the showing. With another group of prisoners camp administration announced that a foreign movie would be shown. A crowd of prisoners gathered; the doors were locked, and a lecture on the beauties of the Soviet regime followed.[36]

In one camp, the Poles simply boycotted the movies, to the chagrin of the camp administration. Finally, the movie house was closed because of lack of attendance.

Public address systems blared Soviet propaganda throughout the camps. There was no escape from it. Installations were fixed inside the living quarters, outside, and even in the public bath.[37] The propaganda talks and Soviet programs were generously interlaced with recorded music of Chopin. The nostalgic, soul-searching melodies which only enhanced feelings of misery were rudely interrupted with announcements of the new achievements of the "glorious Soviet Union." Soviet papers were distributed in the camp and were used by the prisoners for purposes quite removed from reading. Many of these papers were found in the Katyn graves.

Direct verbal communication was also used in this process of indoctrination. From time to time lectures were arranged during which the prisoners were told about benefits of the communist society as contrasted with the other kinds of social and political systems. Such lectures were delivered by the Soviet staff. As a rule Polish culture and its by-products were attacked in the process. The response of the officers had three stages: first they heckled the speaker; after several lectures they tried to engage him in debates or discussion; ultimately they resigned themselves to more or less passive listening.

The prisoners' only direct contact with the outside world was confined to the N.K.V.D. staff of the camp administration. On every level of this contact, formal or informal, the ultimate purpose of the N.K.V.D. activities was to elicit information and to change the Poles' political attitudes. This was done by the simultaneous application of systematic techniques affecting the psychology of the prisoners. The interviews served also as a check on the progress of indoctrination.

Camp Kozelsk (from which came the victims found in the Katyn graves) had its "mystery person"—a General of the N.K.V.D. by the name of V. M. Zarubin. (It could not be established whether there is any connection between the names of General Zarubin and that of Georgi Zarubin, former Soviet Ambassador to the United States and Canada.) He was the highest ranking man in the camp, and it was evident to the prisoners that, although not the camp commander, he wielded the reins. He was the locus of official power. His position in the camp was never defined, nor was his function. By implication he was managing the team of N.K.V.D. investigators, yet he kept himself rather aloof from them.

This man, in contrast to the personnel of the camp, was by all criteria an unusual individual. Very polished and proper in social contacts with prisoners, he behaved with the dignity and sophistication which is usually the result of broad experience of a sensitive man. He was well-educated, and spoke German, French, and some English. Zarubin, by his behavior and these qualities, won the respect of the Polish officers to the point that, contrary to the rule of not saluting any of the Soviet staff, the men saluted the N.K.V.D. general whenever they saw him, causing him some inconvenience for he meticulously returned every salute.

At random, seemingly, he would invite a prisoner for a chat. There was usually another N.K.V.D. officer from the camp's intelligence section present. Tea and good cigarettes would be served. Sometimes even oranges were available, which by Soviet standards (not to speak of the prisoners' conditions) were a real luxury, particularly during the Russian winter. In such comfort a prisoner would "thaw"—physically and mentally. The men would engage in a lively discourse sprinkled generously with opinions on philosophy, political theory, and foreign relations. These opinions were voiced usually by a prisoner.

General Zarubin had brought with him a library of about 500 volumes in French, German, and English languages and was willing to lend the books, allowing the officers to make their own choices. Books—these had greater value for the prisoners than bread. The officers eagerly made choices. (Churchill's *The World Crisis*, published in 1931, was the most popular.) The general was never involved directly in any propaganda activity, but was an exceedingly good listener.

The Polish officers had found someone among the Russians with whom they could communicate. Here was, intellectually speaking, a kindred spirit, interested in their views and attentive to their opinions.[38] In Zarubin's office the men had a sense of self-respect. One does not need profound psychological insight to understand that under these circumstances the prisoners were willing to talk freely to relieve anxiety. They talked as "an officer to another officer," not to an N.K.V.D. "flunky." Emaciated and imprisoned as they were, they were honorable men guided by the concept of an "Officer Honor" rooted in the faraway times of medieval knighthood. One has to know something about pre-1939 Polish officers to understand this.[39]

Yet, to the senior Polish officers in the camp Zarubin's interviews revealed some pattern. There were guesses that he was checking on something which the men could not precisely define. Polish generals in Kozelsk were worried. One of them, General Minkiewicz, decided to find out something about Zarubin's intentions and to quell the wild gossip which swept the camp, increasing the anxiety of the men. He went to Zarubin himself. The Polish general pleaded with the N.K.V.D. man:

Minkiewicz: "Do not make us nervous as all the rumors are spreading around, but tell us. What do you want to do with us?"

Zarubin: "I do not think it would be right.... You would ... [go] mad if I told you. I assure you it would be inhuman. I assure you, General, it is better for you not to know what we want to do with you." [40]

On March 4, 1940, General V. M. Zarubin left Kozelsk Camp. On April 3 the first group of Polish officers was assembled for departure into the unknown. From 15,570 only 448 were selected to live.

Were all of those survivors communists? No. Only twenty to thirty of them ultimately landed in a suburb of Moscow in an indoctrination center called by the Poles "Villa Bliss," and declared themselves to be communists. What were the criteria used for their selection? Because the files of the N.K.V.D. concerning the prisoners are still not available we can only speculate.

It seems probable that the N.K.V.D. selected the survivors on the bases of three criteria: those who already manifested overtly their communistic sympathies (relatively few, several dozen), those who in terms of the N.K.V.D. assessment were susceptible or ready for further indoctrination, and finally, those who had something in their background or personalities which struck a sympathetic note in the "life-savers."

There was a small group of communist sympathizers who were selected, of course. Also there were some prisoners who acted as undercover agents for the administration of the camp. Those men may have been among the survivors, although it is quite possible that with its shrewdness the N.K.V.D. would have shipped them to their death when they became useless. It must be understood that to be classified as "susceptible" in terms of N.K.V.D. operational procedures is not necessarily a slander or reflection on a man's character or his values.

A psychiatric study which was made of the Chinese Communist indoctrination program for prisoners-of-war can, in one respect, be applied to the men in Grazovec. That study classified prisoners who collaborated with the communists into five basic types: weaklings, opportunists, bored or curious intellectuals, those who felt they had "low status," and communist sympathizers.[41] It is not unlikely that the N.K.V.D. men had some sort of guiding criteria according to which personality traits and attitudes were classified. Although the survivors could not be classified outright as "communist sympathizers," yet their personal characteristics or attitudes revealed them to be potential material for further indoctrination efforts. In many instances the more strongly that high ethical values were entrenched in a prisoner, the more susceptible to propaganda he might appear. There is an explanation of this apparently paradoxical statement.

Two American psychiatrists operating as a team studied communist interrogation and indoctrination of "enemies of the state" and arrived at the conclusion that

> persons who carry with them strong feelings of guilt associated with a highly organized system of moral values likewise become ready targets for the persuasion of the interrogator. Very few people are entirely free of guilt feelings, but often such feelings are found in the highest degree in those in whom they are least appropriate. For example, many strongly religious people have a profound sense of sin. They constantly see themselves as trans-

gressing their own moral code, and are in need of forgiveness for doing so. Skilled interrogators make use of this. They point out that many of the ostensible ideals of communism are the same as the ideals to which the prisoner himself subscribes.[42]

The same scientists point out in their work that it is difficult for the person with a highly developed moral code to tell a lie.

The process of selection and classification had to be sensitive and quite flexible in judging the men. For example, two members of the Polish aristocracy, Prince Radziwiłł and Prince Lubomirski, who because of their social origin could surely be deemed "class enemies," were spared and found themselves in Camp Grazovec. Later through the surprising personal intervention of the King of Italy they were released from this camp.[43]

As to the decisions which in all probability reflected preferential values of the interrogators themselves, we may cite the case of the only surviving Polish general from Camp Kozelsk. There were five officers with the rank of general in this camp: Minkiewicz, Smorawinski, Bohatyrewicz, Wołkowicki, and Admiral Czernicki. All except Wołkowicki were found in Katyn Forest. Why did General Wołkowicki (presently in England) survive? His guess was that one event in his life attracted his interrogators' attention and led them to take a favorable attitude toward him.

As a youth, he was an officer in the Russian Navy during the Tsar's regime. As a naval officer he participated in the famous battle of Tsushima between the Japanese and Russian fleets, which ended with disastrous results for the Russian fleet. In General Wołkowicki's words he "was on the ship which was surrendered by a Russian admiral to the Japanese. I was the only officer who opposed the surrender of this ship. . . . "[44] It is quite possible that this was the sole, or an additional, factor in the N.K.V.D.'s decision to spare this elderly gentleman. At Camp Starobelsk there were eight generals, all with outstanding combat or service records: S. Haller, Skierski, Łukowski, F. Sikorski, Billewicz, Plisowski, Kowalewski, and Skuratowicz. All perished.

To cite another instance, Lieutenant Zygmunt Miter (Mitera?) was killed. This man's most conspicuous trait was his enthusiasm for the United States. Prior to 1939 he spent some time in America as a Fellow of the Rockefeller Foundation. In the camp he was most eager to talk about his visit, the country, and the people. According to his acquaintance, Captain Czapski, he was a harmless individual and earned a nickname of "Gondolier" because it was his function to stir the soup in the camp's kitchen. This he did with an oversized ladle, always ready with a smile and lively description of the country of his dreams—the United States.

In all, 448 men were given the chance to live. The underlying idea was to work with them further toward the goal of complete indoctrination. The rest were incorrigible—they were shot. The fate of the survivors is known from the preceding chapter. About twenty to thirty of the survivors ultimately declared themselves to be communists. Only thirteen from this group were accepted as such by the Soviet authorities. Even these joined the Polish Army under General Anders, which was formed as the result of the German-Soviet war and re-establishment of Polish-Soviet diplomatic relations in 1941. The story of these thirteen requires separate treatment.

The men of Kozelsk, Starobelsk, and Ostashkov were dead. In Grazovec, 400 survivors trampled the mud of the camp, gradually losing hopes of going anywhere. Only the occupants of the "Red Corner" behaved with the purpose and preoccupation of new converts who had arrived at the end of the search for an ideal.

On October 10, 1940, seven high-ranking officers chosen from among those the N.K.V.D. thought were communist sympathizers, left for Moscow. This time they traveled in a passenger train and relative luxury. The group consisted of two colonels, four lieutenant-colonels, and one major.[45]

The next day from Camp Kozelsk twenty-one junior officers departed for the same destination. About 2,500 men, after the campaign of 1939, had sought the protection of neutral countries, crossing the borders into Lithuania and then Estonia to be interned there. After the seizure of these countries by Soviet forces, these prisoners were brought to Kozelsk, already empty, most of its original occupants being in the graves of the Katyn Forest, the rest imprisoned in Grazovec. The twenty-one junior officers came from this second group. An interesting and significant incident took place when, after six weeks in Kozelsk, all the remaining prisoners were told to be ready for departure. The men speculated as to where they were going. They tried to probe the camp administration—as usual, without results, except for one incident.

Among the prisoners was a well-known Polish pediatrician. He had saved the life of a child whose mother was the official doctor of the camp. She happened to be a gracious and gentle Chinese lady. After that a subtle thread of professional and human amity existed between these two. When the time for departure came, the Polish doctor asked the Chinese woman whether she knew the place of their destination. Her response was quite unusual. She broke into hysterical sobs, and the Pole had great difficulty in calming her, but she did not say a word. Evidently the Chinese doctor knew what had happened to the previous internees in Camp Kozelsk. Ultimately, however, these prisoners did go to Grazovec and eventually to the Polish Army.

The twenty-eight officers from the two parties arrived in Moscow. Here they were told that they were "guests" of the N.K.V.D. It was reiterated that they were no longer prisoners. They were given "excellent bread, real butter" and even "six lumps of sugar each," and yet even with the status of guests they were locked in Butyrki prison in Moscow. Each party was kept separately.[46]

At Butyrki the men were interviewed individually and in groups by the officers at the highest administrative level of the N.K.V.D.—Merkulov, Raikhman, and Yegorov. Merkulov ranked second only to Beria. Raikhman held the rank of General of the N.K.V.D. (This general is the man who successfully dodged Captain Czapski's inquires about the missing Poles.) Yegorov was a colonel. The talks centered more or less around these questions: Were the Poles willing to fight Germans? Did they recognize that the Polish Government-in-Exile was a fiction? Were they friendly toward the Soviet Union and the communist ideology?

Of the seven men from Grazovec one did not "make the grade." He was separated from the others and placed in a solitary cell. The other six were sent to Lubianka prison in Moscow. Here they met the man who could decide their fate —the Peoples' Commissar for Home Affairs (the Chief of the N.K.V.D.), Mr. Beria himself. Long and frequent conversations took place at Lubianka prison, all bent toward an aim which now was made very clear to these Polish officers—they were to form Polish units fighting under the auspices and command of the Soviet Army. After interviews with Beria and conversations in their cells, the six officers agreed.

The troops would be raised from the over one million Poles deported from the Eastern Polish territories occupied by the Soviet Army. The deportees populated the labor camps and underdeveloped northern areas of the Soviet Union, and being under N.K.V.D. surveillance could volunteer or be drafted for such an army. But what about the officers? It ordinarily requires years to produce a good combat officer. This troubled the future leaders of the Red Polish Forces, particularly since all of them had been promised advancement in rank and commands of large units. The problem appeared even more acute when it became known that of the twenty-one junior officers still kept at Butyrki prison, only eleven had "graduated" to Lubianka prison and interviews with Beria. To accentuate the problem even further, from these eleven only five appeared promising to the N.K.V.D. at Lubianka. The remaining six junior officers were sent back to Butyrki.

The Polish Colonel Berling was not happy about the numerical strength of the nucleus of his "Polish Forces": six high-ranking officers and five junior ranks. That would not be enough officers for an infantry battalion. In addition, Berling discovered that the junior officers, although having been at Butyrki and Lubianka from October to December, still did not know that they were slated to become officers in Polish forces under Soviet command. When on Christmas Eve, 1940, Colonel Berling dressed himself in full Polish uniform and went to pay Christmas visits to the "juniors," one of them, hearing what was in store for them, forgot the customary respect for higher rank and told the colonel what he thought of him and the idea of serving the Soviet Union. The man was taken back to Butyrki. Now the ratio of staff to junior officers was six to four.

Of particular importance is the fact that during the conversations at Lubianka and in connection with the problem of getting officers for the projected forces, two comments were made by N.K.V.D. officials which shed some light on the missing officers from Kozelsk, Ostashkov, and Starobelsk.

Soon after the arrival of the officers at Lubianka, Beria, upon conclusion of a discussion, invited Berling, Gorczyński, Bukojemski, and Tyszyński for supper at which "even cognac was served." [47] During the evening Beria mentioned his intention to organize first a Polish armored division. Hearing this,

> Berling asked. . . . "And where will we get officers? I would like to have my officers from Starobelsk and Kozelsk." . . . To this

Beria replied. . . . "We have committed a great blunder"; and he repeated that twice; "We have made a great mistake; we have made a great mistake." [48]

Two weeks later the reference to the missing men came up again. According to one of the six officers who was interviewed by the Beria second-in-command, Merkulov:

> He (Merkulov) asked me if I could command an artillery brigade. I told him "Yes." I told him that the number of cannon in a brigade like that of artillery would not make too much difference to me; but I asked him, "From where will we get other officers, since there are no artillery officers in Grazovec." I asked him if we could not get any Polish officers from either Starobielsk or Kozielsk [Polish spellings]. To this I received a reply from Merkulov: "We have committed an error. . . . These men are not available. We will give you others." [49]

On November 1, 1940, the six officers were transferred to a private house in a suburb of Moscow, Malachovka. It was dubbed "The Villa of Bliss." To men who for over a year had known the deprivation of the camps and prisons, it was bliss. The house was about twenty-five miles from the center of Moscow. It was a modern building with steam heating and warm showers. It had seven rooms and a kitchen.

The furnishing of the home was luxurious by prison standards—feather pillows, soft armchairs, quilted bedspreads and soft mattresses. The house was maintained by two very attractive young Russian chambermaids. Two cooks prepared excellent food. However, the men were not allowed to leave the house during the night. One of the colonels, Morawski, enjoyed these privileges for only a few days. When asked to write a memorandum pertaining to the creation of a "Polish Committee" under Soviet auspices and expounding his views on the future Polish-Soviet frontier, the colonel did so. What he wrote was evidently not to the liking of the N.K.V.D. guardians. No more pork chops and caviar— back he went to Butyrki prison.

During December, "reinforcements," amounting to eleven officers, came from the Red Corner of Camps Grazovec and Kozelsk. The total number of the pensioners at the "Villa of Bliss" in the winter of 1940 was between twenty and thirty.[50]

Although the men had full stomachs, this was not by any means a happy family. Tempers flared, men eyed each other with suspicion, and there was very little communist brotherly love. The quarrels and clashes usually centered around Polish symbols and values which, in spite of the N.K.V.D. hopes, some officers shed very slowly.

On December 31, 1940, a New Year's Eve party was arranged. Brandy, fresh fruits, and a cold buffet on a spotless white-covered table almost guaranteed a good time. Almost. . . . When midnight struck, the radio blared the "Internationale." The majority of the officers stood at attention, but several hardy souls remained seated. In spite of authoritative glares from the high-ranking officers, they did not budge.

After this incident, the members of the party withdrew into their own thoughts. But when a toast was proposed, "Long live the Communist Party," the scene became chaotic. Many men refused to drink, one crashed his glass to the floor. The next day Colonel Berling gave a one and one-half hour speech to the officers, "trying to smooth out the incident."

On another occasion someone proposed hanging portraits of the Soviet leaders on the walls of the "Villa." Again some men, although in the minority, would not agree. A vote was taken and the minority was overridden. The portraits were hung on the walls.

Tension mounted within the group in proportion to the pressures to become communist collaborators. On one occasion Captain Łopianowski, looking at a map of Europe on which the Soviet mapmaker already had shown half of Poland as belonging to the Soviet Union, burst out with scathing criticism. Berling responded by calling him "a swine and a fascist." A fist fight followed. Later when being encouraged to sign a declaration for a Polish communist paper, Łopianowski stood up and declared that he wanted to be sent back to prison.[51] He did not wait long. On March 25, 1941, he was sent back to Butyrki prison with another uncooperative officer.

Although the number of officers at "Villa Bliss" diminished progressively, indoctrination went on without any particular changes or adjustments. The officers listened to the Soviet radio, attended lectures given by Soviet political officers, and organized discussion groups among themselves. The Soviet press was also available to them.

From time to time the men were obliged to deliver lectures. The topics of the lectures had to be related to the following problems: ideological values of the future leaders of the Polish Army, organization of educational centers among the Polish population, and "Red Poland—the Seventeenth Republic of the Soviet Union." After delivering lectures another two men were taken back to prison.

Ultimately, after six months, the "Bliss Academy" produced thirteen alumni who satisfied their N.K.V.D. supervisors. All of them were former officers of the Polish Forces. Dressed in civilian clothing, these men were taken to Red Square to watch the annual military parade on May 1, 1941.

Four days after the outbreak of the German-Soviet war the ever-suspicious N.K.V.D. officers took the remaining thirteen to Moscow and placed them under guard in Apartment 16, No. 11/12 Neapolitan Street. They were forbidden to leave even to go to a shelter during air raids. But in July 1941, each of the men received 1,000 rubles from the N.K.V.D., Soviet passports, and permission to move freely about the city.[52] There were no other officers coming either from Grazovec or from Kozelsk, and frustrated Colonel Berling announced that since there were no volunteers, no Polish Army would be organized, but why not join the Soviet Army? This did not appeal immediately to the remaining men. Rumors were spreading about the approaching re-establishment of Polish-Soviet diplomatic relations. The men knew that there were already thousands of Poles in uniform fighting on the side of the Allies. Where there are soldiers, there is a need for officers. They were Polish officers.

This reasoning must have prevailed among them because, on July 31, 1941, when the Sikorski-Maisky agreement was announced, the officers formally declined to join the Soviet Army. Instead, they applied to join the new Polish forces under General Anders.[53] All thirteen were accepted. At approximately the same time, the rejects from the "Villa of Bliss," Lubianka and Butyrki prisons were released and sent back to Grazovec camp. They also volunteered for General Anders' forces and were admitted. There are some indications that the Poles, although accepting the men from the "Villa of Bliss" and from the camp's Red Corner, kept them under subtle surveillance. (Colonel Berling, according to General W. Anders, in " . . . September 1942, deserted, stealing documents and papers under his care.")

When, in 1943, the Union of Polish Patriots with the N.K.V.D.'s assistance started to organize Polish units under Soviet auspices, some of the alumni of the "Villa of Bliss" again crossed the lines.[54] They had already left General Anders' units, which pledged their loyalties to the Polish Government-in-Exile, and moved to the Polish forces organized by the Polish communists. This group was headed by Colonel—subsequently General—Berling, who emerged again on the communist side.

In 1942 General Anders' units, within which the old traditional Polish regiments were reactivated, left the Soviet Union for the Middle East to join the British 8th Army. As a component of this army they fought with distinction in the Italian campaign, suffering heavy casualties, particularly among the infantry, in the successful fight for Monte Cassino. A platoon of the 12th Polish Armored Lancers' Regiment—*12sty Pułk Ułanów Podolskich*—was first to put its regimental colors on the ruins of the monastery. (This regiment has been famous for its discipline and for "doing the impossible" since Napoleonic times. Its flag is in London and many of its officers and men live in exile scattered all over the earth.) General Berling's forces fought side by side with the Red Army and played a brave part in the offensive on Berlin.

To return to the massacre itself, there are some facts which give a basis for speculation about the personal responsibility for the atrocity committed on the prisoners. General Zarubin, upon completion of his investigation, went to Moscow. The selection of men for death was made in Moscow and telephoned to the camp administration—in the case of those from Camp Kozelsk, at any rate.

According to the survivors, as reported in Polish sources, the procedure of selection was as follows: Around 10 a.m. a small crowd of officers eager for departure would gather in front of the administration building near the window (of which one pane was always open) of the office where the telephone was located. They could hear the exchange of the names. The N.K.V.D. man at the telephone had difficulties with the Polish names and in many instances some shouting into the phone followed for the purpose of verification. To enumerate thousands of names and to exchange long distance identification of the parties on the phone took time, and gave opportunities to learn that the calls were coming from Moscow.

While the shouting into the phone was going on, the crowd of prisoners increased, listening intently to learn whether their names were coming up for the road to liberty. The optimists believed that some Allied commission in Moscow was acting on their behalf. The pessimists thought the names were "drawn by a parrot in the service of the N.K.V.D."

The evacuation of the three camps was synchronized in time and was obviously centrally directed. This fact suggests that an office in Moscow decided and planned the extermination. Since the prisoners, as has been clear throughout this book, were up to this time under the complete surveillance of the N.K.V.D., we may safely assume that the main office of the N.K.V.D. in Moscow was directly involved.

In the spring of 1940 (at the time of the mass executions) the chain of the N.K.V.D. command on the highest level, in all probability read as follows: Beria, Merkulov, Kruglov, Fedotov, and Raikhman—all these men having the rank of a general of the N.K.V.D. Beria held highest authority.

Who gave the order? Was the decision made collectively? Did anyone object? There is no way of saying. It is this writer's hypothesis that either Stalin or Beria initiated and/or approved the idea of executing the prisoners. The Soviet Government executed Beria and Merkulov in 1953. Kruglov and Fedotov have disappeared from public life. Raikhman was arrested in 1951, released, then arrested again in 1954. His whereabouts have been unknown since that time. Still, through research, it has been possible to establish a list of forty-three N.K.V.D. officials who certainly were connected with the planning, processing, guarding, and the execution of 15,000 Polish prisoners-of-war. The list appears in the Appendix.

Were these N.K.V.D. men complete degenerates or beasts who murdered, disregarding Soviet law? Not necessarily either. What is difficult for Western man to comprehend is the fact that the mass extermination of prisoners could have been done within the legal prerogatives of the N.K.V.D. Milovan Djilas, a man who knows communism, makes a pertinent statement in this connection. "From theory and practice, Communists know that they are in conflict with all other classes and ideologies, and behave accordingly. They are fighting against not only actual but also potential opposition." [55] The Soviet security police (known in 1940 as the N.K.V.D.) has been the shield and sword of the Soviet State for fighting the enemy from within. There was no limit to its exercise of vigilance during Stalin's era. It was both judge and executioner as illustrated by the purges in 1921, 1929, and 1933. The N.K.V.D. classification as "enemy of the people," "class enemy," or whatever nomenclature one prefers to use, led naturally to the death penalty. To the N.K.V.D., destruction of this kind of "anti-social element" was a duty and they went about it with professional detachment.

It might be pertinent to mention here that two former officers of the Soviet security police, now residing in the United States, were asked by the writer to express their opinion about responsibility for the Katyn Massacre. One stated that he heard on several occasions from his fellow officers that the N.K.V.D. shot the prisoners. The other categorically refused to talk on this subject.

The survivors from the three camps said repeatedly that the Soviet administrative personnel, other than the N.K.V.D., was rather humane. Soviet doctors and nurses in practically all instances won the respect and affection of the prisoners. They were doing their duty in the best tradition of service to humanity and with typically Slavic overt compassion and empathy. The N.K.V.D. was also doing its duty, but in its job there was no place for compassion, even for Russians, to say nothing of Poles.

In the spring of 1942 a German prisoner-of-war camp in Lübeck was electrified with the newest gossip passed by word of mouth among the Polish and Belgian prisoners inhabiting the camp. The Germans brought in a new prisoner, a Russian. The only Russian in the camp, he was placed in a separate room and a guard was posted at his window.

After a while the identity of the prisoner became known. He was none other than Jacob Dzugashvili, Stalin's son. This obviously created quite a sensation in the camp. Both Polish and Belgian officers crowded to see him and to talk to him. The German authorities even installed a "guest book" which had to be signed prior to a visit. Polish First Lieutenant Lewszecki, who spoke fluent Russian, became rather well acquainted with Dzugashvili. When, in 1943, the news of the discovery of the Katyn Forest graves was announced, Lewszecki went to Stalin's son to inquire about this affair. Dzugashvili's comments were typical: "What is all that noise about 10,000 or 15,000 Poles being killed? During the collectivization of Ukraine about three million people perished! Why be concerned about the Polish officers. . . . Those were intelligentsia, the most dangerous element to us, and they had to be eliminated." He evidently believed they were incorrigible, could not be "converted," and therefore had to be liquidated. He reassured Lewszecki that they were exterminated "with a humanitarian method unlike the brutal tactics of the Germans." [56]

If the N.K.V.D. men in the eyes of some were brutal, in the eyes of the Soviet elite they were merely doing their job. However, Stalin himself was not "fair" to the N.K.V.D. when in 1944 he ordered the Soviet Special Commission to produce evidence of German guilt for the Katyn murder. The Special Commission and the N.K.V.D. had to accomplish an impossible task. They fabricated the famous *Soviet Report*, but the product of their labor could not withstand testing against the facts.

One would think that the story of the "fixing" of the *Soviet Report* could never be known. However, in June 1950, in one of the journals published in Russian by Soviet exiles in America, a letter to the editor appeared. The letter sheds considerable light on the work and findings of the Soviet Commission in Katyn and is worth summarizing here.

The author of the letter, named Ol'shansky, was a former associate professor at the University of Voronezh and was drafted into the Red Army in 1941. He fought at Stalingrad and on the Bielo-Russian front as an officer. After the war was over, he was employed in an official capacity in the Soviet Zone of Germany from where he escaped to the West. The letter gives a strong impression of veracity and sincerity. It deals with Ol'shansky's friendship with the academician, Dr. Nikolay Burdenko, who was the Chairman of the "Special Commission for Ascertaining and Investigating the Circumstances of the Shooting of Polish Officer Prisoners by the German Fascist Invaders in the Katyn Forest."

Burdenko and Ol'shansky's father (also a doctor) had been very good friends since 1919. The strength of the friendship is shown by the fact that, although the senior Ol'shansky died in 1929, Burdenko still maintained contacts with the deceased's family and helped them financially on many occasions. Ol'shansky junior looked up to Burdenko, who was making a career in Moscow. He was an excellent surgeon and became Stalin's personal physician, also treating Molotov and other prominent Soviet personalities. In 1939 he became a member of the Communist Party.

Ol'shansky, while fighting on several fronts, maintained correspondence with such an important friend. After the war, in 1946, he went to Moscow to pay him a visit. At that time Burdenko lived on Tverskaya Street. He was ill; he had had two strokes and had withdrawn from public life and practice. The old friends talked. The discussion touched upon Burdenko's chairmanship of the Special Commission for investigating the Katyn graves. The old doctor made a nervous gesture saying,

> There is no doubt such 'Katyns' were and will be happening.... If you start digging our Mother Russia you will find quite a few such excavations.... We had to make a complete denial of the widely spread German accusation. On personal orders of Stalin I went to the place where the graves were found. It was a spot check and all bodies [in the graves] were four years old. Death took place in 1940.... Actually, for me as a doctor, the question is clear and there is no argument about it. Our comrades from the N.K.V.D. made a great blunder.[57]

Burdenko died in 1946, the same year in which the conversation took place.

Ol'shansky wrote the letter to the press for two reasons: he felt sorry for the "suffering" Poles, and he believed that many Russians were disgusted with this crime. The fact that his friend Burdenko was already dead and could not be held responsible for the betrayal of state secrets helped him to make up his mind. Undoubtedly there are many people in the Soviet Union who have knowledge of the circumstances of the murder of the prisoners-of-war. But they are silent for readily understandable reasons.

Soviet authorities, when approached for an explanation concerning the Katyn Massacre, invariably refer to the report of the Soviet Special Commission, chaired by Dr. Burdenko in 1944. The *Report* has passages which would be funny, if they did not deal with gruesome subject matter. For example, one of the most important Soviet witnesses, a woman by the name of Moskowskaya, testified that in *March* 1943 she encountered a Russian soldier who told her that he was compelled to work under German surveillance in Katyn Forest. His job was to remove the documents from the bodies of the murdered men, replace them with other sets of documents and to shovel the bodies back into the graves. At the beginning of *April* the Germans started to shoot the Soviet prisoners who were engaged in the substitution of documents. This Russian soldier escaped.

Of particular importance in this story are the dates. According to the Soviet protocol, the Russian soldier told Moskowskaya in *March* what happened to him in *April!* [58] Subsequently Polish sources pointed out this silly discrepancy. Yet, it took the Soviet authorities eight years to take corrective action. *Pravda*, March 3, 1952, repeating the findings of the Soviet Commission, "improved" only one detail—Moskowskaya's testimony. In this new version, she met the soldier in April and not in March as the previous report stated. *Pravda* did not state whether Moskowskaya changed her testimony. One thing, however, is sure. Someone in the Soviet Union still is interested in reading whatever is written about

Katyn and tries to patch up the *Soviet Report* here and there. The report seems to be still under revision in order to make it as effective as possible.

Within the framework of the N.K.V.D. assignment, one can say that their work with the Poles was not entirely wasted. They exterminated approximately 15,000. Yet, about 400 could be worked with further. The N.K.V.D. could not anticipate as early as spring 1940 that there would be war with Germany and that these 400 Poles would become allies and be taken from N.K.V.D. hands. Nevertheless, dealing with the Poles provided the N.K.V.D. a valuable initial experience in conditioning and manipulating attitudes of captive prisoners-of-war. They learned that indoctrination of such a group is very difficult, and requires an adjustment to cultural backgrounds.

One has a distinct impression that, generally speaking, the N.K.V.D. indoctrination of the Poles failed miserably. Allowing for the cultural peculiarities of the Poles (which made them less susceptible to communist propaganda), this might be explained in the initial "intellectual" approach of the N.K.V.D. When "the battle for the mind" was kept on the level of the exchange of ideas, the Poles not only held their own but their values were strengthened by the inability of the N.K.V.D. men to fence intellectually and to undermine prisoners' beliefs.

Katyn apparently convinced the N.K.V.D. that mass executions are also failures, and carry serious dangers of later exposure because of the difficulties of concealing an action of such dimensions. The need to continue the doctoring of the report, already shown, is a further evidence of the risks of such an action. There seems to be no evidence, so far discovered, of a "Katyn" performed on Germans or Japanese. The death of the Poles was considered to be a "mistake" among the N.K.V.D. leaders. The steel fist of the N.K.V.D. had to be veiled a little when employed in propaganda work.

Conditioning became, above all, more adjusted to cultural differences. This is illustrated by the change of approach in treatment of German, Hungarian, and other pro-German troops captured after the outbreak of the German-Soviet war.

It took the N.K.V.D. *18 months* to produce thirteen presumably "Red Poles" from among the prisoners (the Villa of Bliss alumni). With some refinements of approach, *three months* after the outbreak of the German-Soviet war hundreds of newly-captured German, Hungarian, and Slovak prisoners were already indoctrinated and employed by Russian propaganda machinery, issuing communist-inspired appeals to their respective countrymen. But they were not officers. It is possible that N.K.V.D., as a result of work with the Poles, shifted the emphasis from officers to the enlisted men. This does not mean that the officers were left alone. But the propaganda approach toward this group was more deliberate and more time was allowed for its penetration.

With the German prisoners the work of indoctrination was progressing quite successfully. The Soviet-German war started on June 21, 1941. On October 8 of the same year the First Conference of German Prisoners (privates and non-commissioned), 158 in number, took place. The first speaker was Private Helmut Fleschner: "Comrades! We have all experienced the hardships of lying in the mud, under a hurricane of fire: and more than once when the situation became critical we have seen our officers running to take cover and then yelling at us. . . ." [59] The objectives were the same as before— first of all to destroy former loyalties and the structure of affiliations.

The Free Germany Committee was set up on July 8, 1943. The "German Officers Corps" also came into existence. German officers of all ranks participated. They were given more time than the Poles for the purpose of indoctrination. Of course, not all the German soldiers joined. The story of those who did, and who did not, and why, does not belong here.[60]

The only point is that the N.K.V.D. evidently was making good use of its experience with the Polish prisoners-of-war in its subsequent work with prisoners, Germans and Japanese in particular.[61]

It is possible that the Chinese learned from N.K.V.D. experience (it has been established that Soviet advisors were supervising and directing Chinese indoctrination programs in some cases for the American prisoners captured in Korea). In any case the Chinese did avoid the N.K.V.D. policy of plain and direct mass murdering of prisoners. In their dealings with the prisoners-of-war they supplied a relatively more sophisticated staff for direct contacts during the interviews. (General Zarubin, who was a sophisticated man, called on only one Polish camp, Kozelsk, possibly to "sample" the prisoners' attitudes.) But above all, the Chinese stressed even more the environmental conditioning, in many instances attacking the men on the level of their reflexes. They did so with the skill and incisiveness of a surgeon, and with a considerable insight into the cultural values of Americans.[62]

NOTES TO CHAPTER VIII

1. A word of mouth version persistently circulating at one time was that Stalin, referring to the whole problem of the three camps for the Poles, said, "Liquidate," which was interpreted by Beria in the most literal sense and applied to the prisoners themselves. The executions followed. This story cannot be substantiated and, therefore, is not used here as evidence, although its circulation is reported.

2. Stanisław Mikołajczyk, *The Rape of Poland: Pattern of Soviet Aggression* (New York: Whittlesey House, 1948), p. 36.

3. Winston S. (now Sir Winston) Churchill, *The Hinge of Fate* (Boston: Houghton Mifflin Co., 1950), p. 758.

4. For this interpretation of Lenin's view the author is indebted to Professor T. A. Taracouzio.

5. T. A. Taracouzio, *The Soviet Union and the International Law: A Study Based on the Legislation, Treaties and Foreign Relations of*

the *Union of Socialist Soviet Republics* (New York: The Macmillan Co., 1935), p. 32.

6. *Ibid.*, p. 322. "Cheka" is one of the names for a predecessor of the N.K.V.D.

7. *Ibid.*, p. 323.

8. *Zbrodnia Katyńska w Świetle Dokumentów* (The Katyn crime in light of documents). Z przedmową Władysława Andersa. 2-gie wydanie (London: Gryf, 1950), p. 17.

9. Roman Umiastowski, *Poland, Russia and Great Britain 1941-1945: A Study of Evidence* (London: Hollis and Carter, 1946), p. 55. In Camp Krivoy Rog fifty officers were hiding among 6,000 Polish rank and file; in Camp Yelenovka twenty-five officers among 4,000 ranks. In another camp forty-six officers—among them several staff officers and a chaplain—were hiding among the privates. Although the privates knew that the officers were among them, there was not even one instance of betrayal to Soviet authorities. *Polish Report*, p. 17, note 1; Zygmunt Szyszko-Bohusz, *Czerwony Sfinks* (The red sphinx) (Rzym: Polski Dom Wydawniczy, 1946), p. 128.

10. *Zbrodnia Katyńska w Świetle Dokumentów* (The Katyn crime in light of documents), *passim*.

11. *P.S.Z.*, III, 33-34.

12. The Union of Soviet Socialist Republics, however, at least on two occasions, announced the recognition (with reservations) of the Hague Convention of 1907, Respecting the Law and Customs of War on Land.

13. Bronisław Kuśnierz, *Stalin and the Poles: An Indictment of the Soviet Leaders* (London: Hollis and Carter, 1949), p. 91; Jan Kazimierz Umiastowski, *Przez Kraj Niewoli* (Through the land of slavery) (London: Biblioteka Pamiętników, 1947), p. 15.

14. *Hearings*, part 6, Exhibit 32, p. 1648.

15. *Hearings*, part 2, pp. 68, 181; part 3, p. 351.

16. Józef Czapski, *Wspomnienia Starobielskie* (Memoirs of Starobelsk) (Italia: Oddział Kultury: Prasy 2 Korpusu, Biblioteka Orła Białego, 1945), p. 8.

17. In practice even scoutmasters were considered "enemies of the Soviet Union."

18. *Polish Report*, pp. 79-80; *Death at Katyn: An Account of a Survivor.* 3rd ed. (New York: National Committee of Americans of Polish Descent, 1944), p. 22.

19. When in Camp Kozelsk more than 300 Polish doctors signed a petition and delivered it to camp authorities requesting to be treated according to the international conventions concerning medical personnel (they were assigned to clean latrines in the camp), the N.K.V.D. informed them that "bourgeois" rules were not observed in

the Soviet State. *Hearings*, part 6, Exhibit 32, p. 1648. According to a reliable and competent Polish source, the total number of doctors in Camps Kozelsk and Starobelsk was more than 800. Czapski, *Wspomnienia Starobielskie* (Memoirs of Starobelsk), p. 7.

20. For an historical development of the Soviet security police consult Simon Wolin and Robert M. Slusser, *The Soviet Secret Police* (New York: Praeger, 1957), pp. 3-61; for the sections dealing with the period 1939-1945 (N.K.V.D. and N.K.G.B.), see pp. 18-21.

21. For major legislation defining the structure and jurisdiction of the security agencies, see *ibid.*, pp. 46-47, note 70.

22. The information collected from survivors. *Hearings*, part 6, Exhibit 32, p. 1648.

23. *Ibid.*, p. 1674.

24. *Ibid.*, p. 1659.

25. Czapski, *Wspomnienia Starobielskie* (Memoirs of Starobelsk), p. 42; *Death at Katyn: An Account of a Survivor*, p. 30.

26. *Hearings*, part 6, Exhibit 32, p. 1649, *Polish Report*, pp. 31-38.

27. See Ivan Petrovich Pavlov, *Conditioned Reflex: An Investigation of the Physiological Activity of the Cerebral Cortex* (London: Oxford University Press, 1927), pp. 1-430. For a pertinent interpretation of Pavlov's theories consult William Sargant, *Battle for the Mind* (New York: Doubleday, 1957), chapter I; also see chapter VII, dealing with brainwashing in religion and politics, and chapter VIII, concerning brainwashing in ancient times. For findings dealing specifically with prisoners see Joost A. M. Meerloo, *The Rape of Mind: The Psychology of Thought Control, Menticide, and Brainwashing* (Cleveland and New York: The World Publishing Company, 1956), pp. 1-320. Dr. Meerloo had personal experiences relevant to the topic of his book. The same author wrote "Pavlovian Strategy as a Weapon of Menticide," *The American Journal of Psychiatry*, CX (May 1954), 809-813. For the reaction of American prisoners-of-war to "conditioning" see Harvey D. Strassman, M.D., Margaret B. Thaler, Ph.D., and Captain Edgar H. Schein, MSC, "A Prisoner of War Syndrome: Apathy as a Reaction to Severe Stress," *The American Journal of Psychiatry*, CXII (June 1956), 998-1003, and Edgar H. Schein, "The Chinese Indoctrination Program for Prisoners of War," *Psychiatry*, XIX, no. 2 (May 1956), 149-172; also U.S. Senate. Report No. 2832 of the Committee on Government Operations made by its Permanent Subcommittee on Investigations. *Communist Interrogation, Indoctrination and Exploitation of American Military and Civilian Prisoners*. 84th Cong., 2nd Sess., 1956 (Washington: U.S. Government Printing Office, 1957), pp. 1-24.

28. *Polish Report*, p. 33, note 1; *Hearings*, part 6, Exhibit 32, p. 1649, note 1.

29. *Polish Report*, p. 35.

30. Czapski, *Wspomnienia Starobielskie* (Memoirs of Starobelsk), pp. 18-19.

31. *Ibid.*, p. 41; *Polish Report*, pp. 81-82.

32. Czapski, *Wspomnienia Starobielskie* (Memoirs of Starobelsk), p. 31.

33. One of them was N.K.V.D. officer Aleksandrovitch, a "lively character attempting to gain popularity . . . helpful in mailing letters." From a private letter of a survivor to Prime Minister Mikołajczyk. Mr. Mikołajczyk's private files.

34. *Hearings*, part 6, Exhibit 32, p. 1670.

35. Czapski, *Wspomnienia Starobielskie* (Memoirs of Starobelsk), p. 44.

36. *Hearings*, part 6, Exhibit 32, pp. 1650-1651; Umiastowski, *Przez Kraj Niewoli* (Through the land of slavery), p. 42.

37. Czapski, *Wspomnienia Starobielskie* (Memoirs of Starobelsk), p. 18; *Polish Report*, pp. 38-39.

38. Zarubin evidently stood out clearly as compared with other N.K.V.D. men. The survivors are unanimous in praising his level of intelligence and sophistication. Kenneth Mark Colby, M.D., a psychiatrist and my colleague at the Center for Advanced Study in the Behavioral Sciences at Stanford 1961-1962 comments that . . .

"It is doubtful that attempts to break down the men derived from any systematic theory of personality or psychopathology. The N.K.V.D. probably used only their everyday knowledge of human psychology to frighten and disorganize the men by whatever means seemed intuitively—and later from experience—to produce disturbances.

"The result of these crude attempts was to keep the men in a state of anxiety and hostility, not allowing them to progress to states of apathy and detachment which might serve as effective defenses. The soldiers' emotional life was maintained at the level of the first phase of mourning. Separated from their homeland and loved ones, their yearning for reunion with lost objects was repeatedly activated by the playing of Chopin and by the way in which their attachments to dogs were manipulated. Conditions were constantly changed to break up any adaptive reorganizations, such as occur in the normal work of mourning, which might gain stability with time. Only one way out of this dilemma was consistently held open—to become a communist. To make the 'out' more acceptable, Zarubin functioned as an ideal, with which one could identify. By his admirable nature and by his model conduct, he demonstrated that one could still be a cultured man, an officer with a code of honor, and also a communist."

39. In terms of contemporary Polish values, "officer's honor" and the code of formal behavior were very strictly encompassed by

many unwritten rules. Those were further fortified by written statutes. Some insight into the rigidity and complexity of these can be provided by studying Ludomir Brzostowski, *Statut Oficerskich Sądów Honorowych* (Statute of the officers' honor courts) (Warszawa: Główna Księgarnia Wojskowa, 1928), pp. 1-166.

40. General Minkiewicz had been arrested at his home in the Eastern part of Poland. He was brought to the camp in a shabby civilian suit. He felt that this was very humiliating and spent practically all of his time in his room, avoiding appearances out of uniform. From the testimony of a survivor, W. Komarnicki, 9th Field Court Martial, Supreme Command of the Polish Armed Forces, May 21, 1943; cited in *Hearings*, part 4, p. 802. The above-quoted discussion between Zarubin and Minkiewicz was told to Polish Colonel Felsztyn by General Minkiewicz immediately upon his return from Zarubin's office. Colonel Felsztyn survived and testified. *Hearings*, part 4, p. 627. General Minkiewicz's body was found in the Katyn graves.

41. Schein, *op. cit.*, pp. 167-172. Robert Jay Lifton, M.D., in his excellent book *Thought Reform and the Psychology of Totalism: A Study of "Brainwashing" in China* (New York: W. W. Norton, 1961), pp. 19-415, 419-472, contributes considerably to the understanding of the processes involved.

A number of survivors are in the West; it would be most interesting to make a thorough empirical study of this group for the purpose of eliciting the data about the techniques of interrogation. Such a study would be valuable.

42. Lawrence E. Hinkle, Jr., M.D., and Harold G. Wolff, M.D., "Communist Interrogation and Indoctrination of 'Enemies of the State,'" *Archives of Neurology and Psychiatry* (American Medical Association), LXXVI (1956), 141. The authors gathered data from many persons who had undergone imprisonment and "processing" by the Soviet security police.

43. *Hearings*, part 3, p. 356.

44. *Ibid.*, part 4, p. 645.

45. Their names, respectively: Gorczyński, Künstler, Berling, Bukojemski, Morawski, Tyszyński, Lis.

46. Details concerning the subsequent fate of these men were gathered from the testimony in: *Polish Report, passim*; *Hearings*, part 6, Exhibit 32, pp. 1681-1684; also part 4, pp. 807-820.

47. *Hearings*, part 4, p. 553.

48. *Polish Report*, p. 128, note 1; *Hearings*, part 4, p. 555.

49. Witness' testimony, *Hearings*, part 4, p. 553; written deposition, part 3, pp. 440-441.

50. Polish Report, pp. 127-129; compare with Scaevola (pseud.), *A Study in Forgery: The Lublin Committee and Its Rule over Po-*

land. London: J. Rolls Book Co., 1945, p. 31. Scaevola sets the total number of the men who went through "Villa of Bliss" as 74. However, he encompasses a larger span of time: from November 1940 until August 1941. Although this number is quite possible, this writer takes a more cautious position, basing his estimate on the period of winter 1940 and the number of men which can be verified and cross-checked in the primary sources and by witnesses.

51. Written deposition. *Hearings*, part 4, pp. 807-820.

52. *Ibid.*, part 6, Exhibit 32, p. 1683.

53. It is possible that one or two men were "plants" of the N.K.V.D.

54. Scaevola, *op. cit.*, pp. 53-62.

55. Milovan Djilas, *The New Class: An Analysis of the Communist System* (New York: Frederick A. Praeger, 1957), pp. 26-27. Djilas blames the Soviet Government for the Katyn Massacre, *loc. cit.*

56. Lewszecki's testimony. *Hearings*, part 4, p. 777.

57. B. Ol'shansky, "Katyn." Pis'mo v redktsiyu (Katyn. Letter to the editor). *Sotsialistcheskii Vestnik*, XXX, no. 6/633 (June 1950), 114; see also Ol'shansky's testimony, *Hearings*, part 7, pp. 1939-1942.

58. U.S.S.R. Soviet Embassy in Washington. The Soviet Report of Special Commission for Ascertaining and Investigating the Circumstances of the Shooting of Polish Officer Prisoners by the German-Fascist Invaders in the Katyn Forest. *Supplement to the Soviet Embassy Bulletin*, March 23, 1944, p. 10; also *Pravda*, January 26, 1944 reports this version.

59. *First Conference of German Prisoners of War Privates and Non-commissioned Officers in the Soviet Union* (Moscow: Foreign Languages Publishing House, 1941), p. 6; see also other anti-officers statements, pp. 9, 12.

60. German literature on this subject is very abundant and quite enlightening. An interested reader may consult any of these first-hand accounts (only names of the authors given): Reinhart Maurach, Josef Novak, Helmut Bohn, Hans Dibold, Heinrich von Einsiedel [the book by this man is also available in the English language: *I Joined the Russians* (New Haven: Yale University Press, 1953), p. 306], Kurt J. Fischer, Hellmut Gollwitzer, P. Ingebert Franz, Wolfdietrich Kopelke and Fritz Rabe, Joseph Martin Bauer, Assi Hahn, Thoe G. Klein, Helmut M. Fehling (this work includes official documentation concerning the German and Japanese prisoners-of-war in the Soviet Union), Hanno Sörensen, and Robert Kremer.

In this connection, it also might be worthwhile to read some of the accounts of the Italian prisoners-of-war in the Soviet Union; *e.g.*, P. Alagiani, Agostino D. Bonadeo, Franco Fabietti, and Giovanni Brevi. There is also a very discerning interview with a former Soviet prisoner, a German, available at Harvard's Russian Center, *Prisoner* of *War Camps in Russia: The Account of a German Prisoner of War* (Cambridge: 1951), pp. 1-40.

61. Japan. Ministry of Foreign Affairs. Public Information Division. *Announcement of Japanese Foreign Ministry and Letters of Foreign Minister to President of United Nations General Assembly on Repatriation, July 25, 1951,* pp. 1-54; U.S. Army. General Headquarters Far East Command, Military Intelligence Section, General Staff. *Special Report: Japanese Prisoners of War: Life and Death in Soviet P.W. Camps* (n.d.), part 6, pp. 1-4.

62. Those interested in the methods and impact of the Chinese psychological attack on the prisoners-of-war, see a well edited special number of the journal published quarterly by the Society for the Psychological Study of Social Issues (a division of The American Psychological Association): "Brainwashing," *The Journal of Social Issues,* XIII, no. 3 (1957), 1-67. The following articles are most relevant: "Thought Reform of Chinese Intellectuals: A Psychiatric Evaluation," Robert J. Lifton; "Reaction Patterns to Severe, Chronic Stress in American Army Prisoners of War of the Chinese," Edgar H. Schein; "Correlates of Collaboration and Resistance Behaviour among U.S. Army POWs in Korea," Julius Segal.

IX

Problems Caused by Katyn after the War

THIS FINAL CHAPTER deals with several topics. First, an attempt will be made to describe the effects of the Katyn case upon the relationship between Polish public opinion and the contemporary government of Poland. Second, the difficulties encountered with the Soviet Government in this connection will be briefly sketched. Third, postwar policies of the United States and Great Britain will be described. In conclusion, the implications of the Katyn case with regard to current international agreements regulating the treatment of war prisoners will be discussed.

REACTIONS OF THE POLISH AND SOVIET GOVERNMENTS: DISCREPANCIES AND DIFFICULTIES

The present Government of the People's Republic of Poland seems unable to live down Katyn. The evil and injury of Katyn lives on and embitters relations between the people and the government. From time to time a little news trickles out of Poland on this subject. Originally the Polish communists decided to meet the Katyn affair head on. The first step was the visit of Colonel Berling on January 30, 1944, to the Katyn graves with a delegation of Polish units which had been formed under the auspices of Polish communists in the Soviet Union. Colonel Berling was the officer who heard Beria's statement about the "great mistake" made with his 15,000 fellow prisoners. This did not prevent the former graduate of the "Villa of Bliss" from delivering a speech: "Those to whose memory we today pay homage fell into the clutches of the implacable enemy—Germany.... The graves of Poles murdered by Germans cry out for vengeance. It is we who must avenge them. We will avenge them." [1]

An N.K.V.D. major also delivered an eloquent speech on behalf of the dead. A parade was held in front of the graves and a public collection was taken to gather money for a tank unit to be called "Avengers of Katyn." The collection was taken up among Berling's forces, Soviet citizens in general, and the Red Army. N.K.V.D. officers participated actively in the organization of collection and even contributed some money. Whether the tanks were purchased and if they acted as "avengers" cannot be established.

After the war, the American and the British governments ceased to recognize the Polish Government-in-Exile with its domicile in London. Its Prime Minister, Stanisław Mikołajczyk, returned to Poland "to assume the duties of Vice-Premier and Minister of Agriculture in the Provisional Government of National Unity in Warsaw." This government, from the outset, was strongly dominated by the communists. Nevertheless, Mikołajczyk hoped to perform some constructive political action on behalf of the Polish Peasant Party, which he represented. He was then approached by the Polish Attorney General, Jerzy Sawicki, on the subject of Katyn. Sawicki contacted Mikołajczyk in Warsaw in June 1945. He said he was acting in accordance with the wishes of the Minister of Justice, Mr. Świątkowski. Would Mr. Mikołajczyk testify if a public trial were arranged in Warsaw to deal with the Katyn massacre?

Mikołajczyk was most enthusiastic about the trial, stating

that the Katyn affair ought to be settled by a Polish court. Then Sawicki asked, "... and what would you like to tell in such a public trial?" To this Mikołajczyk replied that he would tell all he knew about it and that it also would be desirable to submit all the data gathered by the Germans and by the Poles abroad. Sawicki appeared dissatisfied and terminated the interview. At about this time some preparation of Polish public opinion began with articles appearing in the press.[2]

Subsequently, according to Mikołajczyk, Sawicki and Świątkowski went to Moscow for discussions concerning the possibility of arranging the trial in Warsaw. They argued that a public trial was desirable because Polish public opinion held the Soviet Government responsible for the murder. A public trial proving that German forces were responsible for the atrocity would contribute greatly to better Soviet-Polish relations. Both men supposedly were told in Moscow to drop the whole matter.[3]

To this day no Katyn trial has been held in Poland. The Katyn affair continued to disturb Polish communists. Persons indirectly connected with the murder were approached. In June 1945 Polish authorities demanded that Mr. Goetel, a Polish writer who had visited the Katyn graves during the exhumations by the Germans, "sign a statement that he was kept by force at Katyn and that his main impression in Katyn was that the massacre was done by Germans."[4] Mr. Goetel immediately escaped from Poland.

Two years later a smooth-talking Polish officer who introduced himself as Alex Dobrowolski, an adjutant to the Polish military attaché in Rome, approached Mr. Kawecki, a Pole living in the Italian village of Recceone. As a journalist, Kawecki had visited the Katyn graves. The officer tried to persuade Kawecki to sign a declaration renouncing his formerly expressed views that the massacre was committed by Russians. The officer had two typed declarations in his pocket and presented them to Kawecki. Kawecki noticed while he read them, that the man put a roll of American dollars on the table. Kawecki refused to accept the money or to sign the statements.[5]

On February 13, 1948, a Swedish paper, *Dagens Nyheter*, published a story which supposedly came from Poland. According to this, the Polish Government evidently had recognized how flimsy was the evidence upon which the Soviet defense was built and had decided to conduct an independent and confidential investigation. Dr. Roman Martini had been assigned the task in 1945. Dr. Martini scrupulously gathered data, and came to the conclusion the N.K.V.D. was guilty.

Several weeks later, on March 30, 1946, he was murdered in Kraków by two hotheaded youthful communists—a girl of seventeen, Jolanta Słapianka, and a man of twenty, Stanisław Wróblewski.

A Polish political figure who resides in the U. S. today but who was still in Poland in 1946 corroborates these events in his memoirs. In his book published in Paris by the Polish Literary Institute in 1956, he reports the same story under the entry "April 30, 1946," [6] or one month after the reported occurrence of the murder. Whether the story is true, it is impossible to say. This writer is inclined to doubt its validity. It is reported here as an illustration of the persistence with which Katyn reappears in the press, and as an example of a possible fabrication further clouding the problem.

The Katyn Massacre has been a weak spot of the Polish Communist Government. In fact, it must be so long as the Government refuses to face it. It is evident from the Government's actions that its inability to bring the Katyn affair to an end frustrates even the Polish communists. This frustration is manifested sometimes by outbursts of anger or by silence when the logic of the situation demands some clarifying statement. To illustrate: when the United States Congress initiated an inquiry into the Katyn Massacre in the spring of 1952 (to be discussed below), the official organ of the Polish

Communist Party, *Trybuna Ludu,* exploded with a front-page statement. The title was self-explanatory: "The Polish nation with indignation condemns the cynical provocations of imperialistic Americans preying on the tragic death of thousands of Polish citizens in Katyn. Statement of the Government of the Polish People's Republic." [7] The content of the statement was an attack on the United States, repeating the Soviet version of responsibility for the Katyn Massacre. Protest meetings were arranged in factories. Articles against "imperialist provocation" appeared.[8]

In 1951 the Investigating Committee of the United States Congress invited the Polish Government to present any "evidence, documents, and witnesses it may desire." [9] Through the U.S. Department of State the Polish Government replied that it "does not intend to return to the matter again." [10]

Despite this declaration, under the auspices of the Polish Government a book about the Katyn Massacre was published in Poland under the title, "The Truth about Katyn." [11] Poles bought the book through two editions with understandable eagerness. This book deserves attention because it is the only document of a definitive character on the subject of Katyn printed with tacit approval of the Government of the Polish People's Republic.

In the strictest sense, the work does not deal primarily with an analysis of the Katyn Forest crime. Although the book consists of 218 pages, only 24 pages (pp. 68-91) deal specifically with the problem. The rest (except an appendix) is an attack on the United States. The author concludes that German units committed the Katyn Forest Massacre. Unfortunately, any source which might belie the writer's thesis is conveniently omitted. The testimony of the men from Grazovec is not even mentioned. Omitted in both editions is the wealth of data gathered by the U.S. Congressional Committee and the Polish Government-in-Exile, except for carefully selected points taken out of context.

On the whole the author repeats the Soviet account (discussed in chapter IV) of the affair, adding the following arguments:

(1) The Germans knew long before the Katyn investigation about the Katyn graves, therefore it was they who killed the Poles. This does not necessarily follow, but the argument is worthy of comment. Indeed, passing German combat units, and the men stationed in the area, as early as spring 1942, gathered hearsay from the local population about mass graves of Poles in the forest. Some passing workers of Polish origin employed by German construction and civil engineering firms trampled the forest looking for the graves of their countrymen and found some outlines of the graves at that time. Had the Germans been guilty it seems unlikely they would have permitted this, especially if they had not yet substituted the documents, which the Soviet sources claim was done in March 1943. These men were truck drivers in transit and could not explore further. They built a small wooden cross in the area and left.

On one occasion a German officer saw a wolf dragging out a bone which could have been human. However, during the fighting in Eastern Europe and Russia there was nothing unusual in finding human graves. The investigation really started in the last week of February 1943, when Lieutenant Voss of the German Field Police collated the information, systematically searched for bodies and found them.[12] He then reported to his superiors.

(2) The second argument says that the documents found on the bodies of the slaughtered men were German-fabricated in the concentration camp of Sachsenhausen and then inserted into the uniforms at the graves.[13]

(3) The fact that German ammunition was used is further submitted as evidence of German guilt.

(4) The names of three persons are cited who, according to the author of the book, could not have been in the Katyn

graves. Although the Germans reported finding their bodies, only their documents were there. The author claims that in two instances the men were actually in concentration camps from where their documents were taken and then inserted into the uniforms of the murdered prisoners.[14]

The book has thirty-six pictures. None are of the bodies of the victims or of their belongings. The only picture which deals directly with Katyn is that of a Soviet sign post which says in the Russian language, "Here in the forest of Katyn in the fall of 1941 Hitlerites shot 11,000 Polish prisoners, officers, and soldiers. The men of the Red Army avenge them!" [15]

The remaining pictures are a hodgepodge: Germans committing atrocities in Poland and elsewhere; a meeting of the Ku Klux Klan; containers for "insects infected with cholera and plague dropped by American planes in Korea." The arrangement is not casual. There is a picture of several German policemen standing over bodies prostrate on the ground. The picture which follows is that of a group of American soldiers searching a group of civilians.

The author describes German atrocities in Rawa Ruska, Dęblin and Ostrów Mazowiecki (Polish territories), in each instance describing the method of killing as being "exactly as in Katyn." [16] He offers these as additional proof of the German responsibility for the mass murder in Katyn.[17]

It would have been better had Polish communists not published the book at all, because it proved one thing clearly—that the Soviet Government did not take the Polish communists into its confidence. The writer sponsored by them was not given access to the N.K.V.D. files concerning the Polish officers and men from the camps of Starobelsk, Ostashkov, and Kozelsk. The *Soviet Report* was the only Soviet "primary" source connected with the Katyn affair given to him by the Soviet side. He had to use it, and in doing so magnified the flimsiness of the Soviet stand.[18]

Jerzy Sawicki, the Polish Attorney General in the postwar years, would probably, because of his position and interests, be best qualified to write on this subject. For years he has been concerned with the problem of genocide. Yet he is silent concerning Katyn.[19]

When on March 25, 1957, the Polish Government under the direction of Mr. Gomółka signed the Repatriation Agreement with representatives of the Soviet Union, many Poles held their breath. According to this agreement Poles still detained in the Soviet Union were eligible for return to Poland. Names of those from Camps Ostashkov and Starobelsk who had been missing since the spring of 1940 were known. It was hoped, particularly by the families of the missing men, that among the thousands returning some of them would also return. Their hopes were in vain.[20]

A survey of Polish [21] and Soviet [22] bibliographical sources indicates that, aside from a sporadic reaction to the U.S. Congressional investigation of the Katyn matter in 1952, the literature and press in both countries are relatively silent on this subject. However, this is not the case in Western Germany.[23] German public opinion does not wish Germany to be blamed for this murder. When one recalls the manner in which the Katyn affair was handled at the Nuremberg trial, one can understand why the German press does not consider the Katyn case closed.[24]

From time to time a whispered rumor circulates in Polish society: The government will investigate Katyn. Any political leader who attempts this will achieve considerable popularity at home and a negative reaction from the Soviet Union. This is the reality of the present situation in Eastern Europe. So long as the Soviet Government refuses to deal with the known facts of the matter, the Polish communists have no way to handle the problem. Meanwhile, both governments face an apparent impasse, unless they wish to seem inconsistent.

Polish communists, particularly the leaders, are too well

acquainted with the operations of the Soviet security police during Stalin's era to believe the *Soviet Report*. However, until the Soviet Union gives permission to investigate, the matter has to be pigeonholed. Meanwhile, the version accepted informally by Polish communists is this: The officers in Camp Kozelsk, for one reason or another, revolted. In reprisal the N.K.V.D. executed them. As to the missing 10,000 men from Camps Ostashkov and Starobelsk, the Polish communists have no "line" for an explanation.

The communist parties of other European countries not directly connected with Katyn have at times attempted to intimidate the scientists who participated in the International Commission and visited the graves in 1943. Dr. Markov from Bulgaria and Dr. Hajek from Czechoslovakia, in particular, were subjected to pressure to repudiate their findings.[25] Both men recanted. It is not mere coincidence that Bulgaria and Czechoslovakia have communist governments and both countries lie within the Soviet sphere of influence.

When the communists tried to intimidate scientists living in democratic countries, the results were different. They not only failed, but later some of the men came voluntarily to the U.S. Congressional Committee to testify and to reaffirm their conclusions.

> In October 1946 the Swiss communists introduced a motion in the Grand Council . . . of the Canton of Geneva, concerning the professor of medical jurisprudence, Dr. Francis Naville, and his participation in the European [International] Commission at Katyn. They requested either his dismissal for participating in the "Katyn provocation" or, alternatively, that he should revoke the findings of the Commission. On January 17th, 1947, after the Grand Council had heard an explanatory report by Professor Naville, the chairman of the cantonal Government stated, on behalf of his Government, that Professor Naville's behaviour had been in full accordance with the profession's ethics and principles of honour, and that his new report fully explained the conclusions drawn in his former report of 1943."[26]

The other four distinguished doctors, members of the International Commission—Palmieri in Italy and Tramsen from Denmark, Orsos (formerly from Hungary), and Miloslavitch (formerly from Croatia)—came forward and reiterated their conclusions.[27] The communist parties hastily dropped the affair.

POLICIES OF THE AMERICAN AND BRITISH GOVERNMENTS TOWARD THE KATYN INCIDENT

The massacre of Katyn produced strange effects in the United States. A personal friend of President Roosevelt was assigned to a remote diplomatic post in Samoa; the career of a colonel who did his duty in reporting what he knew about the affair was impaired; U.S. Military Intelligence refused to give the Congress access to its report concerning the matter; ultimately this very report vanished.

The State Department knew the details concerning the disappearance of the men as early as the winter of 1942. Captain Czapski's report, with the names and the data gathered from the survivors from Camp Grazovec, was given to the United States Ambassador in Moscow and dispatched to the State Department in Washington on February 7, 1942.[28] Supplementary information followed.

After the Polish units left Russia for the Middle East, American and British authorities attached their own intelligence officers as liaisons to the Poles. Lieutenant Colonel Szymanski represented the Americans and Lieutenant Colonel Hulls, the British forces. Both men were already compiling material on the missing men by June 1942. As liaison officers they had unhampered access to the Poles, lived with them in the Middle East, and therefore could obtain information covering all possible known aspects of the story. Lieutenant Colonel Szymanski reported his findings to Army headquarters in Washington, including with it the report of his British colleague. Intelligence on this topic was exchanged, as a matter of courtesy between the Allies.[29]

When in April 1943 the Katyn graves were examined, written depositions of the alumni of the "Villa of Bliss," repeating Beria's and Merkulov's statements about the "great mistake" they had made with respect to the missing Polish prisoners-of-war,[30] were delivered by Poles to the Office of the Military Attaché of the American Legation in Cairo. On April 30, 1943, Lieutenant Colonel Szymanski sent an additional report dealing specifically with the Katyn Massacre, to General George Strong, Chief of U.S. Army Intelligence.[31]

By that time material on the Katyn case and the missing men was voluminous and had become important enough politically to require its organization. Consequently, the Head of the Eastern European Section of U.S. Military Intelligence, Colonel Ivan Downs Yeaton, ordered the Polish desk of his section to prepare a special file on "Katyn." The file was compiled in the spring of 1943. All of Szymanski's reports, including that of his British colleague, were in the file.[32]

At the same time Mr. John F. Carter, chief of a small, select research team working especially for President Roosevelt, reported orally to the president on Katyn. The findings of Carter's team (which included experts on Germany) were that Goebbels was telling the truth. Subsequently he dispatched his findings to the president in writing, including also a comprehensive report prepared by Polish military intelligence.[33]

On May 22, 1945, Lieutenant Colonel John H. Van Vliet, Jr., of the U.S. Army reported to General Clayton Bissell, Assistant Chief of Staff, G-2 (Intelligence) War Department, General Staff, on the subject of the Katyn Massacre. Lieutenant Colonel Van Vliet had been captured by the Germans in battle. During his captivity he was taken, with another American prisoner, Captain Donald B. Stewart, to the Katyn graves. It may be recalled that the German authorities insisted on the creation of delegations among prisoners of various nationalities and took them to Katyn Forest. Whatever the purpose of German propaganda, the fact remained that Colonel Van Vliet had a chance to see with his own eyes the manner and circumstances of exhumation, talk to the members of the International Commission and generally make up his own mind about the responsibility for the tragedy.

Upon his liberation, Van Vliet reported to General Bissell, and dictated his report in the office of the intelligence agency. The general ordered Van Vliet's report to be stamped "Top Secret" and told Van Vliet "to remain silent on this matter." [34]

It appears, then, that the United States Government was in possession of the following reliable and well-documented material on this case:

(1) Colonel Szymanski's United States Army report,
(2) British Intelligence reports (including the observations of a British medical officer),
(3) Polish Intelligence reports,
(4) The report of Admiral William H. Standley, the United States Ambassador to Moscow (1941-1943),
(5) John F. Carter's research group report, submitted to the president,
(6) The report of Anthony J. Drexel Biddle, the United States Ambassador to Polish and Belgian Governments-in-Exile,
(7) The report of the Minister, Special Emissary for Balkan Affairs, Mr. George H. Earle,
(8) The report of Colonel John H. Van Vliet, United States Army.

All of these documents either by implication or in plain words blamed the Soviet Government for the massacre.

There was also an additional paper concerning Katyn at the disposal of the State Department. This was a report written by Miss Kathleen Harriman, the twenty-five-year-old daughter of the American Ambassador to the Soviet Union (1943-1946).

It may be recalled that Miss Harriman went to visit the graves during the Soviet investigation and arrived at the conclusion that the Germans committed the massacre.

The United States Department of State seems to have been more inclined to rely on Miss Harriman's account than on the reports of its two ambassadors, one minister, two lieutenant colonels, the results of a study by a presidential research team, and the information supplied by the British and Polish intelligence agencies.

When, from September 21, 1944, to July 5, 1945, Arthur Bliss Lane was in the State Department preparing for his duties as Ambassador to the Polish Government in Warsaw, he was interested in obtaining reliable information on this topic, so important to Poles. According to his own words, the only "document" he was able to see was the paper by Miss Harriman.

Justice Robert H. Jackson fared little better when acting as Representative and Chief Counsel for the United States at the Nuremberg prosecutions. His staff received on February 26, 1946, from the American Military Intelligence, several documents all classified "secret." In his own words, these included "the German report accusing the Soviet, two Soviet documents accusing the Nazis and a paper labeled 'Excerpts of conversations between Sikorski, Anders, Stalin, and Molotov.' "[35]

When the handling of the Katyn affair by the agencies of the United States Government is reviewed, it appears that on the highest policymaking level there were definite attempts to suppress information concerning it, particularly when such information contradicted the Soviet version. Nor was this all, the men who voiced their opinion about the possibility of Soviet guilt seem to have been punished.

On December 19, 1943, the United States War Department expressed dissatisfaction with Colonel Szymanski, charging him with having furnished only a small amount of information, "duplication," and with "bias in opinion in favor of the

Polish group which is anti-Soviet." A telegram sharply criticizing Szymanski was sent from the War Department in Washington to his immediate superiors in the Middle East.[36] It is of great importance to notice that the Washington reaction followed the discovery of the Katyn graves and Szymanski's additional reports on that subject. It is also significant that the War Department had already labeled "anti-Soviet" the Polish units evacuated from the Soviet Union.

It was not the only time an American official suffered for reporting honestly his views on the responsibility for the Katyn Massacre. President Roosevelt himself banished a man with ministerial rank to a remote island in the Pacific for the same reason.

Mr. George Howard Earle, a rather colorful and controversial political figure, had formerly served as Minister to Bulgaria and as Minister to Austria. In 1943 he was Special Emissary of President Roosevelt for Balkan Affairs, assigned to Turkey. He also held an officer's rank in the United States Navy. Earle traveled through the Balkans gathering intelligence useful to the United States Government. Through his contacts in Romania and Bulgaria he received information bearing on the responsibility for the Katyn murder. He also obtained some photographs of the graves and exhumations. Knowing already that the affair was the official reason for the break of Polish-Soviet diplomatic relations, he collated the materials and went to see President Roosevelt personally.

In May 1944, Earle submitted to the president the pictures and his impressions about the case, affirming Soviet guilt. The president's reaction was to the contrary: "George, this is entirely German propaganda and a German plot. I am absolutely convinced the Russians did not do this." [37] Earle was dismayed because he thought he had evidence which was quite convincing. Returning to Turkey, he carried on his duties, but evidently the Katyn affair and the president's general attitude toward it disturbed him, for upon his return to the

United States from his mission, he decided to write "a complete statement about Katyn."

On March 22, 1945, he wrote a personal letter to the president saying that unless he heard from Roosevelt to the contrary by March 28, 1945, he would publish the article on Katyn. In two days he received a letter on White House stationary dated March 24, 1945. President Roosevelt wrote:

> I have noted with concern your plan to publish your unfavorable opinion of one of our allies. . . .
>
> I not only do not wish it, but I specifically forbid you to publish any information or opinion about an ally that you may have acquired while in office or in the service of the United States Navy.[38]

Shortly afterwards Earle got an order transferring him to Samoa.

This was a blow to a man who already had established a network of contacts supplying him with information about Southern Europe, traveled widely, and held responsible positions. Now he was to be sent to the middle of the Pacific Ocean. He wrote another letter to Roosevelt telling him that he did not want to go to Samoa. Roosevelt replied but refused to change his decision.

Earle went to Samoa and was there until Roosevelt's death. Subsequently, he was immediately recalled to the United States, where the Chief of Personnel of the Navy and Commodore Vardaman, the President's naval aide, apologized to him and assured him that his being sent to Samoa was *not* the decision of the Navy Department.[39]

Viewing Roosevelt's attitude toward the Soviet Government from the narrow sector of the Katyn affair, one is forced to the conclusion that the President decided not to be concerned with the truth of the matter.

The policy of muzzling those who blamed the Soviet Government for Katyn extended downward. The Polish, German, and Italian minorities in the United States had their own broadcasting stations and daily programs. Using their native languages, the newscasters explored the issues concerning their respective nationalities in greater depth than the ordinary American newscasters were inclined to do. Some of the sentiments voiced directly or by implication by the foreign-language programs quite often clashed with the interests of the United States. Therefore, it was necessary to establish a federal agency to scrutinize foreign-language press and broadcasts in the United States during the war—the Foreign Language Division of the Office of War Information. The men responsible for this job had difficult problems.

When the news of Katyn was published, a Detroit announcer in the Polish language, Marian Kreutz, an anti-communist by conviction, using materials supplied by a press agency of the Polish Government-in-Exile, condemned the Soviet Government for the Katyn Massacre. A slap from the Foreign Language Division came quite promptly. According to Allen Cranston, former Chief of the Division, the broadcaster "was asked to restrict his activities on the air, . . . to news from reputable American wire services and was requested to avoid making propaganda over the air." [40] The anti-communist broadcaster was silenced at once.[41]

The manner and promptness with which this agency reacted to the Katyn affair when Soviet guilt was implied, as compared with the handling of pro-communist broadcasts—which were not discouraged—is a further illustration of the official position taken by the United States Government in this matter.

In 1944 nine members of Congress, all Americans of Polish descent, disgusted with the manner in which the Katyn affair was being handled in America, requested from the War Department the reports which had been sent from the Middle East by Colonel Szymanski on this subject. The Congressmen were told that the matter was "secret." [42] They did not receive Szymanski's reports.

It is the sad duty of policymakers to make, on behalf of the "national interest," choices between greater and lesser evils. This book is being written in 1962 and not in 1943-1944, when the general climate of public opinion and mood of the leaders were geared first of all to the defeat of Germany. It can be understood why President Roosevelt avoided the issues which could bring about disharmony.

It might be the subject of interesting speculations, however, why *after* the cessation of hostilities in Europe the Katyn affair was still suppressed by governmental officials in the United States?

As has been said above, Lieutenant Colonel Van Vliet submitted his observations concerning Katyn to the American Military Intelligence after the surrender of Germany. It was stamped "Top Secret." In fact, it became so "secret" that it could not be located when searched for later on.

The officer responsible for the classification of the document, Major General Clayton Bissell, was ultimately called before a Congressional Committee in 1952 to explain his position in this matter.

General Bissell was the Assistant Chief of Staff of American Military Intelligence in the War Department between February 1944 and January 1946. He was the man who received Colonel Van Vliet's report in April 1945. The general was placed in an embarrassing position with respect to Katyn, even before Van Vliet appeared in his office.

The Poles in London traced developments concerning Katyn in the United States very diligently, indeed. On the day preceding Van Vliet's appearance at General Bissell's office, the Polish Government-in-Exile awarded General Bissell one of their highest orders (*Krzyż Komandorski Orderu Odrodzenia Polski*).[43] On May 22, 1945, Colonel Van Vliet reported to the general his findings asserting Soviet guilt.

Explaining to the Congressional Committee why he classified Van Vliet's report as "Top Secret," he said, "I saw in

it great possibilities of embarrassment; so I classified it. . . . "
It was the general's opinion that it was the intention of the Commander-in-Chief (President Roosevelt) to induce the Soviet Union to fight Japan. Therefore the general felt he should do nothing to put a strain on Soviet-American relations.[44]

"Poland couldn't participate in the war with Japan. The Russians could participate in it. Those were the factors." [45] Then, he pointed out that the U.N. Charter was already in the process of formulation. The general knew this and, as a matter of fact, in his capacity was asked to comment on its content. "I don't think the Russians would have sat down the first time if that [the Katyn problem in general and Van Vliet's report specifically] had come out. They would have gotten mad. . . ." [46]

Therefore he suppressed the report.

Subsequently the report disappeared.[47]

Even in the postwar years, after President Roosevelt had died, the war with Japan was over, and the U.N. Charter was already in effect—the policy of suppressing the Katyn case was continued by the State Department. The war was over for several years when Mr. Czapski, the man so actively engaged in searching for the missing men in Russia, and himself a survivor of the annihilation, came to the United States for a visit in the early spring of 1950. The Voice of America invited him to make a broadcast in the Polish language to Poland. He submitted a script. From it officials of the Voice of America meticulously eliminated all references to the Katyn Massacre. He was not even allowed to mention the word "Katyn." [48]

Whatever the official position of the United States Government concerning the Katyn affair, many Americans not only abhorred the crime but resented the manner in which knowledge of it was kept from the public. In 1949 a group of distinguished personalities from American public life organized themselves for the purpose of inquiring into the matter. The American Committee for the Investigation of the Katyn Massacre, Inc., came into being.[49] State Department or not, the members started a vigorous campaign to bring the case to the attention of the public. The former American Ambassador to Poland, Arthur Bliss Lane, as the chairman of the organization, made public speeches, wrote articles. So did the other members. By 1951 the United States was involved in the Korean conflict and the treatment of prisoners-of-war created considerable concern. Approaching national elections and a search for political ammunition helped. The United States Congress decided to investigate the affair of Katyn.

A Special Congressional Committee was established. The Committee commenced its hearings on October 1, 1951, in Washington, D.C. Subsequently the hearings were conducted in Chicago, London, Frankfurt, Berlin (subcommittee) and Naples.[50] In total, 81 witnesses were heard, 183 exhibits studied, and more than 100 depositions were taken from witnesses who could not appear at the hearings. "In addition, the Committee staff . . . questioned more than 200 other individuals who offered to appear as witnesses but whose information was mostly of a corroborating nature."[51] Except for one instance when a masked witness, "Joe Doe," appeared, all of the testimony contributed to the clarification of the case. Yet, the atmosphere of the hearings was distinctly not impartial. It was anti-Soviet in its tenor.

The Committee extended invitations to participate in the hearings to the Soviet Government, the Polish Government in Warsaw, the German Federal Republic, and the Polish Government-in-Exile. The Soviet Government and the Polish Government in Warsaw declined.

Having at its disposal staff, money, prestige, and the power to order the submission of appropriate documents from the files of the State Department and the Department of the Army, the Committee did a thorough job in accumulating data bearing on the disappearance of Polish prisoners in the Soviet Union.

The Committee unanimously concluded that the security police of the Soviet Union were responsible for the massacre. It also made recommendations that the

> depositions, this evidence, and these findings should be presented to the General Assembly of the United Nations, with the end in view of seeking action before the International World Court of Justice against the Soviet Union for a crime of violation of the law recognized by all civilized nations.[52]

This statement was subsequently supplemented:

> If the United Nations cannot act, then the President of the United States should seek the assistance of an International Commission of nations other than Germany and Russia to sit as a jury, hear the facts of the Katyn Forest Massacre, weigh the evidence, record its findings, and make such recommendations as it determines are required by justice.[53]

These recommendations were made in 1952; but no action has been undertaken.

The author is painfully aware that the treatment of British policies in regard to the Katyn affair, as compared with the American, is relatively modest, if not inadequate. This is mainly due to the scarcity of available data from British official sources. No public systematic investigation of this affair, to the author's best knowledge was made by the British authorities. Even seven years after the end of the Second World War Sir Winston Churchill refused to comment on the Katyn Forest Massacre.[54] The situation is more fruitful for research in the United States, where the Investigating Committee of the United States Congress unearthed and uprooted the data from the governmental files.

The British and American Governments were not reluctant to investigate and bring about punishment when soldiers wearing British and American uniforms were concerned. To locate the murderers of fifty Allied prisoners from Sagan, a manhunt continued through postwar Germany for several years. According to Colonel Scotland, the Chief of the British War Crimes Investigation Unit, "more than 200,000 people altogether were questioned before the search finally ended," and thirteen of the guilty were hanged in 1948. Also, a hunt of equal intensity was carried out for the German assassins who with two machine guns wiped out company "A," 2nd Battalion, Royal Norfolk Regiment, on May 27, 1940, at Paradis, in the area Pas de Calais. The ninety men of this company were shot down after they had already surrendered and stacked their weapons. The man responsible for the order was identified, searched for, captured, tried on October 11, 1948, and subsequently hanged.[55]

The Americans sought and brought to justice—after the war was over—those who massacred their soldiers at Malmedy.

But there has been no judicial consideration of the case of the murder of 15,000 Polish prisoners.

> Justice is a two-way street. In fact, the doctrine of universality of jurisdiction authorizes even third states, not parties to the conflict, to judge and to punish war crimes committed in a war between others which peculiarly offend against the whole of mankind.[56]

It is not vengeance which is desirable in connection with the Katyn Massacre but an open recognition of the mass murder of prisoners-of-war and establishment of an ironclad Prisoners-of-War Protection Agreement aiming at a degree of effectiveness far beyond that provided by the rules of the Geneva Convention of August 12, 1949.[57] Realistic rules and sanctions shielding captured soldiers—the most helpless victims of any conflict, regardless of the side on which they fight—can and should be created.

The International Red Cross or the United Nations Organization probably would be best qualified to undertake it. There are several other possible ways to secure the protection of prisoners-of-war based upon self-interest of the warring nations, which might be even more effective than the punitive sanctions. The exploration of these means needs further research. It is quite possible that the present Soviet and Chinese governments, when approached without malice and by such an institution as the International Red Cross or the United Nations Organization, would co-operate in such a project, which ultimately would be to their advantage, also.

This problem is of particular importance to the military leaders of the United States, because judging by Korean experiences, Americans probably would be most affected by communist treatment of prisoners-of-war.

To illustrate: American prisoners, Army and Air Force, who died in German captivity during the Second World War were only 1.2 per cent of the total captured. During the Korean War the death rate of the American prisoners-of-war in Communist captivity was 38 per cent.[58] This may be an indication of things to come.

It is useful to notice in connection with the Katyn affair that the standards of behavior of sovereign states yield to consideration of power-relations. This was so during the Second World War and in peacetime. The leaders of states behaved accordingly. When faced with ethical and power considerations as alternatives, they chose the latter. It was more important to Roosevelt to maintain the Soviet Union in the anti-German camp than to be preoccupied with Katyn. Churchill, although greatly disturbed with the evidence (particularly the trees on the graves) pointing to the Soviet Government as the culprit, also believed victory to be the overriding consideration. Both leaders suppressed the truth when the winning of the war was at stake. When the war was over, in terms of power-relations it was still more important to secure the co-operation of the Soviet Government in the United Nations Organization than to take up the Katyn case.

It is a hard task to formulate rules which will control action of sovereign states. Yet few rules of war have been established and constant effort should be made to sustain, strengthen, and extend them. At least defenseless prisoners-of-war should not be murdered. Here lies the lesson of the Katyn affair.

Perhaps in the future, nations will have the courage and wisdom to establish a court to examine all crimes—those of the victorious as well as the defeated. It may be that this is the only means of insuring the protection of prisoners-of-war.

NOTES TO CHAPTER IX

1. U.S.S.R. Soviet Embassy in London. *Soviet War News*. February 5, 1944, p. 4; *Hearings*, part 6, Exhibit 32, p. 1784.
2. "Katyń dziełem Niemców. Oświadczenie Prof. Dra. Hajeka" (Katyn—a German deed. Statement of Professor Dr. Hajek), *Zielony Sztandar*, no. 28 (1945); "Katyń dziełem Niemców" (Katyn—a German deed), *Głos Ostrowski*, no. 27 (1946); "Nowy Dowód Zbrodni Niemieckich w Katyniu" (New evidence of German crimes in Katyn), *Robotnik Mazowiecki*, no. 5 (1946); "Katyń dziełem Himmlera" (Himmler's job—Katyn), *Głos Ostrowski*, no. 2 (1946); *Prawda o Katyniu* (The truth about Katyn) (Poznań: Wojewódzki Urząd Informacji i Propagandy, 1945), pp. 1-40.
3. Personal interview with former Polish Prime Minister Stanisław Mikołajczyk in Washington, D. C., April 1, 1958; see also *Hearings*, part 7, p. 2159.
4. Mr. Goetel's testimony. *Hearings*, part 4, p. 768.
5. Mr. Kawecki's testimony. *Ibid.*, part 5, p. 1504.
6. Stefan Korboński, *W. Imieniu Kremla* (On behalf of Kremlin). (Paris: Instytut Literacki, 1956), pp. 100-101.
7. *Trybuna Ludu* (Warsaw), V, no. 61 (March 1, 1952), 1; *Dziennik Polski* (Kraków), no. 56 (2519) (March 5, 1952), pp. 3-5.
8. Stefan Arski, "Propaganda Ludobójców" (The genocidist propaganda), *Trybuna Wolności*, no. 10 (1952); Leopold Infeld, "Sprawa Katyńska—Nowa Nikczemna Prowokacja Imperialistów Amerykańskich" (The affair of Katyn—a new disgraceful provocation of the American Imperialists), *O Trwały Pokój, o Demokrację Ludową*, no. 12 (1952); K. A. Skalski, "Haniebna Prowokacja" (Disgraceful provocation), *Życie Słowiańskie*, VII, no. 3 (March 1952), 3; Zbigniew Szalawski, "Reżyserzy Prowokacji Katyńskiej" (The stage-managers

of the Katyn-provocation), *Poprostu*, no. 11 (1952); W. A. "Prawda o Katyniu" (The truth about Katyn), *Trybuna Ludu* (Warsaw), V, no. 160 (June 9, 1952), 3, (a book review); "Zbrodnia Katyńska Przed Sądem w Norymberdze" (The Katyn crime at the Nuremberg trial), *Zielony Sztandar*, no. 11 (1952).

9. For the content of the letter see *Hearings*, part 4, pp. 503-504.

10. *Ibid.*, p. 504.

11. Bolesław Wójcicki, *Prawda o Katyniu* (The truth about Katyn), Wydanie drugie (Warszawa: Czytelnik, 1953), pp. 1-218. For a laudatory review of the first edition of the book published in an official Polish Communist Party newspaper see *Trybuna Ludu* (Warsaw), V, no. 160 (June 9, 1952), p. 3.

12. *Polish Report*, p. 229; *Hearings*, part 6, Exhibit 32, p. 1802; *German Report*, pp. 25-26.

13. Wójcicki, *op. cit.*, pp. 124-126, 77-79. He omits, however, that the documents were analyzed meticulously by Poles in Kraków, while they were stored there, although it is obvious that he knew about it, because he used the sources which make a point of this. Mr. Wójcicki simply skipped over this most important factor, for the Poles in Kraków had assessed the documents to be original beyond any doubt. Neither does he mention that Dr. Robel, the man responsible for the analysis of the documents, was subsequently arrested by the Polish communist security police.

14. *Ibid.*, pp. 79-81. This argument is very neatly disposed of by Józef Mackiewicz, "Pierwsza Bolszewicka Książka of Katyniu" (The first bolshevistic book about Katyn), *Wiadomości*. VII, no. 28 (July 13, 1952), 2.

15. *Ibid.*, p. 40.

16. *Ibid.*, pp. 30-31.

17. Using the same reasoning one could as well build a case against the Soviet Government on the basis of the murder of 9,432 persons, among them 169 women, mainly Ukrainians. These people were found in 1943, each shot in the back of the head by a small-caliber weapon. They had been murdered between 1937 and 1939 in the town of Vinnytsia and dumped into 91 mass graves. A public park with dance floor and swings for children was built over the graves. Hands of the male victims were tied with knots identical to those which restrained the hands of the Polish prisoners. This kind of "evidence' can be used by both sides, and appears to be worthless. Germany. *Amtliches Material zum Massenmord von Winniza* (Official material concerning the Vinnytsia massacre). Im Auftrage des Reichsministers für die besetzen Ostgebiete auf Grund urkundlichen Beweismaterials zusammengestellt, bearbeitet und herausgegeben (Berlin: Zentralverlag der NSDAP. Franz Eher Nachf. GmbH.,

1944), pp. 1-228; M. Seleshko, "Vinnytsia—the Katyn of Ukraine," *The Ukrainian Quarterly*, V, no. 3 (Summer 1949), 238-248.

18. Even a false argument concerning the date of the use of German names for Polish towns taken from a letter to an editor was offered as evidence. Wójcicki, *op. cit.*, 84; see also *Der Spiegel*, VI, no. 4 (January 23, 1952), 35, columns 2 and 3, point 4; also *Völkischer Beobachter*. Süddeutsche Ausgabe. April 15-19, 1943. Compare *Ostdeutscher Beobachter*. December 7, 1939, p. 7. Note the change of names Książ-Tiefenbach at this date. Consult Erlass des Reichministeriums des Innern vom 29. Dezember 1939.

19. Dr. Jerzy Sawicki i Dr. Bolesław Walawski, *Zbiór Przepisów Specjalnych Przeciwko Zbrodniarzom Hitlerowskim i Zdrajcom Narodu z Komentarzem* (Collection of special regulations against Hitler's criminals and the traitors of the nation, with commentary) (Warszawa: Czytelnik, 1945), pp. 1-63; Jerzy Sawicki, *Ludobójstwo. Od Pojecia do Konwencji, 1933-1948* (Genocide. From the idea to the convention, 1933-1948) (Kraków: L. J. Jaroszewski, 1949), pp. 1-244; Tadeusz Cyprian i Jerzy Sawicki, *Sprawy Polskie w Procesie Norymberskim* (Polish affairs at the Nuremberg trial) (Poznań: Instytut Zachodni, 1956), pp. 1-814, particularly pp. 245-249 and 574-604.

20. In fact several hundred thousand Poles deported into Russia in 1939-1940 are still missing.

21. Poland. Biblioteka Narodowa. Instytut Bibliograficzny. *Przewodnik Bibliograficzny. Urzędowy Wykaz Druków Wydanych w Polskiej Rzeczypospolitej Ludowej*. (A bibliographical guide. An official list of prints published in the Polish People's Republic), vols. I-XV (Warszawa, 1945-1959); Polska Akademia Nauk. Instytut Historii. Komisia Koordynacji Badań nad dziejami II Wojny Światowej. *Materiały do Bibliografii Okupacji Hitlerowskiej w Polsce 1939-1945* (Materials for a bibliography of Hitler's occupation of Poland 1939-1945). Wł. Chojnacki, K. M. Pośpieszalski, E. Serwański (Warszawa: Państwowe Wydawnictwo Naukowe, 1957), pp. 1-63; J. Kosicki i W. Kozłowski, *Bibliografia Piśmiennictwa Polskiego za Lata 1944-1953 o Hitlerowskich Zbrodniach Wojennych* (A bibliography of Polish literature 1944-1953 concerning the Hitler war crimes) (Warszawa: Wydawnictwo Prawnicze, 1955), pp. 1-177. It is worthwhile to notice that in 1958 a book appeared in Poland (sold out within a few days) which cites without distortion excerpts from the memoirs of General Anders, Churchill, Cordell Hull, Ambassador Ciechanowski and Goebbels dealing with the Katyn case. The author does not pass judgment as to the responsibility for the massacre. Polski Instytut Spraw Międzynarodowych. Dział Bieżących Zagadnień Międzynarodowch. *Sprawa Polska Podczas II Wojny Światowej w*

Świetle Pamiętników (Polish cause during World War II in the light of memoirs). Opracowł Stanisław Zabiełło (Warszawa: "Prasa," 1958), pp. 330-336.
22. Vsesoyuznaya Knizhnaya Palata. *Knizhnaya Letopis'* (Bibliographical yearbook) (Moscow, 1943-1958); Vsesoyuznaya Knizhnaya Palata. *Letopis' Gazetnykh Statei* (Bibliographical yearbook of newspaper articles) (Moscow, 1943-1958); Vsesoyuznaya Knizhnaya Palata. *Letopis' Zhurnal'nykh Statei* (Bibliographical yearbook of periodical literature) (Moscow, 1956-1958).
23. *Bibliographie der deutschen Zeitschriftenliteratur mit Einschluss von Sammelwerken* (Bibliography of German periodical literature including collective entries). Hrsg. von Reinhard Dietrich. Bd. 43/1943-Bd. 115/1957 (Osnabrück: Felix Dietrich, 1944-1958); *Bibliographie der fremdsprachigen Zeitschriftenliteratur* (Bibliography of foreign periodical literature). Unter wissenschaftlicher Mitarbeit von Dr. Th. Adamczyk und Dr. H. Kumerloeve bearbeitet und herausgegeben von Reinhard Dietrich. N.F. Bd. 21/1940-1941-Bd. 42/1956-1957 (Osnabrück: 1944-1958); *Deutsche Bibliographie. Halbjahres-Verzeichnis* (The German bibliography. Half-year index). Bearbeitet von der Deutschen Bibliothek Frankfurt a. M., Bd. (1)/1952-(7)/1958 (Frankfurt a. M.: Buchhändler-Vereinigung GmbH, 1952-1958); *Jahresverzeichnis des deutschen Schrifttums* (A yearly listing of German literature). Bearbeitet und herausgegeben von der Deutschen Büchereri und dem Börsenverein der Deutschen Buchhändler zu Leipzig. Jg. (149)/1945-1946-159/1956 (Leipzig: VEB Verlag für Buch- und Bibliothekswesen, 1948-1957); *Jahresverzeichnis der deutschen Hochschulschriften* (A yearly list of dissertations at German universities). Hrsg. von der Deutschen Bücherei. Jg. 61-(1945)-Jg. 71(1955) (Leipzig: VEB Verlag für Buch- und Bibliothekswesen, 1951-1958); Thilo Vogelsang, *Bibliographie zur Zeitgeschichte* (Bibliography of contemporary history). Beilage der Vierteljahrshefte für Zeitgeschichte. Jg. 1, 1953-Jg. 6, 1958. It is interesting to note that the flow of publications on this topic is quite voluminous, as compared with the Soviet press.
24. "Ein anderes Katyn. Urteil im Polnischen Offiziersprozess" (Another Katyn. Verdict in the Polish officer-trial). *Ost-Probleme*, III, no. 39 (September 29, 1951), 1216-1220; Leopold Caprivi, "Katyn." *Monatschefte für Auswärtige Politik*. X, no. 5 (May 1943), 396; Julius Epstein, "Das Geheimnis der Polnischen Massengräber bei Katyn. Das Ergebnis wissenschaftlicher Untersuchungen auf Grund neuer Zeugnisse und Aussagen" (The mystery of the Polish massgraves of Katyn. The result of scientific research on the basis of new statements and reports), *Die Zeit*, IV, no. 23 (June 9, 1949), 3; "Der Fall Katyn" (The case of Katyn), *Die andere Seite*, II, no. 10 (1951-1952), 4-10; Robert Haerdter, "Katyn," *Gegenwart*, VII, no. 5

(March 1, 1952), 137-140; "Die heutige Wahrheit von Katyn" (Today's truth about Katyn), *Unser Oberschlesien,* VI, no. 20 (1956), 3; "Hintergründe des Katyn-Mordes enthüllt" (The background of the Katyn murder unveiled), *Industriekurier,* V, no. 180 (1952), 2; G. F. Hudson, "Die Toten von Katyn. Zu den neuesten polnischen Geschichtsquellen" (The dead of Katyn. The newest Polish sources), *Der Monat,* IV, no. 40 (January 1952), 403-407; "Katyn und Nürnberg" (Katyn and Nuremberg), *Christ und Welt,* V, no. 19 (May 8, 1952), 2; "Katyn," *Ost-Probleme,* II, no. 29 (July 20, 1950), 917; "Katyn—ein Verbrechen der Sowjets" (Katyn—a Soviet crime), *Der Spiegel,* VI, no. 1 (January 2, 1952), 17-19; "Katyn: Ein schrecklicher Missgriff" (Katyn: a terrible blunder), *Der Spiegel,* X, no. 34 (1956), 28-29; Jürgen Kempski, "Katyn und England" (Katyn and England), *Monatshefte für Auswärtige Politik,* X, no. 10 (October 1943), 674-675; Harald Laeuen, "Die Dialektik von Katyn" (The dialectic of Katyn), *Die Zeit,* VII, no. 18 (May 1, 1952), 3; "Moskauer Entrüstung" (The Moscow exasperation), *Ost-Probleme,* IV, no. 14 (April 5, 1952), 418-420; Hans Thieme, "Katyn—ein Geheimnis?" (Katyn—a secret?), *Vierteljahrshefte für Zeitgeschichte,* V, no. 4 (October 1955), 409-411; "Die Toten von Katyn" (The dead of Katyn), *Christ und Welt,* V, no. 7 (February 14, 1952), 1-2; "Und wieder Katyn" (Again Katyn), *Hamburger Allgemeine Zeitung,* IV, no. 13 (1949), 1; "Die Verschollenen von Kozielsk" (The missing ones from Kozielsk), *Christ und Welt,* IV, no. 43 (October 25, 1951), 4; W. Zietz, "Ein erschütterndes Dokument: Katyn" (A shocking document: Katyn), *Deutsches Ärzteblatt,* LXXIII (1943), 138.

25. *Contra:* Wójcicki, *op. cit.,* pp. 213-215.
26. Bronisław Kuśnierz, *Stalin and the Poles: An Indictment of the Soviet Leaders* (London: Hollis and Carter, 1949), p. 125. Julius Epstein, "Das Geheimnis der Polnischen Massengräber bei Katyn. Das Ergebnis wissenschaftlicher Untersuchungen auf Grund neuer Zeugnisse und Aussagen" (The mystery of the Polish mass-graves of Katyn. The result of scientific research on the basis of new statements and reports), *Die Zeit,* IV, no. 23 (June 9, 1949), 3.
27. *Hearings,* parts 3 and 5, *passim.*
28. *Ibid.,* part 7, pp. 2059-2060.
29. *Ibid.,* part 3, p. 489.
30. These were gathered within the period the alumni served with General Anders' units.
31. *Hearings,* part 3, p. 431.
32. Colonel Yeaton's testimony. *Hearings,* part 7, p. 2294.
33. Mr. Carter's testimony. *Ibid.,* part 7, pp. 2246-2250.
34. Colonel Van Vliet's testimony. *Ibid.,* part 1, p. 51.
35. Ambassador Arthur Bliss Lane's testimony. *Ibid.,* part 7, p. 2217; Mr. Justice Jackson's testimony. *Ibid.,* part 7, p. 1948.

36. U.S. War Department to U.S. Army Forces in the Middle East. Radiogram No. 8623 for AMSME from War. December 19, 1943. Classification changed to "unclassified" by authority of the Assistant Chief of Staff, G-2, June 1952. *Hearings*, part 7, p. 1938.
37. Mr. George Howard Earle's testimony. *Ibid.*, part 7, p. 2204.
38. For a photostatic copy of President Roosevelt's letter see *ibid.*, part 7, p. 2202.
39. *Ibid.*, part 7, pp. 2203.
40. Testimony of Mr. Alan Cranston, Chief of the Foreign Language Division, Office of War Information. *Hearings*, part 7, p. 2292.
41. Mr. Kreutz' testimony. *Ibid.*, part 7, pp. 2012-2019.
42. Statement by Congressman O'Konski. *Ibid.*, part 3, pp. 498-499.
43. *Ibid.*, part 7, pp. 2324-2325.
44. General Bissell's testimony. *Ibid.*, part 7, pp. 2302-2303.
45. *Ibid.*, part 7, p. 2306.
46. *Ibid.*, part 7, p. 2324.
47. For the details read Julius Epstein, *The Mysteries of the Van Vliet Report. A Case History* (Chicago: Polish American Congress Inc., 1951), pp. 1-16. See also *Hearings*, part 2, pp. 51-67; part 7, pp. 1839-1914, 2298-2327.
48. 82 Cong. Rec. 5390 (1952). Verified by Mr. Czapski: his letter of December 26, 1959.
49. The officers and committee members: Arthur Bliss Lane, Max Eastman, Dorothy Thompson, Montgomery M. Green, Julius Epstein, Constantine Brown, George Creel, Rev. John F. Cronin, William Donovan, Allen Dulles, James Farley, Blair F. Gunther, Sol M. Levitas, Clare Booth Luce, Charles Rozmarek, George Sokolsky, Virginia Starr Freedom, and James A. Walsh.
50. U.S. House of Representatives. Select Committee on the Katyn Forest Massacre. *The Katyn Forest Massacre*. Hearings before the Select Committee to Conduct an Investigation of the Facts, Evidence and Circumstances of the Katyn Forest Massacre. 82nd Cong., 1st and 2nd Sess., 1951-1952 (Washington: U.S. Government Printing Office, 1952), 7 parts. 2362 pp. This source has been cited throughout the book as *Hearings*.
51. Interim Report of the Select Committee. H.R. Rep. No. 2430, 82nd Cong., 2nd Sess. 3 (1952).
52. 82 Congr. Rec. 8864 (1952).
53. *Ibid.*, p. 9240, amendment "b."
54. "Mr. Churchill does not wish to make a statement on this subject. . . ." Mr. Churchill's reply to the letter of inquiry from Mr. Julius Epstein. The reply delivered through the British Embassy in Washington in a letter dated February 18, 1952 and signed by K. D.

Jamieson, Second Secretary of the Embassy. 82 Congr. Rec. A1599 (1952).

55. A. P. Scotland, *The London Cage* (London: Evans Brothers, Ltd., 1957), pp. 108, 139, *passim*.

56. Morris Greenspan, "International Law and its Protection for Participants in Unconventional Warfare" in "Unconventional Warfare," *The Annals* of The American Academy of Political and Social Science, CCCXLI (May 1962), p. 39.

57. United Nations. Treaty Series. *Treaties and International Agreements Registered or Filed and Recorded with the Secretariat of the United Nations.* Geneva Convention Relative to the Treatment of Prisoners of War of August 12, 1949, LXXV, no. 972 (1950). Article 85 of the Convention states: "Prisoners of war prosecuted under laws of the Detaining Power for acts committed prior to capture shall retain even if convicted, the benefits of the present Convention." *Ibid.*, p. 202.

58. Sen. Rep. No. 2832, 84th Cong., 2d Sess. 13 (1956); *The Army Almanac: A Book of Facts Concerning the United States Army*. 2nd ed. (Harrisburg: The Stackpole Company, 1959), p. 380.

Appendix

A PARTIAL LIST OF THE N.K.V.D. PERSONNEL WHO IN THE SPRING OF 1940 PARTICIPATED IN (OR HAD KNOWLEDGE OF) PLANNING AND EXECUTING 15,000 POLISH PRISONERS OF WAR IN THE SOVIET UNION

Captain * Aleksandrovich
General L. P. Beria (shot December 23, 1953)
Colonel Bereshkov
First Lieutenant Bogdanovich
Bomsovitch
P. Borodynsky
First Lieutenant A. Borisovets
Buryanov (?)
Major Khodas
Captain Demidovich
Major Elman
"Commissar" P. F. Fedotov
Ch. Finsberg
Filipovich
First Lieutenant Gubayev
Captain Ivanov
Major Kadishchev
"Commissar" Kirshin (or Kirskin)
General S. N. Kruglov
Colonel B. Kutchkov (?)
Koralev
General P. Y. Kosynkin (sudden death, 1953)
Colonel Kupriyanov
Major Lebedev
First Lieutenant Leibkind
Colonel Lebedevsky
Lisak
Major Paweł Mazur
General V. N. Merkulov (shot December, 1953)
Colonel Mironov
Agent Morski

* The rank cited for this man and for all others on this list (whenever it is known) is as of 1940. It is possible that the spelling of the names is distorted or that some are pseudonyms.

General L. F. Raikhman (promoted Ltn. Gen. 1945; arrested 1951; released; arrested again 1954)
Driver Yakim Rozuvaiev (Smolensk N.K.V.D.)
Colonel L. Rybak
"Commissar" I. A. Serov (chairman, State Security Committee, 1953; transferred to "other duties," December 1958)
Agent Sirotky
Second Lieutenant Starikovich
Tartakov
Colonel Urbanovich
Captain Vasilevsky
Colonel Volkov
Major S. Y. Yegorov (promoted to Major General 1945)
General V. M. Zarubin (promoted to Major General 1945)

Bibliography

ONLY THE SOURCES cited or quoted in the book are included in the bibliography. The foreign materials are entered in a standardized manner approved by the scholastic standards in the United States and not according to the academic customs of the countries of their origin.

The above mentioned procedures were adopted for the sake of brevity, consistency, and clarity.

Primary Sources

1. Interviews

Interviews with Stanisław Mikołajczyk, former Prime Minister of the Polish Government-in-Exile in London, 1943-1945; Vice Prime Minister and Minister of Agriculture in the Provisional Government of National Unity in Warsaw, 1945-1947. Princeton, March 1956; Washington, April 1958.

One hundred fifty interviews with officers and soldiers of the 2nd Polish Corps, 8th British Army, all former Soviet prisoners-of-war. Cingoli, Rome, 1946; Shobdon Camp, Herefordshire, 1947; London, 1948.

2. Documents

Germany

Germany. *Amtliches Material zum Massenmord von Katyn* (Official material concerning the Katyn massacre). Im

Auftrage des Auswärtigen Amtes auf Grund urkundlichen Beweismaterials zusammengestellt, bearbeitet und herausgegeben von der Deutschen Informationsstelle. Berlin: Zentralverlag der NSDAP, F. Eher Nachf., 1943. 331 pp. [International Medical Commission Report, full text, pp. 114-135.]

Germany. *Amtliches Material zum Massenmord von Winniza* (Official material concerning the Vinnitsa massacre). Im Aufrage des Reichsministers für die besetzen Ostgebiete auf Grund urkundlichen Beweismaterials zusammengestellt, bearbeitet und herausgegeben. Berlin: Zentralverlag der NSDAP. Franz Eher Nachf. GmbH., 1944. 288 pp.

Germany. *Reichsführer SS und Chef der deutschen Polizei. Persönlicher Stab. Schriftgutverwaltung* (Reichsführer SS and Chief of the German Police. Personal staff. Document administration). Himmler Files 3. Photostatic copies. Folder no. 277, pages numbered 7217-7229.

Germany. *Verordnungsblatt für das Generalgouvernement* (Regulations for the occupied area). Krakau, nos. 1-97. January 6-December 18, 1943. Published in Poland by the German occupation administration during World War II.

Great Britain

Great Britain. *Parliamentary Debates* (5th series). (Commons.) Vols. CCCLII-CCCXCIV, 1939-1943. London: His Majesty's Stationary Office, 1940-1943.

International Military Tribunal

International Military Tribunal. Secretariat. *Trial of the Major War Criminals before the International Military Tribunal. Nüremberg, 14 November 1945-10 October 1946*. Nüremberg, Germany, 1947. Vols. I, II, III, IV,

V, VII, IX, X, XIV, XV, XVII, XVIII, XXII, XXIII, XXIV.

Japan

Japan. Ministry of Foreign Affairs. Public Information Division. *Announcement of Japanese Foreign Ministry and Letters of Foreign Minister to President of United Nations General Assembly on Repatriation*, July 25, 1951. 54 pp.

Poland. (*Polish People's Republic*)

Poland. Rząd R.P. "Naród polski z oburzeniem piętnuje cyniczne prowokacje amerykańskich imperialistów, żerujących na tragicznej śmierci tysięcy obywateli polskich w Katyniu." Oświadczenie Rządu R.P. (The Polish nation with indignation condemns the cynical provocations of imperialistic Americans preying on the tragic death of thousands of Polish citizens in Katyn. Statement of the Government of the Polish People's Republic.) *Trybuna Ludu.* Vol. V, no. 61, March 1, 1952, p. 1.

Poland. (*Polish Government-in-Exile*)

Some of the Polish sources used in this work were originally classified as "secret" or "top secret." These were declassified in the years following the end of the Second World War.

Poland. Komisja Historyczna Polskiego Sztabu Głównego w Londynie. *Polskie Siły Zbrojne w Drugiej Wojnie Światowej.* Tom 1: *Kampania Wrześniowa 1939*, cz. 1, 2; Tom 3: *Armia Krajowa* (Polish forces in the Second World War. Vol. I: The September campaign of 1939, parts 1, 2; Vol. III: The Home Army). London: Instytut Historyczny im. Generała Sikorskiego, 1950-1951.

Poland. Ministerstwo Spraw Zagranicznych. *Stosunki Polsko-Sowieckie od Września 1939 do Kwietnia 1943. Zbiór Dokumentów* (Polish-Soviet relations from September 1939 to April 1943. Collection of documents). London: 1943, 317 pp. (Najściślej tajne—Top secret.)

Poland. Polish Government-in-Exile, Council of Ministers. (Author, Dr. Wiktor Sukiennicki). *Facts and Documents Concerning Polish Prisoners of War Captured by the U.S.S.R. during the 1939 Campaign.* (Strictly confidential.) London, 1946. 454 pp.

Poland. Polish Government-in-Exile. *Official Documents Concerning Polish-German and Polish-Soviet Relations 1933-1939*. London and Melbourne: Hutchinson and Co., Ltd., 1940. 222 pp.

Poland. Polish Government-in-Exile, Polish Embassy in Washington. *Polish-Soviet Relations, 1918-1943. Official Documents.* 1944. 249 pp.

Poland. Polish Government-in-Exile. *Report on the Massacre of Polish Officers in Katyn Wood. Facts and Documents.* For private circulation only. London, 1946. 51 pp.

Skarżyński, Kazimierz. Secretary General of the Polish Red Cross 1939-1945. *Krótki Zarys Losów Polskiego Czerwonego Krzyża w Polsce Podczas Okupacji Niemieckiej* (A brief outline of the history of the Polish Red Cross during the German occupation of Poland 1939-45). Manuscript from the personal archives of Mr. Skarżyński. Made available to the author in January 1961. 3 cards.

Skarżyński, Kazimierz. *List do por. Heizmana w Sprawie Projektu Roztoczenia Sprawy Katyńskiej na Forum Publicznym* (A letter to Ltn. Heizman concerning presentation of the Katyn Affair to the general public). Manuscript from the personal archives of Mr.

Skarżyński. Made available to the author in January 1961. 4 cards.

Skarżyński, Kazimierz. *Oświadczenie, Złożone Przezemnie w Sądzie Polowym Polskim w Londynie, we Wrześniu 1946 r.* (Testimony submitted by me to the Polish Military Court in London, September 1946). Manuscript from the personal archives of Mr. Skarżyński. Made available to the author in January 1961. 11 cards.

Skarżyński, Kazimierz. *Polish Czerwony Krzyż w Katyniu* (The [mission of the] Polish Red Cross at the Katyn [Forest]). Manuscript from the personal archives of Mr. Skarżyński. Made available to the author in January 1961. 82 cards.

United Nations Organization

United Nations. Treaty Series. *Treaties and International Agreements Registered or Filed and Recorded with the Secretariat of the United Nations.* Geneva Convention Relative to the Treatment of Prisoners of War of August 12, 1949. Vol. LXXV, no. 972, 1950, pp. 135-285, 419-468.

Soviet Union

U.S.S.R. Ministry of Foreign Affairs. *Correspondence between the Chairman of the Council of Ministers of the U.S.S.R. and the Presidents of the U.S.A. and the Prime Ministers of Great Britain during the Great Patriotic War of 1941-1945.* 2 vols. Moscow: Foreign Languages Publishing House, 1947.

U.S.S.R. Soviet Embassy in London. *New Documents on Nazi Atrocities.* 1943. 128 pp.

U.S.S.R. Soviet Embassy in London, Press Department. *Soviet Documents on Nazi Atrocities, Illustrated by Some Original Photographs.* London: Hutchinson and Co., Ltd., 1942. 190 pp.

U.S.S.R. Soviet Embassy in Washington. *The Soviet Report of Special Commission for Ascertaining and Investigating the Circumstances of the Shooting of Polish Officer Prisoners by the German-Fascist Invaders in the Katyn Forest.* Supplement to the *Soviet Embassy Information Bulletin*, 23 March 1944. 16 pp.

U.S.S.R. Spetsial'naya Komissiya po Ustanovleniyu i Rassledovaniyu Obstoyatel'stv Rasstrela Nemetsko-Fashistskimi Zakhvatchikami v Katynskom Lesu Voennoplennykh Pol'skikh Ofitserov (Special commission for ascertaining and investigating the circumstances of the shooting of Polish officer prisoners by the German-Fascist invaders in the Katyn Forest).

Nota Sovetskogo Pravitel'stva Pravitel'stvu SShA; Soobshchenie Spetsial'noi Komissii (Note of the Soviet Government to the Government of the U.S.; communication by the Special Commission). Moscow: Supplement to *Novoe Vremya*, no. 10, 1952. 20 pp.

United States

U.S. Army. General Headquarters Far East Command, Military Intelligence Section, General Staff. *Special Report: Japanese Prisoners of War: Life and Death in Soviet P.W. Camps.* n.d. 27 pp.

U.S. *Congressional Record.* 82nd Cong., 2nd Sess., 1952, Vol. XCVIII, 13 parts. Washington: U.S. Government Printing Office, 1952.

U.S. Department of Defense. Office of Public Information. *Katyn Case.* Release no. 1141-1150, September 1950. pp. 8.

U.S. Department of State. *The Department of State Bulletin.* Vol. IX, no. 228, November 6, 1943. 307-337 pp.

U.S. Department of State. International Organization and Conference, ser. II: European and British Commonwealth, 1. *Report of Robert H. Jackson United States*

Representative to the *International Conference on Military Trials, London 1945*. Washington: Division of Publications, Office of Public Affairs, 1945. 440 pp. Released February 1949.

U.S. Department of State. *Nazi-Soviet Relations, 1939-1941: Documents from the Archives of the German Foreign Office*. Edited by Raymond James Sontag and James Stuart Beddie. Washington: U.S. Government Printing Office, 1948. 362 pp.

U.S. House of Representatives. Select Committee on the Katyn Forest Massacre. *The Katyn Forest Massacre*. Hearings before the Select Committee to Conduct an Investigation of the Facts, Evidence and Circumstances of the Katyn Forest Massacre. 82nd Cong., 1st and 2nd Sess., 1951-1952. Washington: U.S. Government Printing Office, 1952. 7 parts. 2362 pp.

U.S. Office of Chief of Counsel for Prosecution of Axis Criminality. *Nazi Conspiracy and Aggression*. Supplement A and B. Washington: U.S. Government Printing Office, 1947.

U.S. Report No. 2832 of the Committee on Government Operation made by its Permanent Subcommittee on Investigations. *Communist Interrogation, Indoctrination and Exploitation of American Military and Civilian Prisoners*. 84th Cong., 2nd Sess., 1956. Washington: U.S. Government Printing Office, 1957. 24 pp.

Bibliographies

German

Bibliographie der deutschen Zeitschriftenliteratur mit Einschluss von Sammelwerken (Bibliography of German periodical literature including collective entries). Hrsg. von Reinhard Dietrich. Bd. 43/1943-Bd. 115/1957. Osnabrück: Felix Dietrich, 1944-1958.

Bibliographie der fremdsprachigen Zeitschriftenliteratur (Bibliography of foreign periodical literature). Unter wissenschaftlicher Mitarbeit von Dr. Th. Adamczyk und Dr. H. Kumerloeve bearbeitet und herausgegeben von Reinhard Dietrich. N.F. Bd. 21/1940-1941-Bd. 42/1956-1957. Osnabrück: 1944-1958.

Deutsche Bibliographie. Halbjahres-Verzeichnis (The German bibliography. Half-year index). Bearbeitet von der Deutschen Bibliothek Frankfurt a. M., Bd. (1)/1952-(7)/1958. Frankfurt a. M.: Buchhändler-Vereinigung GmbH, 1952-1958.

Jahresverzeichnis der deutschen Hochschulschriften (A yearly list of dissertations at German universities). Hrsg. von der Deutschen Bücherei. Jg. 61(1945)-Jg. 71(1955). Leipzig: VEB Verlag für Buch- und Bibliothekswesen, 1951-1958.

Jahresverzeichnis des deutschen Schrifttums (A yearly listing of German literature). Bearbeitet und herausgegeben von der Deutschen Bücherei und dem Börsenverein der Deutschen Buchhändler zu Leipzig. Jg. (149)/1945-1946-159/1956. Leipzig: VEB Verlag für Buch- und Bibliothekswesen, 1948-1957.

Vogelsang, Thilo. *Bibliographie zur Zeitgeschichte* (Bibliography of contemporary history). Beilage der Vierteljahrshefte für Zeitgeschichte. Jg. 1, 1953-Jg. 6, 1958.

Polish

Poland. Biblioteka Narodowa. Instytut Bibliograficzny. *Przewodnik Bibliograficzny. Urzędowy Wykaz Druków Wydanych w Polskiej Rzeczypospolitej Ludowej* (A bibliographical guide. An official list of prints published in the Polish People's Republic). Vols. I-XV. Warszawa, 1945-1959.

Kosicki, J. i W. Kozłowski. *Bibliografia Piśmiennictwa Polskiego za Lata 1944-1953 o Hitlerowskich Zbrodniach*

Wojennych (A bibliography of Polish literature 1944-1953 concerning the Hitler war crimes). Warszawa: Wydawnictwo Prawnicze, 1955. 177 pp.

Polska Akademia Nauk. Instytut Historii. Komisja Koordynacji Badań nad dziejami II Wojny Światowej. *Materiały do Bibliografii Okupacji Hitlerowskiej w Polsce 1939-1945* (Materials for a bibliography of Hitler's occupation of Poland 1939-1945). Wł. Chojnacki, K. M. Pospieszalski, E. Serwański. Warszawa: Państwowe Wydawnictwo Naukowe, 1957. 63 pp.

Russian

Vsesoyuznaya Knizhnaya Palata. *Knizhnaya Letopis'* (Bibliographical yearbook). Moskva, 1943-1958.

Vsesoyuznaya Knizhnaya Palata. *Letopis' Gazetnykh Statei* (Bibliographical yearbook of newspaper articles). Moskva, 1943-1958.

Vsesoyuznaya Knizhnaya Palata. *Letopis' Zhurnal'nykh Statei* (Bibliographical yearbook of periodical literature). Moskva, 1956-1958.

Books

Anders, Władysław. *Bez Ostatniego Rozdziału. Wspomnienia z Lat 1939-1946* (Without the last chapter. Memoirs of the years 1939-1946). Newton, Wales: Montgomeryshire Printing Co., Ltd., 1949. 447 pp.

The Army Almanac: A Book of Facts Concerning the United States Army. 2nd edn. Harrisburg: The Stackpole Company, 1959. 797 pp.

Brickhill, Paul. *The Great Escape.* New York: W. W. Norton and Co., 1950. 264 pp.

Brzostowski, Ludomir. *Statut Oficerskich Sądów Honorowych* (Statute of the officers' honor courts). Warszawa: Główna Księgarnia Wojskowa, 1928. 166 pp.

Carroll, Wallace. *Persuade or Perish*. Boston: Houghton Mifflin Co., 1948. 392 pp.

Churchill, Winston S. (Now Sir Winston). *The Second World War*. 6 vols. Published in association with the Cooperation Publishing Company, Inc. Boston: Houghton Mifflin Co., 1948-1953.

Cyprian, Tadeusz i Jerzy Sawicki. *Sprawy Polskie w Procesie Norymberskim* (Polish affairs at the Nuremberg Trial). Poznań: Instytut Zachodni, 1956. 814 pp.

Czapski, Józef. *Na Nieludzkiej Ziemi* (The inhuman land). Paris: Instytut Literacki, 1949. 320 pp.

Djilas, Milovan. The New Class: *An Analysis of Communist System*. New York: Frederick A. Praeger, 1957. 214 pp.

du Prel, Max Freiher. *Das Deutsche Generalgouvernement Polen* (The German government of Poland). Krakau: Buchverlag Ost G.m.b.H., 1940. 344 pp.

Fainsod, Merle. *Smolensk under Soviet Rule*. Cambridge: Harvard University Press, 1958. 484 pp.

General Sikorski Historical Institute. *Documents on Polish-Soviet Relations 1939-1945. Vol. I, 1939-1943*. London, Melbourne, Toronto: Heineman, 1961. 625 pp.

Gilbert, G. M. *Nuremberg Diary*. New York: Farrar, Straus and Co., 1947. 471 pp.

Glueck, Sheldon. *The Nuremberg Trial and Aggressive War*. New York: A. A. Knopf, 1946. 121 pp.

The Goebbels Diaries, 1942-1943. Edited and translated and with an introduction by Louise P. Lochner. 1st edn. Garden City, N. Y.: Doubleday Co., 1948. 566 pp.

Goebbels, Joseph. *The Goebbels Diaries, 1942-1943* (in German). Microfilm copy of typewritten manuscript. Made by University of California. Library Photographic Service. Positive. Collation of the original: 6792 pp. On 6 reels. (Original manuscript in the

Hoover Institution on War, Revolution, and Peace. Stanford University, Stanford, California).

Jackson, Robert H. *The Nuremberg Case.* New York: Alfred A. Knopf, 1947. 269 pp.

Korboński, Stefan. *W Imieniu Kremla* (On behalf of Kremlin). Paris: Instytut Literacki, 1956. 381 pp.

Kot, Stanisław. *Listy z Rosji do Gen. Sikorskiego* (Letters from Russia to Gen. Sikorski). London: Jutro Polski, 1956. 576 pp.

Kot, Stanisław. *Rozmowy z Kremlem* (My conference with Kremlin). London: Jutro Polski, 1959. 336 pp.

Kuśnierz, Bronisław. *Stalin and the Poles: An Indictment of the Soviet Leaders.* London: Hollis and Carter, 1949. 317 pp.

Lifton, Robert Jay, M.D. *Thought Reform and the Psychology of Totalism: A Study of "Brainwashing" in China.* New York: W. W. Norton, 1961. 510 pp.

Mackiewicz, Joseph. *The Katyn Wood Murders.* London: Hollis and Carter, 1951. 252 pp.

Malaparte, Curzio. *Kaputt.* New York: E. P. Dutton and Co., Inc., 1946. 407 pp.

Meerloo, Joost A. M. *The Rape of Mind: The Psychology of Thought Control, Menticide, and Brainwashing.* Cleveland and New York: The World Publishing Company, 1956. 320 pp.

Mikołajczyk, Stanisław. *The Rape of Poland: Pattern of Soviet Aggression.* New York: Whittlesey House, 1948. 309 pp.

Molotov, V. *The Molotov Paper on Nazi Atrocities.* New York: The American Council on Soviet Relations, 1942. 31 pp.

Moszyński, Adam. *Lista Katyńska. Jeńcy Obozów Kozielsk, Starobielsk, Ostaszków, Zaginieni w Rosji Sowieckiej* (The roll of Katyn. The prisoners of the camps Kozelsk, Starobelsk, Ostashkov, who disappeared in the Soviet Union). London: Gryf, 1949. 317 pp.

Pavlov, Ivan Petrovich. *Conditioned Reflex: An Investigation of the Physiological Activity of the Cerebral Cortex.* London: Oxford University Press, 1927. 430 pp.

Polski Instytut Spraw Międzynarodowych. Dział Bieżących Zagadnień Międzynarodowch. *Sprawa Polska Podczas II Wojny Swiatowej w Swietle Pamiętników* (Polish Cause during World War II in the light of memoirs). Opracował Stanisław Zabiełło. Warszawa: "Prasa," 1958. 594 pp.

Rothstein, Andrew. *Soviet Foreign Policy during the Patriotic War: Documents and Materials, June 22, 1941-December 31, 1943.* Vol. I, London: Hutchinson and Co., Ltd., 1946. 320 pp.

The Royal Institute of International Affairs. Survey of International Affairs, 1939-1946. *Hitler's Europe.* Edited by Arnold M. Toynbee and Veronica M. Toynbee. London, New York, Toronto: Oxford University Press, 1954. 730 pp.

Sargant, William. *Battle for the Mind.* New York: Doubleday and Company, 1957. 263 pp.

Sawicki, Jerzy. *Ludobójstwo. Od Pojęcia do Konwencji, 1933-1948* (Genocide. From the idea to the convention, 1933-1948). Kraków: L. J. Jaroszewski, 1949. 224 pp.

Sawicki, Jerzy, Dr. i Dr. Bolesław Walawski. *Zbiór Przepisów Specjalnych Przeciwko Zbrodniarzom Hitlerowskim i Zdrajcom Narodu z Komentarzem* (Collection of special regulations against the Hitler's criminals and the traitors of the nation, with commentary). Warszawa: Czytelnik, 1945. 63 pp.

Scaevola (pseud.). *A Study in Forgery: The Lublin Committee and Its Rule over Poland.* London: J. Rolls Book Co., 1945. 123 pp.

Scotland, A. P. *The London Cage*. London: Evans Brothers Limited, 1957. 203 pp.

Szyszko-Bohusz, Zygmunt. *Czerwony Sfinks* (The red sphinx). Rzym: Polski Dom Wydawniczy, 1946. 269 pp.

Taracouzio, T. A. *The Soviet Union and the International Law: A Study Based on the Legislation, Treaties and Foreign Relations of the Union of Socialist Soviet Republics*. New York: The Macmillan Co., 1935. 530 pp.

Umiastowski, Jan Kazimierz. *Przez Kraj Niewoli* (Through the land of slavery). London: Biblioteka Pamiętników, 1947. 133 pp.

Umiastowski, Roman. *Poland, Russia and Great Britain 1941-1945: A Study of Evidence*. London: Hollis and Carter, 1946. 544 pp.

Umiastowski, Roman. *Russia and the Polish Republic 1918-1941*. London: Aquafondata, 1945. 319 pp.

Wójcicki, Bolesław. *Prawda o Katyniu* (The truth about Katyn). Wydanie drugie. Warszawa: Czytelnik, 1953. 218 pp.

Wolin, Simon and Robert M. Slusser. *The Soviet Secret Police*. New York: A. Praeger, 1957. 408 pp.

Zbrodnia Katyńska w Swietle Dokumentów (The Katyn crime in light of documents). Z przedmową Władysława Andersa. 2-gie wydanie. Gryf, 1950. 455 pp.

Pamphlets

Czapski, Józef. *Wspomnienia Starobielskie* (Memoirs of Starobelsk). Italia: Oddział Kultury i Prasy 2 Korpusu, Biblioteka Orła Białego, 1945. 35 pp.

Death at Katyn: An Account of a Survivor. 3rd edn. New York: National Committee of Americans of Polish Descent, 1944, 48 pp.

Epstein, Julius. *The Mysteries of the Van Vliet Report. A*

Case History. Chicago: Polish American Congress Inc., 1951. 15 pp.

First Conference of German Prisoners of War Privates and Non-commissioned Officers in the Soviet Union. Moscow: Foreign Languages Publishing House, 1941. 55 pp.

Osmańczyk, Edmund Jan. *Dowody Prowokacji. Nieznane Archiwum Himmlera* (The evidence of provocation. Himmler's unknown archive). Warszawa: Czytelnik, 1951. 48 pp.

Prawda o Katyniu (The truth about Katyn). Poznań: Wojewódzki Urząd Informacji i Propagandy, 1945. 40 pp.

Prisoner of War Camps in Russia: The Account of a German Prisoner of War. Cambridge: Russian Research Center, 1951. 40 pp.

Journals

"Brainwashing," *The Journal of Social Issues*. Vol. XIII, no. 3, 1957, pp. 1-61.

Caprivi, Leopold. "Katyn," *Monatshefte für Auswärtige Politik*. Vol. X, no. 5, May 1943, p. 396.

Greenspan, Morris. "International Law and its Protection for Participants in Unconventional Warfare," in "Unconventional Warfare," *The Annals* of the American Academy of Political and Social Science. Vol. CCCXLI, May 1962, pp. 30-41.

Hinkle, Lawrence E., Jr., M.D. and Harold G. Wolff, M.D. "Communist Interrogation and Indoctrination of 'Enemies of the State,'" *Archives of Neurology and Psychiatry*. American Medical Association. Vol. LXXVI, 1956, pp. 115-174.

Kempski, Jürgen. "Katyn und England" (Katyn and England), *Monatshefte für Auswärtige Politik*. Vol. X, no. 10, October 1943, pp. 674-675.

Meerloo, Joost A. M. "Pavlovian Strategy as a Weapon of Menticide," *The American Journal of Psychiatry*. Vol. CX, May 1954, pp. 809-813.

Schein, Edgar H. "The Chinese Indoctrination Program for Prisoners of War," *Psychiatry*. Vol. XIX, no. 2, May 1956, pp. 149-172.

Seleshko, M. "Vinnytsia—the Katyn of Ukraine," *The Ukrainian Quarterly*. Vol. V, no. 3, Summer 1949, pp. 238-248.

Standley, Admiral William H. and Rear Admiral Arthur A. Ageton. "Murder, or High Strategy? The U.S. Embassy, the Kremlin, and the Katyn Forest Massacre," *United States Naval Institute Proceedings*. Vol. LXXVIII, no. 10, October 1952, pp. 1053-1065.

Strassman, Harvey D., M.D., Margaret B. Thaler, Ph.D., Cpt. Edgar H. Schein, MSC. "A Prisoner of War Syndrome: Apathy as a Reaction to Severe Stress," *The American Journal of Psychiatry*. Vol. CXII, June 1956, pp. 998-1003.

Thieme, Hans. "Katyn—ein Geheimnis?" (Katyn—a secret?), *Vierteljahrshefte für Zeitgeschichte*. Vol. V, no. 4, October 1955, pp. 409-411.

Zietz, W. "Ein erschütterndes Dokument: Katyn" (A shocking document: Katyn), *Deutsches Ärzteblatt*. Vol. LXXIII, 1943, p. 138.

Newspapers and Magazines

"Ein anderes Katyn. Urteil im Polnischen Offiziersprozess" (Another Katyn. Verdict in the Polish officer-trial). *Ost-Probleme*. Vol. III, no. 39, September 29, 1951, pp. 1216-1220.

Arski, Stefan. "Propaganda Ludobójców" (The genocidist propaganda). *Trybuna Wolności*. No. 10, 1952.

Czapski, Józef. "Znów Katyń" (Katyn Again). *Kultura*. No. 3/173, Marzec 1962, pp. 5-8.

"Day in the Forest." *Time*. Vol. XLIII, no. 6, February 7, 1944, pp. 27-28.
Daily Worker. London. April-June, 1943.
Dziennik Polski. Kraków. 1952.
Dziennik Polski. London. 1943.
"Der Fall Katyn" (The case of Katyn). *Die andere Seite*. Vol. II, no. 10 (1951-1952), pp. 4-10.
Epstein, Julius. "Das Geheimnis der polnischen Massengräber bei Katyn. Das Ergebnis wissenschaftlicher Untersuchungen auf Grund neuer Zeugnisse und Aussagen" (The mystery of the Polish mass-graves of Katyn. The result of scientific research on the basis of new statements and reports). *Die Zeit*. Vol. IV, no. 23, June 9, 1949, p. 3.
Haerdter, Robert. "Katyn." *Gegenwart*. Vol. VII, no. 5, March 1, 1952, pp. 137-140.
"Die heutige Wahrheit von Katyn" (Today's truth about Katyn). *Unser Oberschlesien*. Vol. VI, no. 20, 1956, p. 3.
"Hintergründe des Katyn-Mordes enthüllt" (The background of the Katyn murder unveiled). *Industriekurier*. Vol. V, no. 180, 1952, p. 2.
Hudson, G. F. "Die Toten von Katyn. Zu den neuesten polnischen Geschichtsquellen" (The dead of Katyn. The newest Polish sources). *Der Monat*. Vol. IV, no. 40, January 1952, pp. 403-407.
Infeld, Leopold. "Sprawa Katyńska—Nowa Nikczemna Prowokacja Imperialistów Amerykańskich" (The affair of Katyn—a new disgraceful provocation of the American imperialists). *O Trwały Pokój, o Demokrację Ludową*. No. 12, 1952.
"Katyń dziełem Himmlera" (Himmler's job: Katyn). *Głos Ostrowski*. No. 2, 1946.
"Katyń dziełem Niemców" (Katyn—a German deed). *Głos Ostrowski*. No. 27, 1946.

"Katyń dziełem Niemców. Oświadczenie Prof. Dra. Hajeka" (Katyn—a German deed. Statement of Prof. Dr. Hajek). *Zielony Sztandar.* No. 28, 1945.

"Katyn: Ein schrecklicher Missgriff" (Katyn: a terrible blunder). *Der Spiegel.* Vol. X, no. 34, 1956, pp. 28-29.

"Katyn—ein Verbrechen der Sowjets" (Katyn—a Soviet crime). *Der Spiegel.* Vol. VI, no. 1, January 2, 1952, pp. 17-19.

"Katyn." *Ost-Probleme.* Vol. II, no. 29, July 20, 1950, p. 917.

"Katyn und Nürnberg" (Katyn and Nuremberg). *Christ und Welt.* Vol. V, no. 19, May 8, 1952, p. 2.

Laeuen, Harald. "Die Dialektik von Katyn" (The dialectic of Katyn). *Die Zeit.* Vol. VII, no. 18, May 1, 1952, p. 3.

Life. Vol. XIV, no. 13, March 29, 1943.

Mackiewicz, Józef. "Czy Nowa Rewelacja w Sprawie Katynia?" (Is this a new revelation concerning Katyn?). *Dodatek Tygodniowy "Ostatnich Wiadomości,"* Vol. X, no. 40, October 12, 1958, p. 3.

Mackiewicz, Józef. "Pierwsza Bolszewicka Książka o Katyniu" (The first bolshevistic book about Katyn). *Wiadomości.* Vol. VII, no. 28, July 13, 1952, p. 2.

Mackiewicz, Józef. "Tajemnica Śmierci Iwana Kriwozercowa, Głównego Świadka Zbrodni Katyńskiej" (The mystery of the death of the main witness of the Katyn crime, Ivan Krivozertsov). *Wiadomości.* Vol. VII, no. 15/16, April 20, 1952, p. 1.

"Moskauer Entrüstung" (The Moscow exasperation). *Ost-Probleme.* Vol. IV, no. 14, April 5, 1952, pp. 418-420.

"Nowy Dowód Zbrodni Niemieckich w Katyniu" (New evidence of German crimes in Katyn). *Robotnik Mazowiecki.* No. 5, 1946.

Nowy Kurier Warszawski. Warsaw. 1943.

Ol'shansky, B. "Katyn." Pis'mo v redaktsiyu (Katyn. Letter

to the Editor). *Sotsialistcheckiĭ Vestnik.* Vol. XXX, no. 6/633, June 1950, p. 114.
Pravda. Moscow. 1939-1959.
Skalski, K. A. "Haniebna Prowokacja" (Disgraceful provocation). *Życie Słowiańskie.* Vol. VII, no. 3, March 1952, p. 3.
Skarżyński, Kazimierz. "Katyń i Polski Czerwony Krzyż" (Katyn and the Polish Red Cross). *Kultura.* No. 9/51, May 1955, pp. 127-141.
Szalawski, Zbigniew. "Reżyserzy Prowokacji Katyńskiej" (The stage-managers of the Katyn-provocation). *Poprostu.* No. 11, 1952.
Times. London. 1943-1959.
"Die Toten von Katyn" (The dead of Katyn). *Christ und Welt.* Vol. V, no. 7, February 14, 1952, pp. 1-2.
Trybuna Ludu. Warsaw. 1949-1959.
"Und wieder Katyn" (Again Katyn). *Hamburger Allgemeine Zeitung.* Vol. IV, no. 13, 1949, p. 1.
U.S.S.R. Soviet Embassy in London. *Soviet War News,* 1944.
U.S.S.R. Soviet Embassy in Washington. *Soviet Embassy Information Bulletin.* 1944.
"Die Verschollenen von Kozielsk" (The missing ones from Kozielsk). *Christ und Welt.* Vol. IV, no. 43, October 25, 1951, p. 4.
Völkischer Beobachter. Süddeutsche Ausgabe. 1939, 1943.
W.A. "Prawda o Katyniu" (The truth about Katyn). *Trybuna Ludu.* Vol. V, no. 160, June 9, 1952, p. 3.
Wiadomości (Weekly published in Polish). Vols. III-XIII. London, 1943-1958.
"Zbrodnia Katyńska Przed Sądem w Norymberdze" (The Katyn crime at the Nuremberg trial). *Zielony Sztandar.* No. 11, 1952.

Index

A

"A" company atrocity, 189
A. F. of L., 42
Ageton, Arthur A., 14*n*
Ahrens (Arnes), Col., 50, 55, 69, 76*n*
Aleksandrowicz, priest, 139
Alexandrovitch, Soviet officer, 119
American Committee for the Investigation of the Katyn Massacre, Inc., 186-187
American Journal of Psychiatry, The, 164*n*
American prisoners of war, 144-145, 162, 168*n*, 190
Amtliches Material zum Massenmord von Katyn, see German Report
Anders, Władysław, 6, 7-8, 10, 32, 71, 72, 78, 113, 123, 153; notes on 13, 76, 97, 125, 163, 193
Annals, The, American Academy of Political and Social Science, 197*n*
Announcement of Japanese Ministry ... on Repatriation, ..., 168*n*
Archives of Neurology and Psychiatry, 166
Ardeatine Caves executions, 94
Army Almanac: ..., The, 197*n*
Arnes, Col., see Ahrens, Col.
Arski, Stefan, 191*n*
Autopsies, 17, 86-87, 93-94
"Avengers of Katyn," 170

B

"B," witness, 107-108
Barge story, 113
Bartys, Jan, 109
Basilevsky, Prof., 67, 69, 75*n*
Battle for the Mind, Sargant, 164*n*
Bayonet wounds, as evidence, 20, 23, 55, 93, 111
Bazilevsky, B. V., 50
Beck, Dr., 61-64, 74*n*, 99*n*
Beddie, James Stuart, 12*n*
Bedenk, Col., 69, 76*n*
Belgium, 17, 20
Beria, 127, 148, 155
 "great mistake" comment, 149-150, 170
Berle, Asst. Sec., 47
Berlin, 62
Berling, Gen., 149-154, 166*n*, 169-170
Bez Ostatniego Rozdziału. ..., Anders, notes on, 13, 76, 97
Bibliographical sources, 99*n*
 German, 194*n*
 Polish, 193*n*-194*n*
 Soviet, 194*n*

INDEX

Biddle, 37, 180, 185-186
Billewicz, Gen., 146
Birkle, Dr., 17
Bissell, Gen. Clayton, 179, 180, 196n
"Bliss, Villa of," 150-153
Bodies
    exhuming of, 86-87
    finding of, 11, 15-16, 78, 174
    grouping of, in graves, 91-93
    numbers of, 24-25, 28n, 51, 55, 94-95
    searching of, 21-23
    Soviet examination of, 52, 53
    see also Graves
Bogomolov, Amb., 9
Bohatyrewicz, Bronisław, 23, 145
Bohle, 31
Böhmert, Capt., 66
Bohusz-Szyszko, Gen., 11, 123
Bologoe, 113, 114
Books, in prisoner-of-war camps, 142
Boots, as evidence, 84-86
Bór-Komorowski, Gen., 125n
Boxes, document, 60-61
Brainwashing of prisoners, 161-162, 164n, 168n
    Chinese methods, 144, 162; notes on 164, 166-168
    N.K.V.D. methods, 136-143
    studies dealing with, 164n, 168n
Breslau (Wrocław), 61, 62, 74n
Brickhill, Paul, 97n
Britain
    atrocities investigations, 188-189
    handling of Katyn affair by, 10, 188
    in Nuremberg trials, 64, 72
    Polish press in, 36
    Soviet-Polish relations and, see International politics and separate countries
    see also Churchill, Sir Winston
Brown, Constantine, 196n
Brzostowski, Ludomir, 166n
Buck, Prof. Philip W., vii
Bukojemski, 166n

Bulgaria, 17, 177
Bullets, as evidence, 17, 19, 23, 174
Burdenko, N. N., 55, 56n, 158-159
Burial, see Graves
Buryanov, 114
Bussoyedov, Capt., 57n
Butyrki prison, Moscow, 148-152
Buzul'uk, 6
Bychowiec, Capt., 106

C

Caprivi, Leopold, 194n
Carriages, prison, 109, 116
Carroll, Wallace, 41, 47n
Carter, John F., 179, 180, 195n
Center for Advanced Study in The Behavioral Sciences, x
Chałacinski, Lt. Col., 137-138
"Chinese Indoctrination Program . . . ," Schein, 164n, 166n
Chinese psychological conditioning, 144, 162; notes on 164, 166-168
Chojnacki, Wł., 193n
Churchill, Sir Winston, 30, 34, 36-38, 44, 74, 90-91, 128, 188, 190; notes on 46, 47, 76, 98, 162, 193, 196
Ciechanowski, Amb., 193n
C.I.O., 42
Civic leaders, "enemy" category, 133
Civilians, in the graves and detention camps, 24, 132
Civil War, Soviet, prisoner treatment in, 129
Class struggle concept, 155
    effect on treatment of prisoners of war, 128-133
Clogs, as evidence, 85-86
Closing the Ring, Churchill, 98n
Coats of prisoners, as evidence, 83
Colby, Kenneth Mark, 165n
Communism, class war concept, 128-133, 155
"Communist Interrogation and . . . ," Hinkle and Wolff, 166n

INDEX

Communist Interrogations, . . . , Senate Subcommittee on Investigations, 164*n*
Communist Party, Polish, 132
 postwar Katyn attitude, 169-171, 177
 in prison camps, *see* Red Corners
 in Russia, *see* Union of Polish Patriots
Communist Party, Soviet, *see* Soviet Union
Conditioned Reflex: . . . , Pavlov, 164*n*
Congress
 Katyn inquiry of *1944,* 184
 Katyn investigation of *1951-1952, see* House Select Committee investigation
Constitution, Soviet, in prisoner-of-war camps, 140.
Cord, as evidence, *see* Rope
"Correlates of Collaboration . . . in Korea," Segal, 168*n*
Correspondence between the Chairman of the Council of Ministers of the U.S.S.R. and the Presidents of the U.S.A. and the Prime Ministers of Great Britain: . . . , *see* Stalin's Correspondence
Correspondents (journalists), at Katyn investigations, 20-21, 89-90
Costedoat, Dr., 17
Cranston, Allen, 184, 196*n*
Creel, George, 196*n*
Croatia, 17
Cronin, John F., 196*n*
Cyprian, Tadeusz, 193*n*
Czapski, Józef, vii-viii, 7-8, 10, 71, 115, 116, 121, 124, 146, 148, 178, 186; *notes on* 13, 14, 96, 126, 163-165
Czechoslovakia, 17, 177
Czernicki, Adm., 145

Czerwony Sfinks, Szyszko-Bohusz, 163*n*
"Czy Nowa Rewelacja . . . ," Mackiewicz, 126*n*

D

Dagens Nyheter, 172
Daily Telegraph, London, 32
Daily Worker, London, 26*n*, 40, 46*n*
Date, of massacre, 24, 26*n*, 84, 90, 93, 95, 159-160
Davies, Joseph E., 42
Davies, of *Toronto Star,* 53
Davis, Elmer, 41
"Day in the Forest," *Time,* 57*n*, 98*n*
Death at Katyn: . . . , National Committee of Americans of Polish Descent, *notes on* 14, 163, 164
Dęblin atrocities, 175
de Burlet, Dr., 17
Denmark, 17
Department of Armament of Warsaw Polytechnic, 132
Department of State Bulletin, The, 47*n*
Deutsche Generalgouvernement Polen, Das, Freiher du Prel, 45*n*
Diaries of prisoners, 60, 88-89, 101, 108-110, 125*n*, 126*n*
Djilas, Milovan, 155, 167*n*
Djugashvili, Jacob, 156-157
Dobrowolski, Alex, 171
Doctors
 Polish, 133, 163*n*-164*n*
 Soviet, 156
Documents on Katyn, 21-22, 174; *notes on* 45-46, 165
 in British files, 43
 as evidence, 54, 86, 87-90
 German efforts to secure, 59-64
 in N.K.V.D. files, 82, 175
 Polish examination of, in Krakow, 59-60
 in United States files, 43, 179, 180, 185-188

see also Bibliographical sources
Documents on Polish-Soviet Relations 1939-1945, Gen. Sikorski Historical Institute, 13*n*
Dodatek Tygodniowy "*Ostatnich Wiadomości*," 126*n*
Dogs, prisoners', 120-121, 139
Don atrocity, 96
Donovan, William, 196*n*
Dowody Prowokacji, Osmańczyk, 12*n*
Dresden, 62, 74*n*
Dulles, Allen, 196*n*
Duncan-Hooper, of Reuters, 53
Dyergatche, 114
Dziennik Polski, London, 46*n*, 125*n*
Dziennik Polski, Kraków, 191*n*

E

Earle, George H., 180, 182-183, 196*n*
Eastman, Max, 196*n*
Eden, Anthony, 37, 40, 44
Ehrenburg, Ilya, 10
Eighth Army, British, Polish units with, 153
Einsiedel, von, H., 167*n*
Eiseley, Loren, ii
"Enemy of the Soviet Union," categories of, 127, 130-133
Epstein, Julius, *notes on* 194-196
Estonia, 5, 147
Exner, Prof., 66

F

Facts and Documents Concerning Polish Prisoners of War Captured by the U.S.S.R. during the 1939 Campaign, Sukiennicki, *see* Polish Report
Fainsod, Merle, 126*n*
Fairman, Prof. Charles, vii
Farley, James, 196*n*
F.B.I., 42
Fedotov, Gen., 155
Felsztyn, Col., 166*n*

Finger, Edwin, 23
Finland, 17
First Conference of German Prisoners . . . in the Soviet Union, 167*n*
Fleschner, Helmut, 161
Foreign Ministers Conference, Moscow (*1943*), 44
France, 17, 64
Frank, Hans, 4, 79, 97*n*
Freedom, Virginia Starr, 196*n*
Free Germany Committee (Soviet), 161
Freiher du Prel, Max, 45*n*
Furtek, cadet, 125

G

Gags, as evidence, 111
Gawiak, 125*n*
"Geheimnis der Polnischen Massengräber bei Katyn, . . . , Das," Epstein, 195*n*
Generals, prisoner-of-war, 19, 105, 145
see also Officers, Polish
Geneva Convention of *1929*, 128
Geneva Convention of *1949* (United Nations), 189, 197*n*
Genschow, Karl, 28*n*
Genschow Co., 23
German Communication Regiment 537, 11
German Engineer Battalion 537, 50, 55
"German Officers Corps" (Soviet), 161
German press, Katyn articles in, 194*n*
German Report, xv, 94; *notes on* 26-28, 75, 97-99, 192
Germans
  in America, 183
  prisoners of war, 167*n*
  Soviet indoctrination of, 161-162
German Signal Regiment 537, 69
German-Soviet break of *1941*, 152

German Special Medical-Judiciary Commission investigation (*1943*), 18, 23-25, 82, 84, 90, 92, 94
   prisoners of war at, 179-180
   see also German Report
Germany, 175
   appeal to International Red Cross, 33, 34
   attack on Poland in *1939*, 3-5, 11*n*-12*n*, 65
   attack on Soviet in *1941*, 121
   effort to retain Katyn documents, 59-64
   evidence against, on Katyn, 16-25, 50-55, 65-71, 79, 81, 86, 87, 93, 94, 173-175
   exchange of Polish prisoners with Soviet, 128
   finding of the graves, 11, 15
   Katyn Forest area seized by, 16
   Polish extermination policy, 73, 79
   propagandizing of Katyn issue, 30-33, 44
   war-time relations with Poland, 18, 21
Gilbert, G. M., 65, 75*n*
Glavnoe Upravlenie Lagerei (Central Administration Office of Labor Camps), 7
Gleiwitz radio station attack, 4
Głos Ostrowski, 191*n*
Gnezdovo, 107-111
Goebbels, 15, 23, 25*n*, 26*n*, 29, 31, 33, 34, 43, 49, 179, 193*n*
Goebbels Diaries, 15; notes on 25, 28, 47, 56
Goering, 65
Goetel, 171, 191*n*
Gomółka, 176
"Gondolier," 146
Gorczyński, 166*n*
"Gorki Rest House," 138
Graves, 15-25, 28*n*, 112, 126*n*
   finding of the, 15-16, 78, 174
   numbers of, 25
   problem of grave no. *8*, 92
   spruce trees on, 24, 55, 90
   system of burial in, 19
   see also Bodies
Grazovec prison camp, 6, 7, 78, 83, 88, 91, 92, 124, 144-147, 151
   list of prisoners in, 126*n*
   release from, 123-124
   see also Survivors
Great Escape, The, Brickhill, 97*n*
Green, Montgomery M., 196*n*
Greenspan, Morris, 197*n*
Grobicki, Col., 125*n*-126*n*
Gundorov, A. S., 56*n*
Gunther, Blair F., 196*n*

H

Haerdter, Robert, 194*n*
Hague Convention of *1907*, 163*n*
Hajek, Dr., 17, 177, 191*n*
Haller, S., Gen., 145
"Haniebna Prowokacja," Skalski, 191*n*
Harriman, Averell, 52, 54, 57*n*
Harriman, Kathleen, 52-54, 67, 75*n*, 89, 180-181
Hearings, House Select Committee, xv; notes on 13, 14, 26-28, 46, 47, 57, 74-76, 96-99, 125, 163-167, 191, 192, 195, 196
Heizman, Lt., 27*n*
Herrmann, Karl, 74*n*
Hess, 65
Heydrich, 3
Hilgard, Prof. Ernest R., vii
Himmler, 30, 31; notes on 12, 26, 191
Himmler Files, notes on 45-46
Hinge of Fate, The, Churchill, notes on 46, 47, 76, 162
Hinkle, Lawrence E., 166*n*
Hitler, 31, 33, 34, 39, 46*n*
   on Polish extermination, 79
Hitler's Europe, Toynbee, ed., 96*n*
Holland, 20

INDEX

Hoover Institution on War, Revolution, and Peace, The, viii, x, 26n
Hopkins, Harry, 42
Hott, Lt., 55
House Select Committee investigation (1951-1952), 13n, 68, 73, 76n, 172-173, 185-188
  Bissell's testimony, 185-186
  Jackson's testimony, 73
  members of committee, 196n
  Polish government reaction to, 172-173
  see also Hearings
Hudson, G. F., 195n
Hull, Cordell, 44, 193n
Hulls, Lt. Col., 178, 179
Hungary, 17, 20, 31

I

I Joined the Russians, von Einsiedel, 167n
I.M.T., xvi, *notes on* 11, 75, 76, 97, 99
Infeld, Leopold, 191n
Intelligentsia, Polish, extermination of, 79-80
International Commission investigation (1943), 16-25, 67, 68, 81-93
  intimidation efforts by communists, 177-178
"International Law . . . ," Greenspan, 197n
International Medical Commission report (1943), 26n, 27n
International politics, 178-186
  Soviet-Polish issue as problem, 30-45
  standards of behavior of sovereign states, 190-191
  see also Britain, Soviet Union, United States
International Red Cross, 81, 93, 189, 190
  German appeal to, 33, 34
  Polish appeal to, 32-36, 38, 44

Investigations
  by American Committee (1949), 186-187
  findings based on investigations of 1943, 19-25
  by German Special Medical-Judiciary Commission (1943), *see* separate item
  by House Select Committee (1951-1952), *see* separate item
  by International Commission investigation (1943), *see* separate item
  international relations and, 186
  by Polish Embassy in Moscow, 124
  by Polish Red Cross (1943), *see* separate item
  postwar efforts for, in Poland, 169-177
  by Soviet Special Commission (1943-1944), *see* separate item
  United States in relation to, 178-186
Italians, 17, 94, 167n, 183

J

Jackson, Robert, 66, 72-74, 181; *notes on* 75, 76, 96, 195
Jaederlunt, 21
Jamieson, K. D., 196n-197n
Japan, 162, 168n, 186
Jaroszyński brothers, 106
Jews, Polish, 30
"Joe Doe" witness, 187
Joint Decree of the Revolutionary Military Council . . . and of the People's Commissariat . . . , 129
Journalists, "enemy" category, 133
Journal of Social Issues, The, 168n

K

Kaczkowski, Jan, 7, 13n, 71, 124
Kaputt, Malaparte, 12n

INDEX

Katyn case in the United States
American citizens of Polish origin, 41
privately sponsored investigations of, 186-188, 196n
public attitude toward Soviet Union in *1943*, 42
see also, for suppression of information, 184
see also, United States Government and the Katyn Case
"Katyn." . . . , Ol'shansky, 167n
"Katyń dziełem Himmlera," 191n
"Katyń dziełem Niemców. . . . ," Dr. Hajek, 191n
Katyn Forest, 15-16, 50, 69, 114
control of, 16, 23-24, 45
persons living near, 17, 26n
Soviet graves in, 20
spruce trees in, 24
Katyn Forest massacre, *passim*
date of, 24, 26n, 52, 84, 90, 93, 95, 159-160
disappearance of prisoners, 5
finding of the graves, 11, 15-16
investigations of, see Investigations
known facts, 77-78
manner of prisoners' death, 19, 111-112
as "mistake," 149-150, 160, 170
numbers killed, 24, 55
Nuremberg trial, see Nuremberg War Trials
Polish reaction to, 29
propaganda aspect, 115, 175
reasons for, 127
selection of victims, 154-155
significance of, 160, 169, 189-191
Katyn Forest Massacre, The, U.S. House of Rep. Select Committee on the Katyn Forest Massacre, see *Hearings*, House Select Committee

"Katyn—ein Verbrechen der Soviets," *Der Spiegel*, 75n
"Katyń i Polski Czerwony Krzyż," Skarżyński, *notes on* 26, 74, 99
Katyn Wood Murders, The, Mackiewicz, *notes on* 27, 75, 98, 126
Kawecki, 171, 191n
Kempski, Jürgen, 195n
Kharkov, 113, 115
Kharkov N.K.V.D., 114
Khrustalov, 110
Kolesnikov, S. A., 56n
Komarnicki, Wacław, 125n, 166n
Korboński, Stefan, 172, 191n
Korean War, 162, 187, 190
Kosicki, J., 193n
Kot, Stanisław, 8, 9, 13n, 33, 46n, 97n, 124
Kowalewski, Gen., 146
Kozelsk (city), 69, 114
Kozelsk prison camp, 6, 8, 24, 28n, 69, 71, 77-78, 83, 87-93, 101-117, 126n, 131, 137, 140, 141, 151
Chinese doctor incident, 147
civilians in, 132
doctors in, 163n-164n
evacuation of, 154-155
generals in, 145-146
mail from, 138
neutral-country internees in, 147
numbers of men in, 96n
officer revolt version, 177
religious leaders in, 131-132
Zarubin in, 141-143
see also Polish prisoners of war
Koźlinski family, 15
Kozłowski, W., 193n
Kraków, 60-62, 74n, 88, 192n
Kreutz, Marian, 184, 196n
Krivoy Rog, Camp, 163n
Krivozertsov, 110, 114, 126n
Kruglov, Gen., 155
Książ-Tiefenbach, 193n
Kuczinska, Irene, 90

226 INDEX

Kuczyński, Stanisław, 90, 98n
Kultura, notes on 26, 74, 99
Künstler, 166n
Kuśnierz, Bronisław, 163n, 195n
Kutchkov, B., 114
Kwolek, Lt., 138

L

Laeuen, Harald, 195n
Lane, Arthur Bliss, 181, 187, 195n, 196n
Laternser, Hans, 70
Lawrence, Lord Justice, 68, 70
Lawrence, of *New York Times*, 53
Lawyers, "enemy" category, 133
Leaflets, Soviet, 130
Lectures, communist, to prisoners, 140-141
Lednicki family, 16
Lenin, 42, 128-129, 162n
Letters, as evidence, 87-90, 138, 165
Levitas, Sol M., 196n
Lewszecki, Lt., 157, 167n
Life, 42, 47n
Lifton, Robert J., 166n, 168n
"Liquidation" order, 127, 162n
Lis, 166n
Lista Katyńska. . . . , Moszyński, 28n, 96n
Listy z Rosji do Gen. Sikorskiego, Kot, 13n, 97n
Lithuania, 5, 147
Lochner, Louis P., 26n
London
  Conference of *1945* on trial of war criminals, 64
  Polish government in, see Polish Government-in-Exile
London Cage, The, Scotland, 197n
Łopianowski, Capt., 151-152
Lübeck prisoner-of-war camp, Stalin's son in, 156-157
Lubianka prison, 148-150

"Lublin government" (Union of Polish Patriots), 61
Lubomirski, Prince, 145
Luce, Clare Booth, 196n
Ludobójstwo. . . . . , Sawicki, 193n
Łukowski, Gen., 146

M

Machleyd brothers, 106
Mackiewicz, Józef, viii; notes on 27, 28, 75, 98, 126, 192
Maisky, Amb., 6, 39
Majdanek, prison camp, 99n
Malachovka, 150
Malaparte, Curzio, 12n
Malmedy atrocity, 189
Markov, Dr., 17, 67, 177
Martini, Roman, 172
Mass extermination concept, 96n, 155-157
  implications of, 189-190
Medical-Judiciary Commission investigation, German Special, see separate item
Meerloo, Joost A. M., 137, 164n
Megerle, 31
Melby, John, 53, 54, 57n, 75n
Melnikov, P. E., 56n
Mementos, of murdered men, 21-22
"Memorandum Concerning the Polish Prisoners of War . . . ," Czapski, 96n
Menshagin, B. G., 50-51
Merkulov, Gen., 148, 150, 155
Mejster, Stefan, 20
Mikołajczyk, Stanisław, viii, 43, 128, 170-171; notes on 47, 56, 74, 125, 162, 191
  private files, 165n
Military Intelligence, U.S., 179, 181, 185
Miloslavich, Dr., 17, 93, 99n, 178
Ministers, "enemy" category, 131
Minkiewicz, Gen., 143, 166n

Minsk N.K.V.D., 110, 113-115
Missing men, *passim*
　barge story, 113
　Beria comment, 149-150
　departure from camps, 104-105, 112-113
　Dzugashvili comment, 157
　failure to return after repatriation, 176
　fate of leaders among, 102
　grouping of, 105-106
　identities, 174-175
　journey to Katyn Forest, 107-111
　life in prison camps, 101-106, 126*n*
　Merkulov comment, 150
　numbers of, 124
　see also Officers, Polish, *and* Polish prisoners of war
Miter (Mitera), Zygmunt, 146
Molotov, V., 10, 13*n*, 36-37, 44, 72, 96*n*, 158
Molotov Paper on Nazi Atrocities, The, Molotov, 96*n*
Monte Cassino, 153-154
Morawski, Col., 150, 166*n*
Moscow, 121
　Foreign Ministers Conference of 1943, 44
　selection of men for death made in, 154
"Moscow group"
　New Year's Eve party, 151
　at outbreak of German-Soviet War, 152-153
　Red Polish forces plan, 148
　treatment of, 147-153
　in "Villa of Bliss," 150-153
　see also Polish prisoners of war
Moskowskaya, 159
Moszyński, Adam, 28*n*, 96*n*
Movies, in prison camps, 140
M.S.Z., xvi; *notes on* 13, 14, 46, 97
"Murder, or High Strategy?" Standley and Ageton, 14*n*

Mysteries of the Van Vliet Report. . . . , The, Epstein, 196*n*

N

National Committee of Americans of Polish Descent, 163*n*
Na Nieludzkiej Ziemi, Czapski, *notes on* 13, 14, 126
Narodnyi Komissariat Vnutrennikh Del, *see* N.K.V.D.
Nasedkin, Gen., 7
Naujock, A. H., 3
Naville, Francis, 17, 68, 87, 177
Nazi Conspiracy and Aggression, U. S. Office . . . for Prosecution of Axis Criminality, 75*n*, 97*n*
Nazis, *see* Germany
Nazi-Soviet Pact (1939), 12*n*, 39, 65
Nazi-Soviet Relations, 1939-1941: . . . , U. S. Dept. of State, 12*n*
Netherlands, 17
Neue Zeit, 56*n*
New Class: . . . , The, Djilas, 167*n*
"New Germans," 117, 119, 123-124
New Soviet Documents on Nazi Atrocities, Soviet Embassy in London, 97*n*
New Year's Eve party, 151
Nikolai, Metropolitan, 56*n*
Nikolsky, Maj., 57*n*
N.K.V.D., 9, 10, 24, 42, 95, 96*n*
　classifying of Polish citizens, 130
　functions of, 127, 133-134, 155-156
　indoctrination methods, 117-123, 134, 160-162
　interrogations by, 131, 133-136, 139
　Katyn Forest villa, 16, 50
　Minsk report, 114-115
　"Moscow group" and, 147-153
　ordered to place guilt on Germany, 157
　postwar Katyn attitude, 170
　records of, 82, 175

responsibility for massacre, 155-157
in search for missing men, 7-8
selection of victims, 154-155
treatment of Polish prisoners, 103-106, 112-123; *notes on* 163-165
Non-Aggression Treaty, German-Soviet, see Nazi-Soviet Pact
Noncommissioned officers, in the death camps, 132
Norway, 20
Nota Sovetskogo Pravitel'stva Pravitel'stvu SShA; Soobshchenie Spetsial'noi Komissii, see Soviet Report
"Nowy Dowód Zbrodni . . . ," 191*n*
Nowy Kurier Warszawski, 45*n*, 126*n*
Nuremberg Case, The, Jackson, 96*n*
Nuremberg Diary, Gilbert, 75*n*
Nuremberg War Trials, 64
   Katyn case, 55, 64-74, 84, 95, 181
   reports on, *see I. M. T.*
Nurses, Soviet, 156

O

Oberhaüser, Gen., 69, 76*n*
Officers, Polish, 9-10
   arrest of, 131
   codes of, 165*n*-166*n*
   "enemy" category, 127, 129, 130-133
   fondness for Gen. Zarubin, 141-143
   generals among, 19, 105, 145
   hiding of, 130, 163*n*
   investigations of, in prison camps, 128
   numbers missing, 78, 95
   shortage of, after Katyn, 148-149, 151, 152
   see also Missing men, Polish prisoners of war, Survivors
Office of War Information (O.W.I.), 41, 42, 184
Official Documents . . . 1933-1939, Polish Government-in-Exile, 97*n*
Ogloblin, Maj., 57*n*
O'Konski, Congressman, 74, 196*n*
Ol'shansky, B., 157-159, 167*n*
Olszyna-Wilczyński, Gen., 131
O'Malley, Sir Owen, 91
"Operation A-B, . . . ," German, 79
Oradour-Sur-Glane, 96
Orsos, Dr., 17, 26*n*, 93, 99*n*, 178
Osmańczyk, Edmund, 12
Ostashkov (city), 114
Ostashkov prison camp, 6, 8, 77-78, 79, 83, 88, 94, 96*n*, 101, 102, 112, 113, 117, 131, 132, 135, 177
   evacuation of, 154-155
Ostdeutscher Beobachter, 193*n*
Ostrów Mazowiecki atrocities, 175
O Trwały Pokój, . . . , 191*n*

P

Palmieri, Dr., 17, 87, 93, 99*n*, 178
Paradis atrocity, 189
Pavelishtchev Bor prison camp, 78, 92, 117-118, 120, 124
Pavlov, I., 137, 164*n*
"Pavlovian Strategy as a Weapon of Menticide," Meerloo, 164*n*
Persuade or Perish, Carroll, 47*n*
Pfeiffer, Albert, 27*n*
Pieńkowski, Stefan, 22
"Pierwsza Bolszewicka Książka of Katyniu," Mackiewicz, 192*n*
Pilsen, 63
Plisowski, Gen., 146
Pohorecki, 131
Pokrovsky, Col., 65
Poland
   attack on, in *1939*, 3-5, 12*n*, 65
   effectiveness of intelligence and counter-intelligence, prewar, 132
   German-occupied, 4, 17, 79-80
   government-in-exile, *see* Polish Government-in-Exile
   Peoples' Republic (communist), *see* Polish Peoples' Republic
   Soviet-occupied, 5, 127

INDEX

Union of Polish Patriots, *see* sepaarate item
"Warsaw (interim) government," 72, 170-171
see also Poles
Poland, Russia and Great Britain 1941-1945, R. Umiastowski, 163n
Poles
  in America, 163n, 183, 184
  classifying of, by N.K.V.D., 130
  communist, *see* Communist Party, Polish, *and* Polish Peoples' Republic
  deportees into Russia, 193n
  elite liquidated, 133
  emigrés, 31, 40
  resistance to indoctrination, 127, 160-162
  war-time aid to Allies, 34
Polish Armored Lancers' Regiment *12*, 153-154
Polish Army (under Anders), 6, 78, 97n, 119, 122, 123, 148, 153
  lack of officers for, 6, 7, 9
  "Moscow group" accepted into, 153
Polish Army Officers' Corps, 9-10
  see also Officers, Polish
Polish Embassy in Moscow, 124
Polish Government-in-Exile (London), 5, 18, 88
  Allied relationships, 30-45; *see also* International politics
  appeal to the International Red Cross, 32-36, 38, 44
  award to Gen. Bissell, 185
  inquiries on Katyn, 35, 124n-125n
  invited to House hearings, 187
  Nuremberg trial and, 66, 73
  postwar, 170
  pressure by Allies on, 37-38
  publications of, 97n
  Soviet *1941* agreement with, 123
  Soviet *1943* break with, 182

Soviet effort to form its own "Polish Government," 38-39
Soviet offer of new relations with (*1943*), 43-44
Polish Institute of Forensic Medicine, Kraków, 60
Polish Institute of Gas Warfare, 132
Polish Literary Institute, Paris, 172
Polish Parliamentary Group, London, 66, 75n
Polish Peasant Party, 170
Polish Peoples' Republic
  book on Katyn published in (*1958*), 173-175, 193n
  effort to investigate Katyn, 169-177
  invited to participate in House hearings, 187
  public opinion on Katyn in, 171, 176
  see also Poland
Polish prisoners of war
  amnesty of *1941*, 6, 123
  class struggle concept and, 128-133
  disappearance of, *see* Missing men
  dog incidents, 120-121, 139
  failure to escape, 83
  indoctrination, 103-104, 120-122, 134, 135-143, 165n-166n
  informers among, 144
  internees from neutral countries, 147
  interviewed by author, 97n
  Katyn Forest visits by, 18
  leaders and officers among, 138, 163n
  letters, 77-78
  morale of, 103
  numbers of, 5, 15, 77, 94-95, 96n
  prison camps, *see* Grazovec, Kozelsk, Lübeck, Ostashkov, Pavelishtchev Bor, Starobelsk
  prison life of, 102-103
  professions and character of, 22-23, 24

sale of effects by, 102-103
Soviet files on, 136
Soviet treatment of, 50, 124, 163n-164n
survivors, see Survivors
woman among, 22
work performed by, 82, 85, 103
Polish Red Cross, 17, 29, 62, 74n, 88
investigation of Katyn, see Polish Red Cross Commission investigation
Kraków examination of documents, 60
Skarżyński manuscripts, 26n-27n
see also International Red Cross
Polish Red Cross Commission investigation, 17-25, 81-94, 192n
German pressure on, 25
medical team, 112
report of, 27n, 28n
Polish Report, xvi, 80, 84, 89; notes on 12-14, 26-28, 46, 47, 73, 91, 96-99, 125, 126, 163-166, 192
Polish search office, 113
Polish-Soviet Relations, 1918-1943, . . . , Polish Government-in-Exile, 12n, 97n
Polish Technical Institute for Armament, 132
Polish Underground, 30, 34, 125n
documents of Katyn and, 59, 60, 62
in search for missing men, 18, 78, 81-82, 88
Polskie Siły Zbrojne w Drugiej Wojnie Światowej, see P.S.Z.
Pośpieszalski, K. M., 193n
Potemkin, V. P., 56n
Pravda, 34, 159; notes on 26, 47, 96, 167
"Prawda o Katyniu," W. A., 192n
Prawda o Katyniu, Wójcicki, 173-175, 191n, 192n
Prayers, prohibited to prisoners, 138-139

Press, German, Katyn articles in, notes on 194-195
Priests, "enemy" category, 131
Prison camps, see Grazovec, Kozelsk, Lübeck, Ostashkov, Pavelishtchev Bor, Starobelsk
Prisoner of War Camps in Russia: . . ., 167n-168n
Prisoner-of-war protection agreement, need for, 189-190
"Prisoner of War Syndrome: . . . , A," Strassman, Thaler, and Schein, 164n
Prisoners of war
accounts by German, 167n
accounts by Italian, 167n
American, see American prisoners of war
brainwashing and indoctrination, 136-143, 161-162, 164n, 168n
death figures, 190
Polish, see Polish prisoners of war
Privates, in the camps, 24, 132
Prochovnik, Col., 66
Professions, "enemy" categories, 131-133
"Propaganda Ludobójców," Arski, 191n
Proprostu, 192n
Prosorovsky, Dr. 67, 69
Provisional Government of National Unity, Warsaw, 72, 170-171
Prozorovsky, V. I., 53, 56n, 99n
Przez Kraj Niewoli, J. K. Umiastowski, 163n, 165n
P.S.Z., xvi; notes on 12, 26, 97, 163
Public address systems, in prison camps, 140
Purges, Soviet, 156
Pushkareva, Lt., 57n

R

Rabbis, "enemy" category, 131
Radebeul, 63, 74n
Radziwiłł, Prince, 145

Raikhman, Gen., 8, 96*n*, 115, 148, 155
Rape of the Mind: . . ., The, Meerloo, 164*n*
Rape of Poland: . . ., Mikołajczyk, notes on 56, 74, 162
Rawa Ruska atrocities, 175
"Reaction Patterns . . . in American Army Prisoners of War . . . ," Schein, 168*n*
Recceone, 171
Red Army, 45, 122, 152
  "Polish forces," 148-153
  treatment of prisoners under class-struggle concept, 129-133
  Union of Polish Patriots (Berling's forces), 153-154
Red Corners, of Polish prisoners of war, 120-123, 146, 151
Red Cross, *see* International Red Cross, Polish Red Cross, Swiss Red Cross
Rekst, Lt., 55
Religious leaders, as prisoners of war, 138-139; *see also* Priests, etc.
Repatriation Agreement of 1957, Polish-Soviet, 176
Report on the Massacre of Polish Officers in Katyn Wood, Polish Government-in-Exile, 13*n*
Report of Robert H. Jackson, . . ., 74*n*
Reuger, 32
Reuters International News Agency, 32, 33
"Reżyserzy Prowokacji Katyńskiej," Szalawski, 191*n*
Ribbentrop, von, Joachim, 4, 30, 31, 34, 44
Ribbentrop-Molotov line, 4
Rintelen, von, Amb., 46*n*
Robel, Dr., 62, 192*n*
Robotnik Mazowiecki, 191*n*
Rockefeller Foundation, 146
Romania, 17

Romer, Tadeusz, 9, 36-37
Roosevelt, F. D., 30, 34, 36, 40, 42, 44, 47*n*, 178, 186, 190, 196*n*
Rope, as evidence, 19-20, 55, 93
Rostov mass murders, 96*n*
Rothstein, Andrew, 12*n*
Royal Institute of International Affairs *survey* . . . , 96*n*
Rozmarek, Charles, 196*n*
Rozmowy z Kremlem, Kot, 13*n*, 14*n*
Rudenko, Gen., 65, 66
Rutkowski, Col. (Redhead), 125*n*

S

Sachsenhausen concentration camp, 174
Sadykov, Lt., 57*n*
Sagan atrocities, 189
Samoa, 183
Sargant, William, 164*n*
Sawicki, Jerzy, 170-171, 175-176, 193*n*
Saxen, Dr., 17
Scaevola (pseud.), 166*n*-167*n*
Schein, E. H., *notes on* 164, 166, 168
Schirach, von, Baldur, 65
Scotland, A. P., 189, 197*n*
Scoutmasters, "enemy" category, 163*n*
Security police, Soviet, *see* N.K.V.D.
Segal, Julius, 168*n*
Seleshko, M., 193*n*
Semenovsky, P. S., 56*n*
Serwański, E., 193*n*
Shvaikova, M. D., 57*n*
7-*Tag*, 113
Sikorski, F., 146
Sikorski, Władysław, 5-6, 31, 37, 47*n*, 72
  in search for missing men, 9-10
Sikorski government, *see* Polish Government-in-Exile
Sikorski-Maisky Agreement of 1941, 5-6, 123, 153
Skalski, K. A., 191*n*

Skarżyński, K., vii, 60; *notes on* 26, 74, 99
  listing of manuscripts on Katyn, 27*n*
Skierski, Gen., 145-146
Skuratowicz, Gen., 146
Słapianka, Jolanta, 172
Slusser, Robert M., 164*n*
Smirnov, E. I., 56*n*, 68
Smolensk, 8-9, 11, 15, 50, 69, 82, 109, 113-114
  N.K.V.D. of, 110, 114
  temperature in area of, 83-84
Smolensk Observatory, 50
Smolensk Under Soviet Rule, Fainsod, 126*n*
Smolyaninov, V. M., 56*n*
Smorawinski, Gen., 145
Sokolsky, George, 196*n*
Solski, Maj., 110, 125*n*-126*n*
Sontag, Raymond James, 12*n*
Sotsialistcheskii Vestnik, 167*n*
Soviet Agreement with Hungary . . . (*1921*), 129-130
Soviet Army, *see* Red Army
Soviet Embassy Information Bulletin supplement, 56*n*
Soviet Embassy in London, 191*n*
Soviet Foreign Policy during the Patriotic War: . . . , Rothstein, 12*n*
Soviet Infantry Regiment *129*, 114
Soviet Infantry Regiment *190*, 114
Soviet Medical Commission, 89
Soviet Report, xvii, 56*n*, 65-69, 82-85, 89, 93, 175, 177; *notes on* 98, 99, 167
  "fixing" of, 159-160
  Ol'shansky's letter on, 157-159
Soviet Secret Police, The, Wolin and Slusser, 164*n*
Soviet Special Commission for Investigation of Katyn (*1943-1944*), 54, 49-55, 82-94, 98*n*, 99*n*, 158-159
Soviet Union
  Allied relationships, *see* International politics
  claim to Polish eastern territories, 43
  in effort to find missing men, 6, 8-11, 81, 82, 159
  Geneva Convention of *1929* and, 130-131
  invasions of Poland, 4-5, 61-63, 131
  invitation to House hearings, 187
  Katyn evidence against, 17-25, 80, 83, 90-95, 180, 188
  military agreement with Polish government (*1941*), 123
  Nazi attack on, in *1941*, 121
  Nuremberg trials *and*, *see* Nuremberg War Trials
  Polish diplomatic break of *1943*, 33-45
  recognition of Hague convention of *1907*, 163*n*
  response to finding of the graves, 15
  treatment of prisoners of war, 5, 127, 128, 163*n*-164*n*
Soviet Union and the International Law: . . . , *The*, Taracouzio, 129, 162*n*
Soviet War News, 26*n*, 191*n*
Spain, 20
Special Congressional Committee for investigation of Katyn, *see* House Select Committee investigation
Special Declaration, Moscow, *1943*, 44-45
Special Report: Japanese Prisoners of War: . . . , U. S. Army, . . . , 168*n*
Speleers, Dr., 17
Spiegel, Der, 75*n*, 193*n*
"Sprawa Katyńska— . . . ," Infeld, 191*n*

Sprawy Polskie w Procesie Norymberskim, Cyprian and Sawicki, 193n
Spruce trees, as evidence, 24, 55, 90
Stahl, Dr. Zdzisław, viii
Stahmer, Otto, 66, 71, 72
Stalin, 9-10, 13n, 34-44, 47n, 72, 127, 128, 155-158
 "liquidation" story, 162n
 son of, as prisoner of war, 156-157
Stalin and the Poles: . . ., Kuśnierz, 163n, 195n
Stalin's Correspondence, xvii, 46n, 47n
Standley, William H., 10, 37, 39, 180; notes on 14, 46, 47
Starobelsk (city), 114
Starobelsk prison camp, 6-8, 77-79, 83, 88, 90, 94, 96n, 101-106, 112-117, 131, 134, 138, 139, 177
 doctors in, 164n
 evacuation of, 154-155
 generals in, 145-146
 religious leaders in, 132
State Department, United States, 178
 position in the Katyn affair, 41-42, 186
State Jewelry Trust, Soviet, 102
Statut Oficerskich . . ., Brzostowski, 166n
Steinberg, Rabbi, 139
Stewart, Donald B., 179
Stockholm Tidningen, 21
Stosunki Polsko-Sowieckie od Września 1939 do Kwietnia 1943. Zbiór Dokumentów, see M. S. Z.
Strassman, H. D., 164n
Strong, George, 179
Study in Forgery: . . ., *A*, Scaevola (pseud.), 166n-167n
Subbotin, Maj., 57n
Subik, Dr., 17
Sukiennicki, Wiktor, viii, xvi, 12n, 47n, 73

Survivors, 104, 106, 109, 118-124
 anti-Semitism charge, 120
 basic types, 144
 communists among, 146
 departure from camps, 116
 "fascist" charge by Soviet, 122
 fate of, 146
 letters received and sent by, 118-119
 list of, 126n
 "Moscow group," 146-154
 "new Germans" among, 117, 119, 123-124
 news sources of, 122-123
 N.K.V.D. treatment of, 101, 116-123
 numbers of, 101, 124
 opinion of prisoner-of-war treatment, 156
 "Red Corner," 120-122
 selection of, 143-144, 154
Sweden, 20, 21, 44
Sweet, Paul, 46n
Świaniewicz, Prof., vii, 71
Świątkowski, Minister of Justice, 170-171
Switzerland, 17, 20, 44, 177
 Polish emigrés in, 31
Szalawski, Zbigniew, 191n
Szymanski, Col., 72, 178-182, 184
Szyszko-Bohusz, Zygmunt, 163n

T

"Tajemnica Śmierci . . . ," Mackiewicz, 126n
Tank unit collection, 170
Tappin, John, 72
Taracouzio, T. A., 129, 162n
Teachers, "enemy" category, 133
Temperature, as evidence, 92
Thaler, M. B., 164n
Thieme, Hans, 195n
Thompson, Dorothy, 196n
Thought Reform . . . in China, Lifton, 166n

"Thought Reform of Chinese Intellectuals: . . . ," Lifton, 166n, 168n
Time, 57n, 98n
Times, London, 45, 47n
Timoshenko, Gen., 130
Tolstoy, Alexei, 56n
Toynbee, Arnold M., 96n
Toynbee, Veronica M., 96n
Tramsen, Dr., 17, 26n, 68, 178
Trial of the Major War Criminals before the International Military Tribunal. Nuremberg, see I. M. T.
Truth about Katyn, The, Wojcicki, 173-175, 192n
Trybuna Ludu, Warsaw, 173, 191n, 192n
Trybuna Wolności, 191n
Turkey, 44
Tyszyński, 166n

U

Ukraine, 157, 192n, 193n
Ukrainian Infantry Regiment 68 (Soviet), 114, 115
Ukrainian Quarterly, The, 193n
Umiastowski, J. K., 163n, 165n
Umiastowski, Roman, 163n
Underground, Polish, see Polish Underground
Union of Polish Patriots (1943), 38, 43
  Berling's forces, 153-154
Union of Soviet Socialist Republics, see Soviet Union
United Nations, 189, 190
  Charter of, 186
  in Katyn case, 188
  prisoner-of-war convention of 1949, 189, 197n
United States Government and the Katyn case
  official inquiries: Nuremberg trials and, 64, 72, see also Jackson, Robert; Special Congressional Committee Investigations, 187-188, see Hearings; State Department, 10, 178; War Department, Military Intelligence, 179-180
  research and evidence: Office of War Information, Foreign Language Division, 41, 184, 196n; Roosevelt, 179, 182; State Department, 178, 180-181; War Department, Military Intelligence, 179-180, 184-186, 195n, see Hearings
  suppression of information: Office of War Information, Foreign Language Division, 41-42, 184; Roosevelt, 182-183; State Department, 41-42, 72-73, 180-181, 186; War Department, Military Intelligence, 72, 181-182, 185-186
  see also International politics
United States Naval Institute Proceedings, 14n

V

Van Dyke, Prof. Vernon, viii
Van Vliet, John H., 72, 179-180, 185, 195n
Vardaman, Commodore, 183
Veliki Luki, 114
Verordnungsblatt für das Generalgouvernement, 45n
Viazma, 113
Vinnytsia, 192
"Vinnytsia—the Katyn of Ukraine," Seleshko, 193n
Voice of America, Czapski's talk on, 186
Völkischer Beobachter, notes on 26, 126, 193
Von Eichborn, 97n
Von Herff, 24
Voss, Lt., 174
Vyropayev, D. N., 56n
Vyshinsky, Andrei, 8, 10, 13n

W

Walawski, Bolesław, 193n
Walsh, James A., 196n
War Department, U. S., 181-182
Warsaw, 30, 72, 80
　public trial efforts in, 170-177
"Warsaw (interim) government," 72, 170-171
Wasilewska, Wanda, 38, 53
Welles, Sumner, 47n
Werth, of B. B. C., 53
West German Federal Republic, 187
　Katyn a live issue in, 176
White Sea, 113
Wiadomości, 126n, 192n
W Imieniu Kremla, Korboński, 191n
Wodzinski, Marian, 27n, 112
Wójcicki, Bolesław, notes on 192, 193, 195
　book discussed, 173-175
Wolff, Harold G., 166n
Wolin, Simon, 164n
Wołkowicki, Gen., 145
Wolna Polska, 53
World War II, 3-4, 63, 130; notes on 11-12
　see also International politics

Writers, "enemy" category, 133
Wróblewski, Stanisław, 172
Wspomnienia Starobielskie, Czapski, notes on 13, 14, 163-165

Y

Yeaton, I. D., 179, 195n
Yegorov, Col., 148
Yelenovka, Camp, 163n

Z

Zabiełło, O. S., 194n
Zalewski, Maj., 102
Zarubin, Georgi, 141
Zarubin, V. M., 115, 141-143, 154, 162, notes on 165, 166
Zbiór Przepisów Specjalnych . . . , Sawicki *and* Walawski, 193n
"Zbrodnia Katyńska Przed Sądem w Norymberdze," 192n
Zbrodnia Katyńska w Świetle Dokumentów, notes on 27, 96-98, 125, 163
Zhukov, G. S., 11, 123
Zielony Sztandar, notes on 191, 192
Zietz, W., 195n
"Znow Katyń," Czapski, 14n
Życie Słowiańskie, 191n